Ireland from the Sea

ANDREW PHELAN first skippered an ancient rowing boat on the River Suir at the age of ten. Later he acquired cruising experience on coasts from Norway to Spain, and frequently wrote and broadcast on sailing and Irish history. He served for several years on the General Purposes Committee of the Royal Yachting Association and was elected a member of the Royal Cruising Club in 1983.

A native of Co. Waterford, he practised at the Bar in England and has now retired after 21 years as a Circuit Court judge. His book, *The Law for Small Boats*, was published in 1974.

He describes *Ireland from the Sea* as a labour of love, and followed his circumnavigation of the island by crewing on a friend's yacht from Cornwall to New England. Living on the Thames riverside at Chiswick, he offers the older of ten grandchildren dinghy sailing from the end of the garden and occasional cruising in his 32-foot sloop *Sarakiniko*. He would like them to grow up preferring anchorages to marinas and hopes that they will yet cross the sea to Ireland, and find that some of the best cruising grounds in Europe still remain unspoilt.

IRELAND
from the SEA

ANDREW PHELAN

Foreword by Dr John de Courcy Ireland

WOLFHOUND PRESS
& in the US and Canada
The Irish American Book Company

Published in 1998 by
Wolfhound Press Ltd
68 Mountjoy Square
Dublin 1, Ireland
Tel: (353-1) 874 0354
Fax: (353-1) 872 0207

Published in the US and Canada by
The Irish American Book Company
6309 Monarch Park Place
Niwot, Colorado 80503
USA
Tel: (303) 652 2710
Fax: (303) 652 2689

Photographs other than the author's are reproduced by kind permission of Wallace Clark and Michael Diggin.

Wolfhound Press receives financial assistance from the Arts Council/An Chomhairle Ealaíon, Dublin, Ireland.

British Library Cataloguing in Publication Data
A catalogue record for this book is available from the British Library.

ISBN 0-86327-663-4

10 9 8 7 6 5 4 3 2 1

Cover Photograph: Oliver Bond
Cover Design: Slick Fish Design
Maps: Eilish Young
Typesetting: Peter Malone
Printed and bound by ColourBooks Ltd.

To Joan, of course

There breathes a living fragrance from the shore
Of flowers yet fresh with childhood, On the ear
Drops the light drip of the suspended oar.

Lord Byron, 'Childe Harold'

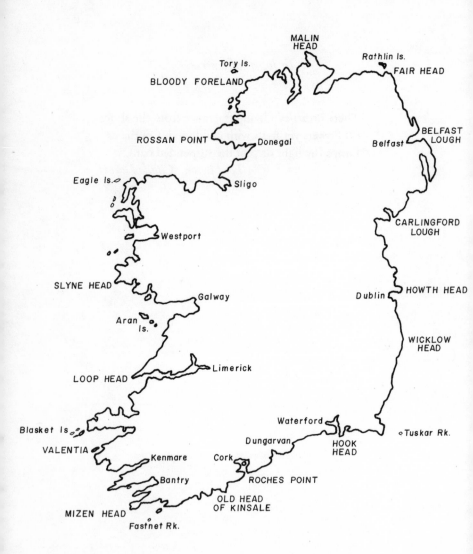

Contents

Foreword

I HAVE NO hesitation in confessing that my first thought on reaching the end of this remarkable volume, so full of incident and information, and adorned with gems of wisdom dropping lightly down the narrative like finely tinted autumn leaves, was: what was this country of mine doing when it allowed this author to slip away from us to use his splendid gifts in another land? Are men of erudition, imagination and insight so common in Ireland that we can afford to make gifts of them to communities across the sea? During the greater part of my lifetime we have been allowing citizens with outstanding qualities to depart to other climes, often without as much as a farewell, and rarely have we had the grace to weigh the full sum of our loss, though we often utter formal lamentations about it. I hope those days are coming to a close.

Andrew Phelan has an ability anything but common, as I know from a lifetime spent with books about the sea. He can bring you from point to point along a coast, not just so you can follow it on a map or chart, but so that you can clearly see with your mind's eye cliffs and rocks and channels as he encounters them, and feel with your very being, rather than just with your mind, what he felt with the appearance of every marine hazard he met on his voyage round Ireland.

The film-maker George Morrisson called the film he made for the Lifeboat Institution about its Irish service *Two Thousand Miles of Peril*. Andrew Phelan encompassed those perilous miles with skill and relish, but also with the humility of the true seafarer who knows how easy it is for even the most experienced navigator to make an error, and how fathomless is the malice of what Masefield called 'the green and greedy seas' and Shakespeare 'the wild and wasteful ocean'.

Foreword

To deck out his story in unforgettable colours, this generous author offers his readers, in light helpings but rich with the sauce of knowledge, tale after little-known tale of events geological, historical, meteorological and theological that have occurred along the coasts of his native country, which – exceptionally – he describes from outside looking in, rather than from the landsman's viewpoint, from inland looking outward.

Dr John de Courcy Ireland
Dalkey, July 1998

Acknowledgements

THIS BOOK COULD not have been written without drawing on the endless patience of Dr John de Courcy Ireland, who has a unique knowledge of our maritime history, and without the inspiring example of Wallace Clark's writings on sailing the Celtic seas. I would add that Wallace Clark has also been more than generous in providing several photographs for the book.

I would also like to thank the following for their kindness and help: David Bedlow, Martin Blake, Jim Deeny, Ray Fielding, Charles Haughey, Reg Jarvis, Lt Com. A. Kehoe, Donal Lynch, Martin McCarthy, Michael McCaughan, Cormac Henry, Paddy O'Leary, Fr Diarmuid Ó Péicín, Jean O'Sullivan, Dr Emer Rogan and Trudie Sly.

The voyage could not have been made without the help of the Irish Cruising Club's excellent *Sailing Directions*, the loan of many charts from the Royal Cruising Club, and of course the endeavours of an ever-cheerful and forgiving crew.

This included my wife, Joan, who could not have anticipated the subsequent task of rescuing me from seas of paper and the shoals of computer-land.

Finally, I thank my publishers and in particular my editor, Peter Malone.

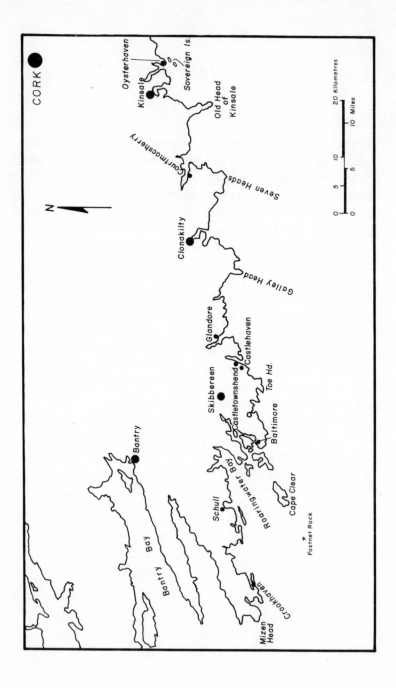

ONE

The Western Approaches

IT WAS 2345 hours. Wriggling with difficulty from my sleeping-bag, I started to dress for the night watch. I staggered as I eased a leg into my oilskin trousers and wondered if the sea had become a little more lively. We had left the Scilly Isles soon after dawn, aiming to make landfall on the south coast of Ireland. Since going to my bunk I had dozed rather than slept, my brain too active for proper sleep. I would put that right tomorrow night when our mooring lines held us snug to a pontoon in Kinsale, but now I wondered if I had judged the tides correctly; all through the evening the ebb pouring from the Irish Sea had been pulling us out into the Atlantic.

A turned-down paraffin lamp spread a dim glow over the saloon – just enough light to find my sea boots – and it was probably unwise now to spoil my night vision by turning on the light at the chart table, but I paused long enough to train the beam on the 'Western Approaches to St George's Channel'. The wells of the Kinsale gas field were clearly marked, and on this course – 330 degrees, north by north-west – we should pass close to their great flaring platforms. They make excellent navigation marks some 26 miles from the coast of Cork.

'Manage to sleep?' Anne asked as I hauled my way into the cockpit. She was hunched near the tiller, dimly lit by the light of the compass.

'A bit,' I said, 'but mostly dozing.' I rubbed a fingertip on the dial of the log. 'Maybe 55 miles to go. I checked the gas platforms; their lights might come up in an hour or so. Anyhow, it's time you were in bed.'

I should have known exactly how far we had to go. The electronic marvels that give you a position picked from the transit of satellites or from radio beams transmitted by land stations are commonplace now, but the performance of ours, a Decca system whose aerial had been damaged, was erratic: immediately the Scillies were out of sight it had started flashing 'Position Suspect'. So I had been relying on old technology, a Walker log, a little rotator hanging from the stern spinning the wavelets into miles. It is a long-tried and accurate system, until it begins to collect too much drifting seaweed.

Left alone in the darkness, I waited until my eyes grew accustomed to the gloom and then struggled into my safety harness. The act seemed a bit pretentious for such a pleasant night, but falling over the side while the boat sailed on is not something you take a chance on. The thought stayed with me as I snapped the end of the harness line to a guard-rail, climbed along the heeling deck, grabbed the forestay at the bow and craned on tip-toe around the edge of the billowing jib. The red and green navigation lights glowed at my knees and a satisfying hiss of black water rose from below. There was nothing at all on the dark horizon. Being based at Portsmouth, our frequent journeys across the Channel had accustomed us to horizons defined by necklaces of lights, shipping lanes where there was a risk of collision, but also companionship of a sort. Tonight the Celtic Sea seemed a lonely place.

Since acquiring *Sarakiniko* in 1985, my wife Joan and I had sailed her as far north as Scotland and south to Spain. *Sarakiniko* was not a name of our choosing: the former owner had called her after a bay in Ithaca, and changing a boat's name is said to bring ill luck. Like all yachts, this 32-foot Westerly Fulmar tended to govern our lives. We found ourselves locked into the annual ritual of laying her up in the autumn, repairing the boat through the winter, varnishing and anti-fouling in the Easter rain. Then, instead of easing ourselves into the season with some gentle sailing in the Solent, we would dash for small harbours and large meals on the Cherbourg peninsula during early May. This year, however, we wanted to get away from the Friday night struggle through London traffic and the ever-more-crowded English south coast. We decided instead that *Sarakiniko* would circumnavigate Ireland.

Some years before we had sailed as far as the Kerry coast, a voyage which brought us to places which seemed uniquely unspoiled. Ireland's coast also hinted at a long maritime history which was largely unexplored, and we felt we could come to understand it better travelling in our own small boat. And perhaps our ambition owed something, too, to the masochism which lurks near the surface of our souls, for a circumnavigation would surely involve some rugged sailing. Our plans emerged by a common understanding, intuitively and without much discussion, until we found ourselves wondering who we could persuade to become the third member of the crew.

Three would be a good number. An optimist might claim that *Sarakiniko* had berths for six, and she has actually sailed five-up without mutiny, but the boat's accommodation is not over-generous. Two companionable people may squeeze into the berths in the vee-shaped forepeak, where they can be hoisted and dropped with insistent regularity in a short head sea. Emerging from the forepeak you squeeze past the heads ('your damp little bathroom', as a non-nautical friend once described it) with two hanging lockers on the other side, one for clothing, the other usually jammed with sea boots and wet oilskins. Beyond lies the saloon, eight feet long and flanked by settee bunks, with bookshelves, pictures, cushions and a swinging net of fruit which hints of the warm landfalls we might one day reach. A few feet further and the gas stove with a two-burner grill and oven rocks on its gimbals. The navigation table stands opposite and, a hand's reach away, a radio and the dial of an electronic depth-finder. Behind the chart table lies the mouth of a rather claustrophobic tunnel, a cubbyhole with a bunk where two very slender mariners could possibly lie together, but for one occupant it is a fine and private place. Joan favours it and had filled a shelf in there with books for the voyage.

Joan and I had spent many years sailing together, crossing the Bay of Biscay three times. She knows how to work *Sarakiniko* and is also a great cook. She wears oilskin trousers against the risk of hot spillage and can get quite fluent if the crew tack unexpectedly when a stew is coming to the boil. On a recent cruise off the

Spanish coast, a sudden squall laid *Sarakiniko* over, and in the boat's rebound to the vertical the kettle lifted past Joan's shoulder. She followed the kettle. Nonetheless the collected wits on board *Sarakiniko* got tea and cake ten minutes later.

A phone-call to Anne Baily's Tipperary home secured our third crew. Involved in equestrian affairs and a demanding garden, Anne can only spare brief intervals away, but she positively enjoys days of tumbling sea when water swills around the deck and sluices into the cockpit. She smiles into it all, hair streaming in the wind. Occasionally Joan or I may suggest that we might be more comfortable if we pulled down a reef – 'comfort' being a euphemism on *Sarakiniko* for easing apprehension – but Anne's early encounters with boats had been in a family Dragon, racing round the buoys in Belfast Lough, and she still seemed happiest in a lightweight speed machine. Migrating south to live in Tipperary, she enjoyed day-sailing with a farmer friend, Pat O'Donnell, on Lough Derg on the Shannon, but we knew she hankered after the salt.

'A circumnavigation; clockwise. How much time do you have?' I had asked her.

'I can go as far as West Cork. But I could meet you again later, perhaps in Mayo or Donegal. Why don't you give Pat a call too; he may be able to join. The farm is not too busy in early summer.'

Anne had joined us at Plymouth, equipped, as the ideal crew will be, with one collapsible bag. Anchoring mid-way at the Helford River in Cornwall, we reached sheltered water in the Scilly island of Tresco, then made a dawn departure for the Irish coast, under motor at first until wind returned with the sun.

We had decided on two-hour watches, and Joan took over at 0200. The moon, which had been drenching our wake in silver, had sunk behind low clouds. We shortened sail for the night, taking in one reef which ties an impressive five feet of mainsail along the boom, and *Sarakiniko* seemed happy with the way she was dressed.

Later, as I drifted into sleep, Joan called down, 'A fishing boat ahead, I think.' The light gradually grew clearer: it was one of the gas platforms. The second came over the horizon a few moments later and, as the north-east sky acquired a suggestion of dawn and the wind fell away, we engined past the towering cradles of lights, dutifully obeying the chart's injunction to keep at least 500 metres clear. The Old Head of Kinsale, rising to 256 feet and jutting three miles south from the mainland, would be our first sight of Ireland. Other headlands thrust out against the prevailing westerly winds, but it is the Old Head which has always been the natural landfall for sea trade with southern Ireland.

For our circling of the island, we had planned in a general way for passages here and stopovers there, and we had gathered information about the many who had rounded Ireland before us. The earliest known non-stop circumnavigation by yacht seems to have been by John Jameson of the whiskey family in the 1880s in his yacht *Irex*. In 1889 Walter Boyd of Howth took the 44-ton yawl *Aideen* around, but the first detailed log dates from 1896 when Howard Sinclair of the Royal Ulster Yacht Club won the Royal Cruising Club Challenge Cup for achieving the circuit in the 6-ton cutter *Brenda*.

There were not many circumnavigations. The next one achieved from an Irish harbour was probably by Humphrey Barton in a 35-foot Fife cutter, *Dauntless*, which sailed without an engine in 1935. Wallace Clark sailed around twice in the 1950s, but most remarkable was the success of the 18-foot sloop *Durward* in 1961, when Kevin and Colm MacLaverty and Michael Clark pushed this boat around from Carrickfergus at an average speed of 3.4 knots.

That record was broken three years later by *Ainmara*, a vessel 136 feet long and, like *Dauntless* and *Durward*, without an engine. So it stood until the first Round Ireland Race in 1975. In subsequent years there were many attempts to set new records in a wide variety of craft. James Cahill used a 13-foot, 6-inch dinghy in 1976. Robin Deasy set the singlehanded record. Bob Henshaw sailed a Laser dinghy round the coast in 1990 and a sailboarder completed the circuit in 1992. Denis Doyle set a record in 1984 which was only broken in 1998, when Colm Bannington established a new sailing record of just under 77 hours. The multihulls, of course, set their own standards. In 1994 a 60-foot trimaran, *Lakota*, covered a 708-mile course in 44 hours 42 minutes and 20 seconds, an average speed of 15.84 knots.

At an average speed little over 4.5 knots, *Sarakiniko* might achieve 100 miles in 24 hours, though we did not intend to sail by night. We were not seeking to set any records. We had come simply to meet Ireland from the sea.

Even the strongest commitment can waver a little in the small hours. So much can go wrong on a boat. 'This damn gas for a start,' I thought grumpily. We had replaced an empty cylinder last evening, but the flame from the new container flickered unless the flow was stimulated by extracting the bottle from the cockpit locker and shaking it.

'Coffee is ready,' I called to Joan; 'you can stop the shaking now. Can you see anything ahead yet? The Kinsale light is two flashes every ten seconds.'

'I've been mesmerised by the platform. It's like a huge Christmas tree; layers of galleries. Wait a moment.' She stood up and peered over the sprayhood. 'There could be something up there; maybe phosphorescence on a wave-top. No, it's a light.'

I climbed the steps to the cockpit and looked out on a very dark sea, for the moon had set now. The horizon seemed to dissolve in the grey murk. The faint light in the north-east was either the dawn or a glow from the clouds over Cork. Probably both.

Anne came up, blinking sleep from her eyes.

'It's very near here, ten miles from the Head, that the *Lusitania* went down,' I said.

'In the First World War?'

'Yes, May 1915.' We sat on the cockpit seats, mugs of hot coffee warming our hands. 'A few years ago they got robot cameras to move all along the hull – nearly 800 feet long. When she dived the bow hit the sea-bed – it's less than 300 feet deep here – while the stern was still tilted 100 feet up. People were afraid to jump. The cameras picked out part of the name – ITAN, I think. Reading a tombstone you could say.'

Anne glanced at me. 'You have all the details. Does it fascinate you so much?'

'I suppose so. In a way it's part of my childhood. My mother's family farmed in Co. Waterford. They were at the Fermoy Races that Friday when the news came through: in the late afternoon, I expect, because the torpedo struck at 2.10 as passengers were finishing lunch. My mother often talked about how the noise of the racecourse became somehow muted. It was something that remained very vivid in her mind.'

At dawn the *Lusitania* had run into fog, which later cleared. In an age of limited navigational aids and dead reckoning, it was usual to make landfall on a headland, and Captain Turner, determined to fix his position precisely, put his ship on a straight course, her speed constant, unchanged by a fraction of a knot, for the 40 minutes required to take a four-point bearing on the Old Head. The German government had warned all shipping that they regarded the waters around Great Britain and Ireland as a war zone, and their submarines were active off the southern coast, but the Admiralty had not told Captain Turner that 23 merchant ships had been torpedoed in his general steaming area off Ireland since he had left New York the previous Saturday.

The target presented from 1.45 pm on was a U-boat captain's dream. Among the displays in Kinsale museum we would see a copy of the U-boat's log: 'The steamer turns to starboard, directs her course towards Queenstown and makes possible an approach for a shot. Ran at high speed to gain position directly ahead.'

The *Lusitania* was a queen of the seas, the most powerful liner afloat. The people of Kinsale, who had been expecting her arrival on that forenoon, flocked to the Old Head: fishermen, coastguards, farmers and villagers sitting on the white stone walls around the lighthouse. Children were left out of school to be there. The ship appeared round Seven Heads and seemed to alter course. Then came the explosion: 'A sort of heavy rumble like a foghorn,' a schoolboy, John Murphy, later said.

Of the 1,959 people who had sailed in the liner from New York, 1,198 perished. For many weeks afterwards, relatives searched the coast, poking in shallow inlets, questioning local people, travelling in ancient steam-driven automobiles or in horse-drawn carts. On Monday, 10 May, at the Old Church cemetery two miles outside of Queenstown, a mass grave received the first group of over a hundred coffins bearing unidentified victims. A few were also buried in the graveyard of the church of St Multose in Kinsale.

Despite the multiple horrors of our century, that day has left echoes rolling down the years. There are memories of the million-aire Alfred Vanderbilt, a non-swimmer, giving his life-jacket to a nurse, and of the death of Sir Hugh Lane, whose unsigned codicil to his will would start an English-Irish struggle over the owner-ship of his paintings which lasted until recent years. Some passengers survived. In a recently taken photograph, Alice Drury and Audrey Johnston stand hand-in-hand; that May, Alice was an 18-year-old English nurse, preparing a bottle for the infant Audrey when the torpedo struck. She tied the baby to her with a shawl and jumped into the sea, where she was grabbed by the hair and pulled into a lifeboat.

The light of the Old Head now lay somewhere abeam, lost in the murk. Outlines of land appeared, definite shapes on the star-board bow which were probably the Great and Little Sovereigns lying near the entrance to Oysterhaven. The entrance to Kinsale, two miles further west, is marked by a rock, the Bulman, with a large buoy near by. I disengaged the automatic steering, gripped the tiller and turned to port. Presently the long shoreline emerged. We saw a speck of light ahead. 'A sleeping seagull near us,' said Joan. 'A fishing boat far off,' Anne thought. I could not decide between them. These optical illusions, born of haze, water and light, put one in mind of landscapes painted by Turner, and dissolve quickly. In a few moments the image became the Bulman buoy, swaying gently in the tide, and we wondered how we could possibly have thought otherwise. We turned into the wind and Anne clawed down the rattling mainsail, Joan shaking its folds into neat lines and tying it to the boom. Soon the walls of Charles Fort, a seventeenth-century system of barracks, ram-parts and bastions, was frowning down on us from the slopes of the Kinsale estuary.

We bowed to progress and secured our lines to a pontoon berth. This after all was one of the relatively few marinas on the coast of Ireland, and we should soon have our fill of anchorages and with them the clattering of anchor-chain over the bow rollers, foot-pumping the dinghy, and wondering whether the distance to shore would be a brief row or justified the rigging of the outboard motor. Inevitably we would sometimes forget to fetch the rubbish ashore or the spare water-can for topping up. We were likely to be overdosed on rocks and gannets, Atlantic swell and anxious pilotage. Let us enjoy the convenience of a marina.

In a post-arrival mood of exuberant confidence, we bent to bacon and eggs in the cockpit. Although this had been no great voyage, we had navigated our way across the Celtic Sea and arrived safely, the first leg of our journey completed.

Joan and Anne went off to clean up, only to find that the showers in the Yacht Club were locked until nine o'clock, but eventually they returned, groomed and shining, and deriding my use of *Sarakiniko*'s low-technology shower unit, a 'Killaspray' sold in gardening shops. I defended it stoutly. A kettle of warm water poured into the can, 30 strokes to build up air pressure, and you have a quarter-hour douche from a telephone-like spray head, although admittedly, you can run out of water while still soaped over. However, by staying aboard the skipper had been on hand when the Marina Master called by. He cast an eye over the gas bottle and examined our stove, and looked taken aback when I asked about the cost of his time. I realised that, no less than the crew, I too needed to adjust to Ireland.

The old fishing town of Kinsale may have an ambition to become a mini-Salcombe, and certainly it now prospers. It has more in common with Cork and points east than the remoter west. Its history, and there is a great deal, is cherished locally and made accessible to the visitor, though I saw no reference to the fact that Alexander Selkirk sailed from here in 1703 on board the *Cinque Ports*. Marooned on Juan Fernandez in the Pacific, he was of course immortalised as Robinson Crusoe.

We avoided the tendency of some cruising boats to regard ports of call only as places with a pub, a launderette and a telephone, and set off through streets whose colourful and slated houses still resisted the prestige development and the shopping mall, but the spreading Lego-like residential terrace spoiling the northern slopes of this tranquil harbour may have been a hint of horrors to come. 'We call them the cash registers,' said the man in the newsagents.

As I passed the manicured lawns by the quay, enticing boutiques, restaurants and teashops – the town now claims with some justification to be the gourmet capital of Ireland – I recalled a Kinsale of 30 years ago, a memory of trawlers on the slip and the racket of welding when, crewing on a friend's yacht, I lowered our anchor into the tide. The narrow winding streets seemed sad and weary then, rusting drainpipes askew, grass invading the gutters, empty warehouses and a great sightless barracks looming on the hill. We had rowed ashore and tied up in solitude where today a forest of masts rises from white plastic hulls. There seemed to be just one hotel, a soothingly shabby, uncompromisingly respectable Acton's. A sleepy waiter took us to a bathroom, twisted huge brass taps to release a torrent of hot water, and presently had time to chat to us as we breakfasted at a fine mahogany table, the hotel cat stroking our shins.

Kinsale's new prosperity has come once again from the sea, though now from its recreational use. Game fishing led the way, and soon scores of yachtsmen made the town's marinas their Irish landfall, the French in particular, sailing with the prevailing south-west winds comfortably on the beam as sailors have done for centuries, and finding the Scilly Isles, where pub prices are sometimes chalked in francs, conveniently on the way. Part of Kinsale's harbour front is called Scilly in memory of the fishermen who came here and stayed.

Possibly the most crucial battle in Irish history was the Battle of Kinsale at Christmas 1601. The Ulster leaders, Hugh O'Neill, the Earl of Tyrone, and his son-in-law, Red Hugh O'Donnell, had for nine years waged a largely successful war which threatened English control of Ireland, and in December 1600 a Spanish fleet with some 4,000 troops stood into the bay and occupied Kinsale in support of the Irish cause. They were besieged by some 6,600 foot and 650 horse under Mountjoy,

Queen Elizabeth's deputy in Ireland.

Ulster lay some 300 miles to the north, and in the depths of winter the Irish troops had to traverse a countryside almost without roads to reach Kinsale. They now encircled the English force surrounding the town, cutting off its supplies from Cork. However, the inlet of Oysterhaven, which had confused us earlier today as we approached Kinsale, lay within the English lines and allowed supplies to be fetched by sea. As the English held on, the undisciplined impatience of O'Neill's colleagues spurred the Irish into attack and they were defeated. There was nothing but surrender for the Spaniards watching from the town. Kinsale was a disastrous defeat for the Irish and marked the end of the Gaelic aristocracy as a power for the English to reckon with.

Kinsale became a completely English town and, given its splendid natural harbour, an important port for the navy. It was noted for its boatbuilding. Later, during the English Civil War, the defeat of the Royalists in Cork in 1652 led to Lord Muskerry's retreat to the fortress of Ross Castle at Killarney. Today the castle sits on a peninsula jutting into Lough Leane, but it was virtually an island fortress in the seventeenth century. An old lay recorded its seeming impregnability: 'Ross which may all assaults disdain/ Till on Lough Leane strange ships shall sail.' And this is exactly what happened. One of Kinsale's shipwrights, Captain Thomas Chudleigh, designed prefabricated vessels and had them taken in pieces across some 50 miles of rough country to Killarney, where they were reassembled and launched against Ross Castle. Perhaps this shocking materialisation of the old prophecy accounted for the sudden laying down of arms by Lord Muskerry's 5,000 troops. So fell the last fortress in Ireland to stand in the way of the final Cromwellian victory.

The Chudleigh family remained well known for their boatbuilding, constructing the royal frigate HMS *Kinsale* in 1700. By the latter part of the eighteenth century, however, ships had become bigger and could no longer be accommodated in Kinsale, and the naval base was moved to Cork. Thereafter Kinsale went into decline until recent times.

OUR DESTINATION tomorrow lay 35 miles west, where we would meet Pat O'Donnell at the small inlet of Glandore. I turned on the Shipping Forecast after an acquaintance on the pontoon told me that BBC TV had shown a severe storm approaching from Newfoundland, but the radio suggested nothing more fearful for Sea Area Fastnet than north to north-westers Force 3 to 4, occasionally Force 5. All are cheerfully listed in sailing manuals as 'breezes' and even Force 6 is no more than a 'strong breeze.' I have never known it to be called that when emotions are recollected in the tranquillity of a yacht club bar.

As sausages curled crisp on our restored gas stove, I opened the *Sailing Directions of the Irish Cruising Club*. 'A race,' it declared, 'extends over one mile from the Head.... This race can be dangerous to small craft. The race can be avoided by rounding the Head close up except in south winds and any strong winds when the broken water extends right up to the Head. Under these conditions give the Head a berth of over 2 miles.' I felt one mile would be enough tomorrow. It might be a little splashy at the Head, but the north-west wind would be coming off the land, making for easy seas. With a long stretch of water between us and Glandore, it was the tides that mattered most. I turned to the *Tables*. The west-going tide would flow in our favour for nearly six hours from about 9.30 am. Sweet news for the crew, and we could probably cut a few miles off by skirting the headland.

The morning wind was fresh but coming off the shore, and we passed under the black-and-white bands of the lighthouse in smooth water and opened up Courtmacsherry Bay. The proximity of Kinsale means that Courtmacsherry is not first choice for yachts making a landfall, but the bay has anchorages well sheltered from westerly weather and they were popular in the days before engines with coasters and lobster boats from the islands to the west.

The Seven Heads came abeam. Seven Castles Head is its true name, though I could see only one ruined tower there now. Clonakilty Bay emerged. Possibly because it suffered brutally in the Famine the town has, or had, the appellation, 'Clonakilty, God help us.' Skibbereen, further west, has been called

'Skibbereen, where they ate the donkey,' and a Famine memory may lie behind that too.

The breeze grew lighter, the sails pulled gently, and *Sarakiniko* was a lullaby rolling in the sun. Joan and Anne dozed on deck, hoping their legs would turn brown. Washing hung drying on the rails. Finally the wind died, and even Anne conceded that the shadows on the water to seaward were false prophets of a returning breeze. Inland lay chequered fields and the powder-blue cones of distant hills, a countryside of modest prosperity running down to narrow inlets and lonely beaches.

Another nine miles to Galley Head and we could consider changing course north-west for Glandore. We could see the white finger of Galley Head lighthouse as we approached the Doolic Rock under engine. The depth there dropped to 14 metres at low tide – no hazard to us with *Sarakiniko*'s twin keels drawing only four feet of water – but we needed to keep clear of the well-named Sunk Rock and the Clout Rock near Galley Head. At spring tides the current runs at three knots towards the Robber Bank three miles to the south-west, and it is not a place to be in rough weather. With depths varying from 14 to 35 metres over a short distance, a tide running against a strong south-west wind can create a tumble of water like a mountain stream magnified a hundredfold.

Now we looked into Glandore Bay. Joan focused the binoculars on the slopes above the creamy line of Rosscarbery Beach.

'It's like a ruined Buckingham Palace. It's enormous!'

'It's Castle Freke,' I said.

It is enormous: an assemblage of walls and towers built from 1780 on by Sir George Evans-Freke in Romantic Gothic style. The Barons of Carbery, whose family name was Freke, were once among the biggest landowners in Co. Cork, with some 14,000 acres. This wondrous pile was gutted by fire in 1910 and rebuilt in time for the coming-of-age ball given in 1913 for the 10th Lord Carbery, one of the first Irishmen to fly his own plane – and indeed perform acrobatics to the astonishment and delight of the countryside. But, as we watched the castellations and towers set in the remains of planted woods, we wondered if His Lordship had tired of West Cork, for he emigrated to Kenya where, I expect, he enjoyed a lifestyle which could not be found around Rosscarbery.

Near the mile-wide outer entrance to Glandore Creek lay an island called Adam and about half a mile further up a smaller one called Eve. The *Sailing Directions* repeat the local saying, 'Avoid Adam and hug Eve,' for there are several rocks beyond it where the entrance narrows. We were trying to pick out Adam's profile against the coastal slopes when Joan spotted a distant yacht, apparently also bound in to Glandore, wheel about and steer towards us. We dutifully bore off to pass them port to port but still they sailed down on us. By the time I could distinguish their shouts of 'Net!' we were close upon a line of floats. *Coriander* had saved us from tangling with our first monofilament drift net.

Drift nets are laid, usually at right angles to the coast, all the way round to Ulster. They can be several miles long and their floats, set a few feet apart, are often no larger than a handball. They can be impossible to see in anything of a chop and the shape of *Sarakiniko*'s twin keels and screw almost guarantees entanglement. The usual advice is to leave one's VHF radio on in the hope of receiving a warning call from the fishing boats tending the nets, but they may be hull down on the horizon. One is also advised to carry a hay-fork to push the net down and ride over it, but *Sarakiniko* had no hay-fork.

Damage to nets is an occupational hazard for fishermen, and they cannot be expected to like it. They have a hard and dangerous living to make while we swan about, taking up valuable space in their harbours. I believe warning shots were fired at a yacht during a Round Britain Race a few years ago, though I have never had a harsh word from a trawlerman.

We dropped anchor in Glandore Harbour and made to go ashore. The dinghy had acquired a slow leak, and as I rowed Joan and Anne across I found that pushing from my feet raised my body and brought the centre of the dinghy up, while my passengers went down at either end. On the return stroke my bulk pressed down on the rubber seat while Joan and Anne rose off the water. Thus we see-sawed to the steps at the pier and disembarked with wet bottoms.

A sleepy, easygoing hamlet climbs the hill above the tiny drying harbour, occupied now by a few launches and some children struggling with an air mattress in the shallows. Through gaps in the fuchsia hedges we gazed across the limpid water, past swans and oystercatchers who were scraping a living on some margins of mud, to Union Hall, the neighbouring village on the opposite side of the creek. Dean Swift had stayed there as a guest of the local rector. He had come, grieving for the death of Stella, 'to hide in the south of Ireland'. Apparently he spent much time sailing around the coast.

The local Church of Ireland rose prettily from amongst the trees. Sylvan Glandore whispers of another age. The nineteenth-century landlord, James Barry, spent much of his 90 years helping this place. A member of one of several West Cork Catholic families who kept their wealth and prospered, he is most remembered for his work in improving fisheries. In 1819 he joined a newly created Board of Commissioners for Irish Fisheries, whose remit extended along the south and south-west coasts as far as the Shannon. He built wharves and quays in this harbour and supervised the construction of a small boatyard at Union Hall as well as a larger yard at Baltimore. As we entered the narrow neck of Glandore Harbour, we had passed a line of four rocks which lurk beneath the surface at high water, unimaginatively but truly called 'The Dangers'. They had once wrecked many vessels tacking through the entrance, and it was Barry who first had them prominently marked. He would surely have rejoiced in the fact that Glandore now hosts an annual Summer School which promotes a better appreciation of Ireland's maritime heritage.

When Pat and his family arrived at the pub we entered upon a session of self-congratulatory chatter. We felt sad at losing Anne, glad at having Pat aboard. His experience of sailing a small boat on Lough Derg had given him a true sailor's caution of the short nasty seas that can build up even on a 20-mile stretch of water, and as a farmer he knew about engines. I touched wood whenever I discussed *Sarakiniko*'s 27 horsepower diesel. It was being very well behaved, but it would do no harm for it to know that there was now one aboard who could soon get the measure of its character. I do try to see that it gets a regular supply of good clean fuel, ample oil and that the alternator gives it a regular dose of amps, and it has not done a nasty on us offshore for a couple of years. I had bought it to replace an older engine for which I had developed a smouldering resentment. That one had needed only a busy harbour or a yacht club verandah to break out in abrupt rebellion.

This present installation was supposed to whistle if it over-heated, and it will readily overheat if weed jams the intake for seawater which must rush around its innards to keep it cool. It last whistled the year before when we were 25 miles out from Milford Haven. We checked everything was weed-free and restarted. The wailing reached a higher pitch. The dying wind conspired with tidal currents not far from the reefs and tidal races aptly named The Bitches and Wild Goose Race, and it took us nine hours to return to our mooring. Next day we discovered that a defective solenoid had started the whistling and the engine was in fact in a normal state of health. Pat, I felt sure, would never have fallen for that.

A good engine is vital on the exposed western coast, where a large swell and awful sea can persist long after the gale which caused them has ceased. The lumpy sea shakes any wind there is out of the sails and makes for miserable conditions aboard a pure sailing vessel. I lay sleepless in tranquil Glandore, considering the treacherous Atlantic coast to which we were about to commit ourselves. The Irish coastal waters forecast claimed that from tomorrow south-west winds would be fresh becoming strong, with widespread rain. The barometer had fallen. All sailing, I suppose, involves acts of faith – in oneself and the crew, the boat, and the weather. I lay on my bunk, making a mental check of our resources. We had ample fuel and water at the moment, a 20 gallon tank for one, 30 for the other, and would take a can ashore at every opportunity to top up. From now on we would usually be anchoring. We had two good anchors, the plough-shaped CQR type and the traditional Fisherman, which gets a good grip on a kelpy sea floor. If we had gear strong enough to lie alongside a rough pier in a bit of a swell without damaging the boat, it might save dinghy work and wettings. I fell asleep wondering if a small plank would solve the problem.

A west wind headed us as we cleared Adam Island next morning and, anxious to get well on towards the big turning point of Mizen Head, we motored into the chop. A group of porpoises greeted us, revolving in the water like a line of semi-submerged motor tyres. Later, I was balancing over a basin in the heads, navigating a razor around some recent scars, when Joan's call of 'Net!' brought me up. A figure waved frantically from a distant fishing boat. We were thudding directly into the bobbing floats and just had time to swing about and run parallel until we reached the large buoy marking the end of the line. 'He should have called us on the VHF,' Pat said crossly. He looked at Joan. 'Mind you, the language isn't all that great sometimes.'

I squinted against the breeze, chilly enough now to bring tears to the eyes. 'I noticed a mark beyond the Stags last evening. Can you see it?'

'It's a buoy,' Pat said. 'It marks a wreck. A bulk carrier, the *Kowloon Bridge*, went on to the reefs a few years ago.'

I recalled it now, that disaster of November 1986. The monster vessel, 190,000 tons of steel carrying many thousand tons of iron ore, ended up on the rocks over there. A British scrap dealer, Sean Kent, bought the lot for £1. Costly as salvage may be, he believed he could make a profit of £1 a ton on the cargo. The *Kowloon Bridge* was a sister ship of the *Derbyshire,* whose loss in a typhoon off Japan in 1980 is under inquiry. Some 300 bulk carriers have been lost at sea in the past 20 years.

From the north the Stags look strangely like ships under sail. We were to see several such named rock formations off the coast. They were once called 'cruach' or 'stuaic'; the Irish was translated into 'stacks' and the word was then slurred to become 'stags'. As we approached the great rocks, we passed the delightful natural harbour of Castletownshend, a place of humpy little fields, open ditches and bogs. Here was the home of Edith Somerville, whose *Some Experiences of an Irish RM*, written with Violet Martin, immortalised a slice of Irish life with patronising accuracy.

The families of the landed gentry, the Somervilles, the Coghills and the Townshends, lived in seigneurial isolation around the Protestant church of St Barrhane which we could see beyond the estuary, its pinnacles rising like spears above the trees. The Catholic church is well out of sight over a mile away towards Skibbereen. Edith Somerville played the organ in St Barrhane's for some 70 years. It is more family shrine than church – one wall is given over to a marble tablet recording at length the history of the Townshends – but I also saw an oar from a *Lusitania* lifeboat resting near the belfry stairs. This simple piece of wood was placed 'in memory of the twenty-seven victims whose bodies were brought ashore in Castletownshend.'

An enterprising shipowning ancestor brought prosperity to the Townshends in the mid-eighteenth century by trading out of here, mainly to the West Indies. The harbour was considered one of the three most important on this coast, comparable to Baltimore or Berehaven in Bantry Bay, and Castletownshend became such a centre of trade and provisioning that it enjoyed its own splendidly built Custom House. It was not just an important base for fishing vessels; in these remote and rocky regions most heavy goods were transported by water. Into the Coal Quay at Castletownshend came the coal boats from Bristol. To the flour mill upriver at Rineen went the flour boats and smaller craft, many made by a local boatbuilding family, the O'Mahoneys, who turned out fishing boats, sailing dinghies and pleasure craft for the quality. The combination of sheltered water and a clutch of houses of the gentry resulted in the Castletownshend Regatta. They called it Calves, the minor edition of Cowes. Calves Week still thrives and in our democratic age is held in the first week of August further up the coast at Schull.

Edith Somerville and her relations sailed in a range of splendid boats. There was Sir Jocelyn Coghill's schooner *Ierne,* called after the name Greek geographers gave to Ireland. *Ierne* broke up on rocks in a storm in 1917. There were yachts like *Thea, Gyneth* and *Haidee,* and delicate little sailing gigs like *Mori Chi.* The latter was a gift to Edith from an importunate swain; its name is

Romany for 'My Girl'. Edith's diary records a cruise to Glengarriff in 1879. She suffered from seasickness. 'On board Gyneth at 11 and peaceful run as far as the Mizen. Fainted in a rough swell after the Mizen. Mrs Warren sick overboard.'

Set against the land near the entrance to Castletownshend, I could see Horse Island, separated from the shore by Flea Sound. A fisherman in a Baltimore pub once assured me that, by the time horses had swum across to pasture on the small island, not a single tick remained on their coats. As the island faded in the distance, I went below to check on our progress. There seemed a good chance now that we would reach the anchorage of Crookhaven, close to the Mizen, before the weather worsened. Ten miles beyond the Stags, near the entrance to Baltimore, lay the Gascanane Sound which divides Clear Island from the mainland. By going through the sound we would reach Long Island Bay, and once across the bay we would find the long inlet of Croookhaven. If the weather held that would be our departure point for Mizen Head tomorrow. Then we would set a course to the north-west.

Approaching these most southerly points of Ireland, the country looked as if were running out of substance, turning into rocky terrain and untidy lumps of land that seem tossed at random towards the sea. The whole weight of Ireland was felt behind one, while ahead were rocks and scraps of islands petering out in an expanse of ocean. The great headlands lay beyond. If I looked at my upturned right hand, the palm could represent inland Co. Cork, the little finger the coast that lies along the north shore of Long Island Bay, with Mizen Head at my fingertip. The bays of Bantry (with Dunmanus Bay beside it) and of Kenmare and Dingle would be the three spaces between my fingers and, out from them, the islands that face the Atlantic. The first is Dursey, then Valentia off the tip of the middle finger and the Blasket Islands off the forefinger. The thumb might even be imagined as a pointer to the great estuary of the River Shannon or, away to the north, the sea cliffs of Co. Clare.

Perhaps the majority of Irish promontories sport ruined towers. There had been one on Toe Point near the Stags; now we could see another as we passed Spain Point, a ruin with gutted windows which was occupied by the army as late as 'The Emergency', as the Second World War was known in Ireland. Many signal towers were built in reaction to the abortive plans for a French invasion during the French Revolutionary Wars; the one on Toe Point dates from shortly after the French attempt to land at Bantry Bay in 1796. The *Cork Remembrancer* records that 'On December 30th, 1803, Captain Maguire R.N. arrived in this city to attend to the erection of Signal Posts along the coast', and the following year it reported that buildings to lodge a naval officer, his assistant and some armed men were placed near the signal posts 'so constructed that they were entered by a ladder from the top'. Each tower on the south-west had a signalling system which kept it in touch with two others, and it was claimed that the whole coast could be alerted within an hour.

Several signal towers had been built in the seventeenth century after the Sack of Baltimore in 1631, when two Algerian ships had sailed into the harbour and taken 117 people, most of whom lived out their lives as slaves on the Barbary coast. In 1649 an envoy sent by the English parliament secured the release of only two, at £30 a head. The poet Thomas Davis wrote of the event:

The yell of Allah breaks above the prayer, the shriek, the roar.

Oh! Blessed God, the Algerine is Lord of Baltimore.

How vulnerable small shore-based communities were when the nearest militia force was a few hour's ride away, while a fresh wind on a galley's sails could bring it over the horizon so quickly.

We passed the great white sugarloaf beacon, shown on old charts as Lot's Wife, which marks the entrance to Baltimore. A few yachts of the Glenans Sailing Centre emerged. The harbour is a nearly ideal sailing ground for small craft, stretching a mile across each way, with its only flaw being a mid-harbour shoal charted as the Lousy Rocks. Time did not allow a nostalgic visit to Baltimore. Years ago I had induced fellow London barristers to have our Bar Yacht Club challenge the Baltimore Sailing Club to a dinghy race and persuaded several members to readjust their holiday plans so that they might come. As hosts the Baltimore Club had choice of weapons. They selected their ten-foot Mirror dinghies, crewed by wily children who grinned at us over their life-jackets. In familiar craft and home water, they beat us hollow, a victory eased only by the condition we were in after the previous night's hospitality from the delightful Musgrave family. Accidents there were none, though in any case two heart surgeons from Dublin, an orthopaedic specialist and several doctors were on holiday in the village that August. Today the defeated would likely be offered counselling.

The history of Baltimore revolves around boats and fishing. It has been calculated that in the sixteenth century the revenue from fishing, boat dues and licences may have reached an annual £1m in modern money. Such a valuable resource was also a source of conflict. Gaelic chiefs like the O'Driscolls charged fees for the right to fish their waters, while the English administration promulgated decrees, such as that of 1465, against 'foreign fishermen without licence fishing among the King's Irish enemies'.

The Sack of Baltimore devastated the town and many people moved inland, but the pilchard fisheries recovered in time. As well as levying fees on the fisheries, the O'Driscolls charged rents on the processing bases ashore, where pilchards were salted, cured and compressed to exude 'train oil' for rushlight lamps and the curing of leather. Traces of curing houses – called 'palaces' locally – still exist, one near the Baltimore Beacon.

The first Earl of Cork introduced the seine net to the southwest, a mesh 600 to 800 feet long and over 40 feet deep, which two boats would help to close between them. In the early eighteenth century, mackerel and herring gradually replaced the pilchard, and they were much sought by the French, despite local people's objections. In May 1770 a Cork newspaper reported a fleet of 300 French vessels off the coast; in April 1786 a Revenue cutter claimed to have sighted 200 French boats fishing between Baltimore and Crookhaven. Mackerel shoals grew sparse through the first half of the nineteenth century, but their reappearance around 1860 created much activity in salting and exporting. The scale of industry all along the coast is hard to grasp now. During the First World War up to 16 trains left Baltimore each day loaded with salted mackerel. In 1925, 20,000 barrels of West

Cork mackerel were exported to America. When America eventually imposed tariffs to protect its own fisheries, this area suffered badly. By the 1960s Irish government subsidies were helping to revive the fishing industry, though in the new age of large-scale trawling, the big boats have moved further along the coast to ports like Berehaven in Bantry Bay.

After that ill-fated contest with the children of Baltimore, I had wandered off to watch the skeletons of new boats taking shape by the harbour slipways. A Fisheries School had been opened in 1886 to teach fishing and boat building to local children, and though it closed in 1951 for lack of boys, there were two ship-building yards in the area and a third lay out on the road to Skibbereen. The famous small-boat sailor, Conor O'Brien, who circled the world in 1923-25 – a remarkable feat at the time – recalls in his book *From Three Yachts* that when seas damaged his earlier boat *Kelpie* off Mayo, he took her to Baltimore for repair. His next boat, *Saoirse*, was built in Tom Moynihan's yard as was later still a third vessel, the 56-foot *Ilen*. O'Brien sailed *Ilen* to the Falklands in 1926 as a Service Vessel. She was bigger than *Saoirse* but, as he wrote, 'of the same general type'. After retiring from the sea, *Ilen* might have mouldered away in Port Stanley, but the *Ilen* Trust was formed in 1997 to buy her. She was shipped to Dublin where she will be restored, and will eventually be based at Limerick and kept in commission, sailing in the waters she regularly used before her migration to the Southern Ocean. Back at Baltimore building continues, a new boatyard having been established in 1952 for the construction of trawlers and lobster boats.

For us Gascanane Sound lay close ahead. In the centre of the half-mile passage lie the Carrigmore Rocks, so we swung from west to north-west through a patch of short, steep sea which threw fans of spray from the bows. Pat stood, eyes half shut, tiller braced against his hip. Treacherous fringes of black rock swept past. We could soon see the western side of Cape Clear and presently the narrow entrance to North Harbour and the road climbing out of it past gorse-covered cliffs. Faced with a forecast of nasty weather, we had no time for a visit, but I had been there ten years earlier.

Cape Clear (only strangers call it Clear Island) is the final survivor in the south-west of the beleaguered Irish-speaking islands. The island's outer harbour is small and the inner one tiny. I remember the crane fixed over its entrance ready to lower a dozen baulks of wood into slots on the walls when local boats crowded in for refuge, and the curious explanation offered by a cheerful Caper that the timber was 'not to keep out the swell but the draw'. The island was disorganised and picturesque: heaps of lobster pots, boats in various stages of decay and the ruined church of Teampall Ciaran, built around 1200 on the site of an earlier monastery. Our island guide took our lines and looked astonished when I asked if there was a pub. He pointed up the hill: 'You can see three from here and that ould shed is the Cape Clear Night Club.' Burke's was the nearest. There was slow talk in the dim interior of the night of the great gale in 1941, and the walls displayed yellowing photographs of vessels with names like *Jasmine Dowlings*, *The Faith* and *Carbery King*.

The travelling clergyman Richard Pococke came to the island in 1758 in critical and perhaps credulous mood. 'The great vice here is drinking Spirits which even some of them they say do to a gallon a day. They were alarmed at seeing our boat, thinking it was the King's, as they had laid in a store of Rum from the West India fleet which had lately passed. They were glad to be undeceived, though when an officer not long ago made a seizure, the women rescued it.'

The old schoolhouse had been converted into a museum which showed how pilchards were compressed and how 'haffity' was made. Haffity was a cheap cotton or calico steeped in linseed and treated with egg yoke to make protective clothing for fishermen before the development of the oilskin. There were photocopies of entries from the Down Survey of Ireland of 1650, and some fine examples of its bureaucratic precision: 'J. Doherty. Ir. Papst. 16.8 acres.' There was something charming in the account of the deception said to have once been used by the English against possible French or Spanish landings: they set lines of stones upright on the cliffs and painted them red to represent redcoated soldiers. The locals called them *Fir bréaga*, the false men.

As we sailed by the island, half a mile west of the harbour we could discern the shattered tower of an O'Driscoll castle, one of the many which lie along this coast. O'Driscoll rule once embraced all of south-west Cork but, even before the Anglo-Norman invasion in the twelfth century, other Irish septs, such as the O'Mahoneys, O'Sullivans and the O'Donovans, encroached on them, and they came to be reduced to the areas around Baltimore.

As we reached a point some four miles beyond the Bill of Clear at the tip of the island, we saw a tall angular rock of granite rising from the sea: the Fastnet. I squinted through the swinging dial of the handbearing compass and, when the great rock and its light-house bore due south, noted 'Fastnet abeam' in the log and marked the time, as if we had crossed the Atlantic. The Fastnet, turning point of so many ocean races. Now we were really on the way.

'A milestone achieved,' I said.

'It's been called that, hasn't it,' said Pat. 'Paddy's Milestone.'

I pointed to the rock. 'It was often the last bit of the country the emigrants saw as they left for America, so it was also called the "Teardrop of Ireland".'

TWO

To the Kingdom of Kerry

THE WIND FAILED and we drifted on the tide. Beer cans hissed open. Joan passed up sandwiches. Presently we turned on the engine and began to make a bowline across Roaringwater Bay. Inshore were more than a dozen islands and islets beyond number spread out like cards on a table. The slopes of Mount Gabriel lay farther back, its summit capped by the domes of aircraft tracking stations. Under Gabriel, tucked away in a corner of a fine natural harbour, was the neat little village of Schull.

I have seen Schull Harbour carrying as many sails as when the French mackerel boats crowded in here before the First World War: the village is on the international race circuit for teenage sailors and the yachting set proper gather here for the regatta season. Angling, windsurfing, dinghy rentals, diving: the sea has proved a recreational asset which the long departed families of the islands in the bay – Carbery's Hundred Isles – could never have imagined.

The three Calf Islands were nearest now – West, Middle and East – each about half a mile across. Pat guided us carefully between some lobster-pot buoys and we edged towards the shallows. We could see the triangular gables of ruined cottages on the islands, some cattle silhouetted like cormorants on spits of the shore. Long Island lay a few miles over the starboard bow. It is the biggest island, a two mile strip of treeless and rather featureless land, but 240 people once inhabited its 160 acres.

They lived a subsistence life. There is a story of a family of eight crossing to Schull at the start of winter to sell their boots to raise money to pay the rent, and they remained without footwear until spring. But the farmer-fishermen have almost all gone now. Some years ago Bernard O'Regan, Honorary Life President of the Mizen Archaeological Society, recorded his recollections of the

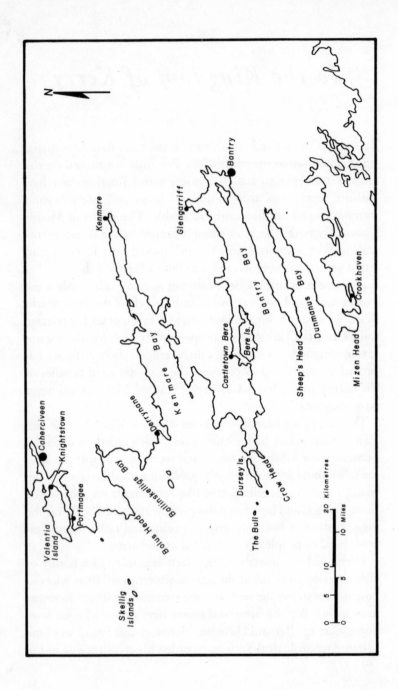

life they led. He could remember the community gathering sea-weed to fertilise the potato crop. 'When I'd be getting up from bed I'd see at least forty boats dredging in the bay. People on the mainland rented stations of weed and cut it themselves.... My grandfather drew a lot of rocks down to one of our strands and the weed grew on them. We would cut sixty horse cart loads of manure every year.'

Shipwreck was a boon. 'The *Savona* in 1890 came in and struck the West Calf in the middle of the night with all sails set and nobody on board. They had been taken off further out at sea. She was laden with timber and, in the morning, you could walk across from the middle of West Calf on timber and the whole bay filled with it. Many of the houses round here were built with it.'

People and goods moved more conveniently on water than over bad roads and rutted tracks. On market day islanders rowed across to the mainland to sell eggs and butter, and to have their farm implements repaired and corn milled. In the autumn they cut sally rods along the inlets and fetched them home to make pots for the lobster season. Boats travelled wherever the tide could reach, up the Ilen river to Skibbereen or along the inlet to Ballydehob. 'People came by boat from Schull and Goleen [near Crookhaven] to do the shopping, especially at Christmas.... The big coal boats and maize boats could come up only as far as Oldcourt. The cargoes were then taken up to Skibbereen on what were called "lighters", pushed up river by six men, three each side, with long poles.' Just two generations ago, cargoes of lime-rich sand and kelp ('ribbons and clouts') were being brought into Skibbereen and Ballydehob to fertilise inland farms, returning with loads of turf to warm the islanders' homes.

Some years ago we had sailed up Skibbereen's river. It was a dreamlike half-hour, helming a sea-going yacht through tranquil narrows, a breath of following wind just filling the jib. Herons lifted reluctantly as we passed and an otter swam across our bow towards a few heathery acres called Quarantine Island, which lies near the much larger Spanish Island on the back entrance to Baltimore Harbour. An excavation carried out in 1990 on one of the smaller islands, Skeam West, revealed shards of Spanish

Merida ware from the sixteenth and seventeenth century. This ware was not traded outside Spain and must have been carried here by sailors or soldiers. The flourishing fishing industry, wine and salt trade, as well as the need for fresh provisions, brought many Continental ships to the area.

The wind returned, coming light and southerly for the moment. Pat wound up the long triangle of white canvas, flogging and rattling before it settled into a smooth curve, and made a final tightening half-turn with the winch handle. *Sarakiniko* heeled. Joan emerged from the companionway holding the book she had been reading in her bunk.

'Look,' I said, swinging an arm, 'we're sailing.'

We could hear the bow wave, bubbling and building. The entrance to Crookhaven emerged from the dull haze and we saw the towering ruin of Leamcon Castle beyond the point of Long Island. Built about 500 years ago by an O'Mahony chief, it stood at the tip of the peninsula, looming over the whole western corner of Long Island Bay. It remained in O'Mahony hands, off and on, until Conor O'Mahony finally lost it when he was proclaimed an outlaw after the Rebellion of 1641.

Many years earlier the land surrounding the castle had been leased to William Hull, a planter who had moved to Cork from Devonshire. He was appointed Deputy Vice-admiral of Munster in 1609 to administer the Laws of Admiralty, the ancient code which governed maritime affairs outside national land boundaries. It ruled on disputes such as damage to ships by collision, rights of salvage, claims for shipwreck and for prize in time of war. In earlier times, Ireland had had its own rules of the sea. The Brehon Laws codified in the *Book of Achill* in the eight or ninth century declared, for example, that articles cast up by the ocean belonged to the owner of the shore, that goods rescued from beyond nine waves belonged to the rescuer and that wrecked ships above a certain value should have the cargo divided between the chief, the clan and the shore owner.

The first known Admiral of Ireland under English rule was appointed in 1335. His courts were jealous of their jurisdiction; indeed a practice developed of hanging pirates on gibbets set in tidal waters in order to avoid conflict with the assize courts ashore. By the seventeenth century, when bands of pirates known as 'pecharoons' infested the coasts, there were four Vice-admiral's Courts, one for each province. Hall's appointment was important, for he had large estates and wide interests. He and Robert Boyle, first Earl of Cork, developed Crookhaven, expanded its pilchard fisheries and exported fish to places as far away as the south of France. We would see the ruins of their fish 'palace' near our anchorage this afternoon.

As Admiralty judge, Hall had the curious title of Commissioner for Treating with Pirates in Munster. It was a position he used in his own interest, taking a commission on the sale of ships' booty as well as buying and selling cargo. The creeks and inlets of this wild and remote coast were a haven for pirates in the first half of the seventeenth century. Some came from Devon and Cornwall when their bases there were threatened by the growth of the Royal Navy. Many were Dutch: our chart showed Amsterdam Rock and Amsterdam Reef close to the Leamcon inlet. The inlet itself dries out, so the pirates would hide not far away beneath the low cliffs of Goleen Creek. A Dutchman, Peter Easton, who assumed command of a pirate ship in 1610 by the simple expedient of throwing his wounded captain overboard, eventually had 13 ships using Leamcon, where his crew set up their women and children in dwellings ashore. His career did not last for long. In 1616 a Dutch ship attacked him at anchor in Crookhaven where he was captured and no doubt hanged.

Another Dutchman, Claus Campeon, used his base in the south-west to waylay the great East Indiamen as they passed by the Spanish and Portuguese coasts. It is said that he may have captured some 100 ships a year; certainly he became extremely rich, rich enough to buy a pardon from the Dutch government, become a respectable citizen, and publish his autobiography before his death. The booty from the East Indiamen was taken either to the small republic of Salee on the north African coast or to Leamcon in Co. Cork. Pirates needed markets. Records show a Mr Boyle of Waterford purchasing tobacco, spice and elephants' teeth, and a man from Kenmare buying bed-coverings and canopies which had come off a ship 'from the Canary Islands'. When some 16 pounds of 'massy gold' was stolen from Campeon by a Cork army officer, the pirate took the unfortunate officer and forced a confession from him.

Campeon and Sir William Hull retained the friendship of the Lord Deputy of Ireland, Lord Falkland, sharing their profits with him in return for information on official moves against pirates. By the 1630s, however, English and other navies had become sufficiently powerful to chase pirates in more distant waters, and Hull decided to become more law abiding. He wrote to the Earl of Cork about seeing the lateen sails of the Algerian ships that had just sacked Baltimore in June 1641, 'plying off and on near Mizen Head' for 'the past eight or nine days'. 'If these pirates are not driven off trade will be ruined and the people will be utterly unable to pay their debts,' he warned officiously.

Hall was attacked by both sides in the Rebellion of 1641 and suffered great losses, and the English officer Captain Cole who burned Crosshaven, Leamcon and Schull, all of them Hull's property, may have been acting under official orders. But Hull's descendants carried on the connection with Leamcon. Pococke reported them in the eighteenth century to be living on the nearby Coney Island, and it was a Mr Hull of Leamcon who, in 1796, saw the French invasion fleet off the coast and sent warning to Mr White of Bantry.

The wind blew blustery as Leamcon fell astern. Such places were notorious centres of piracy in their day, but in the weeks to come we would see many a cove where modern high-speed craft could run ashore undetected and land a cargo of drugs or guns. It would be naive to believe that smuggling does not still happen.

Crookhaven was just ahead. Its entrance faces due east so the inlet has shelter from the Atlantic seas, but wind can sweep down the shallow valley of the inlet and the entrance by Rock Island is no more than 300 metres wide.

'I think we might have the sails down and go in under engine,' I said. 'We don't want to anchor too far off the village quay, but if there are other boats in we may have to jill about looking for a good spot.'

I came head to wind as we approached Rock Island with its two high towers, erected to spot smugglers. Pat pulled down and tamed the thrashing mainsail with four ties around the boom and moved on to the bow.

'How much chain will you need?'

'Probably 20 metres for a start. It's marked in fathoms: red tag at five and another at ten. We can let out more once we grip.'

At high water we should probably find ourselves lying in seven metres and would need at least three times that length of anchor-chain, indeed four times as much in a windy anchorage. Joan hauled on the reefing line and the jib furled itself neatly around the forestay. She switched on the echo-sounder and watched it signal our depth. The ritual exchanges began as to where to drop.

'You're down to eight feet.'

'I can go on further.'

'No. You'll be too close to them.' Two other yachts were in, French and German ensigns stiff in the breeze.

'Not if the wind doesn't shift.'

'Well I think you should drop now!'

Pat was at the bow, well out of reach of the dispute between skipper and first mate. He had the CQR anchor ready to let go.

'Lower it!' The chain clattered over the bow roller. I gave us a burst of reverse to dig the anchor in and we stood in the cockpit for a while to check that we were holding. All was well.

Joan put the kettle on. I unfolded the chart 'Cork Harbour to Dingle Bay' on the saloon table and ran a finger along it. We might have to make a break for it if the weather was going to get worse over the next few days.

'It's about six miles to Mizen Head. Eight from here, allowing for going back down the harbour. Then its north-west and north all the way up to Kerry.'

Pat leaned over. 'To Derrynane?'

'Yes. The most beautiful little harbour in Ireland.' I walked the dividers across the expanse of blue. 'It looks like about 33 miles. Nothing to it.'

'Except Atlantic swell,' said Joan.

Pat turned in mock alarm. 'Is that a fact now, skipper?' He

went on deck to check the wind, which clearly was increasing. 'It's harrowing the water,' he reported.

A brisk walk might put nautical problems in perspective, so we inflated the dinghy and pulled across, getting out on the sandy floor of the old dock, now almost drained by the ebbing tide. The dock would once have been the site of endless bustle as ships' boats hurried to and fro from the windjammers anchored off Crookhaven. It is said that the harbour floor is littered with empty rum bottles.

Bernard O'Regan recalled that 'All the big sailing ships, the tea clippers, when they came across the ocean rounded the Mizen and anchored off Crookhaven. Those deep-sea men would not take their ships up the Irish Sea or the English Channel at all, because they felt they did not know the currents and the tides and these ships could not work their way offshore if they got in too close; they were not good at going into the wind. So the Cape Clear pilots took over the ships at Crookhaven. They might then be six months away. They might have to go to Dublin, Liverpool or Bristol and they would have to wait for another ship to bring them back – or even be piloting the same ship back again.'

Crookhaven had 'agents from every big shipping company, and they gave instructions where each ship would have to go because the cargoes would have been sold while they were at sea'. Lying at the south-western tip of Ireland, this fine harbour had immense significance in the days of sail. As a vital port of call it became a provisioning depot, especially during the Napoleonic Wars, when Britain's need for meat, corn and butter brought prosperity to many Irish farms. And, as elsewhere, fleets of mackerel boats berthed at Crookhaven in the early twentieth century,

We walked to the pier at the far side of the harbour, near which the ruins of quarry buildings and the walls of a pilchard processing plant operated by the notorious Sir William Hall and his partner Sir Richard Boyle stood entangled in briars and nettles. Out of the village then past spongy fields and bony hillocks, and although it was now beginning to rain seriously, a man, surely with hope in triumph over experience, was slowly turning swathes of hay with a pitchfork. The road separated two farming eras: on the other side were dozens of bales of silage, wrapped in black plastic and flagged to deter the crows. 'When they see themselves mirrored in the shiny plastic they attack,' Pat explained. At the end of a wet grassy track lay the little Church of Ireland, shut up, looking unused. It was once the only church in Crookhaven, so Catholics would row across the harbour and walk the six miles to Goleen. We could decipher only one tombstone, deep in the brambles, for a child of six years 'drowned on the morning of 10th. August, 1826 at Rock Island.' On impulse we cleared away the moss growing over the inscription.

As we turned back to the village we could see a caravan park beyond the shallows at the end of the harbour. 'Good cash crop that,' Pat remarked. The caravans and the medley of bungalows offering Bed and Breakfast probably explained Crookhaven's air of neat prosperity, but the bungalows looked sadly alien with their patios and balustrades of reconstituted stone. Before we bemoan the passing of the Paul Henry thatch and whitewash, let us ask which we would wish a family to spend a winter in, but it would be pleasant to see someone building a two-storey dwelling or houses more in keeping with the countryside.

On the outskirts of the village we found Marconi House, now in part a restaurant. It may not have been only geographical location which encouraged Marconi to carry out so much work in Ireland; he had an Irish mother and his second wife, Anna, one of the Jameson distillery family, was born in Co. Wexford. In 1896 he applied for the first patent granted in wireless telegraphy and, two years later, Lloyds of London commissioned him to fix a link between Rathlin Island and Ballycastle in Co. Antrim. By 1907 a massive station, with eight huge masts, a turf-fired generating unit and over 150 employees was set up at Clifden, Co. Galway, and connected to Cape Breton Island, Nova Scotia. It was the world's first fixed point-to-point station. Here in the south, where busy sea lanes ran past the Irish coast, he made contact with a ship 18 miles off shore. That success prompted the building of his station at Crookhaven, which was opened in June 1901. Soon afterwards Marconi succeeded in gaining signals from Cornwall, 225 miles away. He was confident now of bridging the Atlantic, and did so six months later.

One survivor of the Marconi days remained in Crookhaven long after the communications revolution which brought him here had passed into history. Arthur Nottage came from England in 1904 as a telegrapher on the Morse code apparatus, which he worked until 1914. Thereafter he became landlord of the Welcome Inn and, on occasion, would show visitors like us his original handwritten logs. He died in 1974, aged 90.

The tide had risen and the wind too. Pat emerged from a phone-box, having spoken to his wife Madeline and her sister, Aline, who were having a short holiday in the south-west. On the off-chance that we might be weatherbound tomorrow, they would drive over from Schull in the morning. We hurried for the dinghy to catch the forecast at 6.23 pm. The rain had diminished, but it was a stiff wet crabbing row back to *Sarakiniko*.

The Irish forecast for coastal waters is preceded by a review of farming stock prices.

'The barometer has fallen,' I said, pulling off my oilskin and reaching for pencil and pad.

'So have lamb prices,' Pat muttered glumly.

When we heard that the Force 6 to 7 winds were set to become 8, a full gale, it seemed fitting to open the gin. The demon hidden in boats – we call him Murphy – waited until we were sitting comfortably before setting the rigging clattering against the mast. It felt as if one was in the sound-box of an out-of-tune harp. Back into oilskins and a clamber to the bow to tighten lines even more. Anticipating weather like this when fitting out, I had shaped a piece of rigid transparent plastic to fit the companion-way opening so we could keep our daylight and shut out the cold. The swinging brass lamp and the aroma of Joan's stew raised the temperature, a bottle of Merlot added to our comfort, and the evening grew quite cosy. I had let more chain out and, despite the clunks from the cable and *Sarakiniko*'s slew and stumble, I was confident that she would remain firmly attached to Crookhaven. The boat gyrated in the wind like a skittish horse, but we slept well. I woke just once to see Pat snoring gently, lying on the saloon bunk, hands folded on his chest like the tombstone effigy of a Norman knight.

By morning the wind had moderated but visibility was now very poor. The ship's company agreed that the view of the rollers off Mizen Head would look better today from the cliffs than from sea level, so we squeezed into the O'Donnell car and set off for the lighthouse buildings.

Mizen was established in 1910 as a fog signal station. In pre-foghorn days, the keepers set off a charge of explosive at three-minute intervals as a warning to ships, and a fog signal continued to sound here up until 20 years ago when sonar and satellite navigation took over. Mizen acquired a light in 1959. At that time there were nearly 200 lighthouse keepers and over 100 light-ship men along the Irish coast. As we made our tour, only three lights remained manned: the Baily at Howth, the Hook near Waterford and the Mew in Co. Down, and they would soon be fully automatic. When the last lighthouse keepers left the Mizen in 1993, a local community group signed a lease with the Commissioners of Irish Lights and re-opened the lighthouse to the public, an imaginative move which brought some 27,000 visitors to 'The Mizen Vision' in 1994.

Lights along the coast matter a great deal to local boats and to ships coming in from the Atlantic. In 1782, the MP for Kilkenny complained that there was no lighthouse between the Shannon and Kinsale, some 150 miles of coastline which was a landfall for ships in the Hudson Bay, Quebec, Newfoundland, North American and West Indies trade. Regularly they would outrun their reckoning and sail into bays on dark nights, imagining themselves miles from land. The 'prodigious indraft and western swell' threw ships on to the coast, and though sometimes the appearance of a Revenue officer with a guard of soldiers or the arrival of a naval ship with the hated press gang aboard would deter the locals from rushing to the scene, usually, the Kilkenny MP concluded, masts and rigging were cut away and the cargo carried off.

In response to such complaints, the first light on the south coast – apart from the ancient Hook Tower at the entrance to Waterford – was built on Cape Clear in 1810, but it was set so high that in thick fog its beam was obscured. When in 1847 an American ship, the *Stephen Whitney*, sank on a reef off Cape Clear with the loss of 100 lives, the tragedy impelled a decision to select the Fastnet Rock, eight miles south-east of Mizen Head, as the new site for a lighthouse.

A cast-iron tower built on the rock was ready by 1854, but it was found to need regular repair and strengthening. That pioneer among small boat sailors, R.T. McMullen, whose voyages around our coasts in the nineteenth century are sailing classics, records in *Down Channel*: 'July 16th 1869... at 2.40 pm passed Cape Clear. There was evidently some great work being carried on at the Fastnet Rock. I have since been informed that they have been engaged nearly three years filling up a gap which endangered the lighthouse.'

Work on a new structure began in 1899. Sheltering near the telephone-box the previous evening, I had met Stephen O'Sullivan, a former lighthouse man at Mizen, who told me the project was completed without a fatality. It was an enormous undertaking. Over 2,000 interlocking blocks of granite, weighing three to five tons each, were carved and fitted in Cornwall, numbered and loaded on to a specially built ship, the *Irene*, for transportation to Ireland. The jigsaw was put together for checking on Rock Island at Crookhaven, dismantled again, taken out to the Fastnet and finally assembled.

From the top of the Mizen cliffs we peered down on the swirl of foam sucking at the rocks 200 feet below us. Mr Charles Haughey, former Taoiseach, had come onto these rocks in thick weather in 1985. 'Engine failure?' I asked an old man who was charming some tourists near by.

'I expect so,' he replied. 'Sure, he had the luck. By the time the lifeboat came they were over an hour in the life-raft.' He raised a finger and glared at me. 'One hour and 20 minutes.'

Since then Mr Haughey has shown me a photograph he took at a party to mark the anniversary of the incident, with his crew and rescuers standing at the railings where we were now. I craned my neck for another look at the turbulence below. It would have been impossible to climb the cliffs.

BACK ON *Sarakiniko* the radio spoke of Force 5 and 6 winds from the south-west, 'locally Force 7'. I lost myself in the small print of Reed's *Nautical Almanac.* Tomorrow we faced a difficult passage. During spring tides a four-knot current runs off the Mizen, causing a dangerous race when the wind sets against the tide. The fortnightly springs would have eased by tomorrow, but the *Tables* showed the tide flowing east against us until about noon. As we were aiming to leave early, we would have to plug into it for about six miles under engine until we could turn the corner and get the south-westerly on our beam as we crossed the mouths of Dunmanus and Bantry Bays. That should fetch us to the sound between Dursey Island and the mainland, a short-cut to Kenmare Bay and the landlocked anchorage of Derrynane waiting on the far side.

The narrow sound was a problem. We might meet a different wind on either side and had to be prepared for sudden changes as we went through, especially at the northern end where heavy squalls can come off the high ground. Salmon nets were often laid just north of the north entrance, and it would be very dangerous to get on to one.

My notebook became a tangle of speculation as I explored more and more conjunctions of wind and water. The main thing would be to have a favourable tide pushing us through Dursey Sound, and we would have that from midday onwards. I surfaced from the books and charts and said we should leave at six in the morning. The crew took it well.

Madeline and Aline had left for Schull, promising to look out for us in Kerry. We were on deck, putting one reef in the mainsail against the likelihood of fresh winds tomorrow, when the topping lift came adrift. This is the line from the top of the mast to the end of the boom and is normally kept taut in harbour. It was entirely my fault: I had ineffectively spliced the fitting that secures the line to the boom. The wind carried it aloft, all 45 feet of it, writhing like a pennant from the masthead. In a calm it would have hung vertically and been readily recaptured; now I had to sit into the bosun's chair and be hoisted until I was far enough aloft to catch it with a boathook. Perhaps we were being overcautious to first raise the anchor and nose in alongside the dock, but the boat was rolling and pitching in the wind. At least the sight of a sheepish skipper waving to the sky with a boathook cheered up the locals in O'Sullivan's Bar.

The wind was a light westerly as we thudded towards Mizen Head next morning. The race was having a Sunday morning lie in, showing itself only by little wavelets running here and there and circles of curiously smooth water. In fact we stood a few miles to the west before making our turn: by motoring out for a few more miles we could get the wind at a better angle and lay Dursey Sound on one tack. *Sarakiniko,* with her twin keels, should concede that she is a cruiser-racer rather than a racer-cruiser, and her owner, with reluctant honesty, that she begins to get moving only at 50 degrees to the wind.

With the sails up, the big headlands began to draw past. Three Castles Head, with the triple tower structure which gives the promontory of Dún Locha this Anglicised name, bore yet another O'Mahony castle, in remarkably sound condition considering that it has faced the Atlantic weather since the thirteenth century or earlier. Sheep's Head loomed ahead of us, edged in foam. It bears a monument to those who died when an east-bound Air India jet was destroyed by a terrorist in 1985. A schoolfriend of Pat's niece had lost her family that night.

Bantry Bay, scene of a fateful moment in Irish history, was opening up to starboard. On 21 December 1796 a French fleet arrived here, 35 ships with 12,000 battle-hardened veterans who had slipped past the blockading British squadrons off Brest five days before. Dreaming of an Irish republic, Dublin barrister Wolfe Tone had persuaded the French Directory to attempt a mass landing. The plan was to expel the British from Ireland with the help of Tone's United Irishmen. For the French it would be a preliminary to the invasion of England.

Tone was on board the 80-gun flagship, but as the Commander-in-Chief, General Hoche, had become separated from the main body and had not yet arrived, it was decided to wait for him off Bantry. All that day the fleet lay waiting, the wind light and the sea calm. Conditions were ideal for a landing. The military and naval base at Cork lay almost undefended only 90 miles away.

A longboat went ashore, but it was captured at Lonehort Cove on the south-east corner of Bere Island. The following day an east wind resumed, freshening into squalls of rain and snow. The fleet began to lose contact. Square-rigged ships do not lie as close to the wind as modern yachts, and looking up this bay now, long but usually only three miles wide, one could see why the French could not beat against the wind into the shelter of the bay's coves. 'I am now so near the shore,' Tone wrote, 'that I can in a manner touch the sides of Bantry Bay with my right and left hand; yet God knows whether I shall ever tread again on Irish ground.' By Christmas Eve the gale had become a storm. The admiral signalled to the 14 remaining ships to cut their cables and run.

On the night of 27 December, as they fled towards France, a hurricane blew. Tone was woken by a sea smashing into the great stern gallery. When a window caved in the cabin filled with water and he was resigned to death. The ship survived, however, as did Wolfe Tone, who recorded that England had not been in such peril since the Spanish Armada. He was probably correct. The demands of the French War meant that there were perhaps no more than 5,000 regular infantry and cavalry in Ireland and fewer than 10,000 troops of any sort available to muster against the French.

The longboat captured at Bantry may be seen today, the red, white and blue still visible on its hull, at the National Maritime Museum in Dun Laoghaire. It is probably the only surviving example of an eighteenth-century French admiral's barge. The ten-oar vessel had three masts, each with a lug sail, and carried a crew of 13. In the 1980s, French, Norwegian and American enthusiasts built several replicas of this 38-foot boat for inter-national challenges between young seamen and women. The Danes and the Irish joined the event in Duarnenez in 1988, and in 1996 the longboats returned for a competition at Bantry, 200 years after the prototype went ashore.

Presently Joan produced a second breakfast, bacon and eggs, and the motion was just easy enough for us to take turns sitting at the saloon table if we kept a very sharp eye on the coffee pot.

As I took my turn Pat called down: 'A big sailing craft coming south.'

Ten minutes later Ireland's sail-training brigantine, *Asgard II*, was abeam, its green hull and full sails a glorious sight as it dipped and lifted to the slight swell, a moustache of creamy water at the bow. It passed in a rush of sails and rigging, bringing an image of the French fleet vividly to mind.

Had we time we could have gone up to Bantry and tasted the first whiff of the moist luxuriance which reaches its peak in the gardens of Glengarriff and Parknasilla, but a cruise of all of Ireland's coast would take a lifetime of summers. It has been calculated at 3,500 miles long, more than 1,000 miles longer than that of England and Wales and exactly 1,000 miles more than the Scottish coast. The Irish Cruising Club was founded in Glengarriff on 13 July 1929, when five Irish yachts cruising independently happened to meet there. After dinner in Roche's Hotel, Harry P. Donegan proposed the idea, and the 19 men present put up half a crown each to get it started.

Away to the north-east a white speck against the land was a yacht emerging from the shelter of Bere Island. The island, at the mouth of Bantry Bay, shelters Berehaven, one of the largest natural anchorages in northern Europe. The ship that carried Wolfe Tone had anchored there. Narrow at each end, it was easy to protect with forts and gun emplacements, and it became one of Britain's most strategic ports in Ireland, along with Cobh in Cork and Lough Swilly in Donegal. They were only handed over to Ireland in 1938, having been excluded from the transfer of power in the Anglo-Irish Treaty of 1921.

The decision was long delayed, and one can understand why: reliance on Irish defences as protection for Britain, the possibility of foreign landings (the French attempts at Bantry were a vivid historical lesson), distrust of the Irish government and fear of subversion. By 1938, however, Prime Minister Neville Chamberlain could tell the House of Commons that 'a friendly Ireland was worth far more to us, in peace and war, than these paper rights'. And as the ports were returned to Irish control, *The Times* wrote that their defence was 'an onerous and delicate task' from which Britain had been released. Churchill, however, regarded the transfer as a colossal blunder. If the navy, he said, were denied Berehaven and Cobh (Queenstown) and had to work instead from Pembroke Dock in Wales, 400 miles would be cut from its radius out and home. But for Taoiseach Eamon de Valera, Irish possession of the ports was not just a symbol but an essential requirement if the country were to pursue an independent foreign policy in a European war.

I had sailed into Berehaven past the great mooring buoys some years ago. The gun embrasures lay overgrown, the water tanks broken, and few memories remained of the Royal Navy. No pictures of warships hung in the old sailors' pubs of nearby Castletown. No British officer had attended matins in the Anglican church for many years.

I believe you can still find bits of iron stanchions in the rocks above the narrows where a hawser was suspended in the nineteenth century as a harbour boom, claimed to be the strongest ever made. It was laid to test the ramming power of an extraordinary craft, the 2,640-ton *Polyphemus*, built as an innovation in naval warfare. Driven by 7,000 horsepower engines, it had a bulbous hull culminating in a long underwater ram; it was, in effect, a huge steam-driven battering ram, a modern version of the weapon which the ancient Greeks had used. On a July day in 1885 she sped down the Berehaven narrows and successfully smashed through the boom, but no ship like her was ever built again. However, her exploit inspired H.G. Wells, who gave her the alias 'Thunder Child' and in *The War of the Worlds* made her the superweapon which would defeat the Martian machines – until their Heat Ray did for her.

The yacht we had seen earlier and *Sarakiniko* each closed on Dursey Sound, apparently on a converging course, but, by the time she was close enough to distinguish that her ensign was French, I had to concede she would get through first. I consoled my competitive crew with the opinion that she was bound to have better winds close to the shore.

Off Dursey we could see islands and rocks lying further to the west, the bigger ones called the Bull, the Cow and the Calf, but even after his second beer we could not persuade our farmer crewman that they bore any resemblance to these animals. The Bull is the big one, 600 feet across and half that in height, with a tunnel running right through it. McMullen, in his 1869 cruise, heard that boats could enter the cavern and, despite a seven-foot-high Atlantic swell, he 'pulled in between the points of entrance upon which the sea broke with considerable violence... The interior, which is about fifty feet high from the surface of the water, forty feet wide, and 500 feet through, is like a grand hall with an undulating floor.' The cavern's sides were smooth and lined, a few feet below high water mark, 'with little mussels in such myriads that the rock looks as if it were covered with black velvet'.

I suspect the Bull's Passage is not a tourist attraction, and for our part we were content to traverse the sound which divided Dursey Island from the mainland. Motoring to combat the fluky wind, we had to watch out for lobster-pot buoys, swing around them and yet avoid the Flag Rock which lurks in mid-channel, covered by one foot of water at low tide. The sound is only 220 yards across at its narrowest point, and the treacherous tidal race, running through it like rapids, would often cut the islanders off for long periods, especially in winter. Now, however, a cable car swings across overhead, its little cabin taking up to six passengers or one man and a cow. Dursey had only 50 inhabitants left by the time it got this lifeline, but now that its isolation has ended the island community's future is, hopefully, more assured.

The Slieve Miskish mountains lay scarfed in cloud to starboard as we began to cross the bay of Kenmare. Kerry lay ahead. Up the bay in Parknasilla I knew anchorages like that under the lovely island of Garnish where masses of rhododendron brush the peaty water and an ebbing tide reveals reefs of orange seaweed. It is a place of subtropical lushness, a landscape of myrtle, arbutus and fern trees. Our course lay north, however, and presently the windswept islands of Scariff, Deenish and Twoheaded Island which guard the approach to Derrynane grew on either side of the bow. We wondered if today's light swell would have permitted a landing out on Skellig, for now we could also see its towering crags: Skellig Michael, the great fortress of the Gaelic Church, rising 700 feet out of the Atlantic eight miles offshore, and its neighbour Little Skellig, home of seals, puffins, fulmars and perhaps 20,000 pairs of nesting gannets.

Derrynane entrance was easy today, a sea-saw ride in with the swell sucking the rocks close by on either side, then a sharp turn to starboard and we were there. All was smooth. All was calm. Sand dunes on one hand, mountain slopes on the other. We moved on to anchor clear of some floating lobster tanks. The French yacht was in, two of her crew already up to their thighs in the shallows, probing at the rocks with long poles. 'Probably collecting a delicious supper,' Joan said reflectively.

Suddenly the VHF burst into speech. 'Pan! Pan! All Ships! All Ships! This is Bantry Radio. A 32-foot motor launch has broken down one mile off Mizen Head and is drifting on shore.' A jumble of messages crackled over the airwaves as Bantry tried to stay in contact with the launch. When it seemed that the boat was coming within half a mile of the cliffs the calls were upgraded to 'Mayday', and it cannot have been cheering news for the distressed boat to hear that the lifeboat had been launched at Baltimore with an 'ETA one hour ten minutes'. The situation was growing desperate when help arrived from the naval vessel *Aisling*. Its inflatable sped inshore, sighted the drifting launch, and towed it clear of the breakers.

We had been absorbed in this acute drama and now sat down to a late tea in the cockpit. Derrynane must be the most lovely anchorage in Ireland. Traces of an indigenous forest of stunted oak, alder and hazel stretch to the water, a feature rarely found on the west coast. Derrynane's greatest charm is its diversity of small features: little hollows floored with sand or starred with the powder grey of sea holly and separated by rock ridges crowned with furze. There is bog myrtle and foxglove and, in the shallows, white sand where the water shines emerald green between purple patches of weed-grown rocks. In few places can you bring a boat so quickly in from the Atlantic to an environment such as this.

Derrynane House, home of Daniel O'Connell, lay just up the road. Son of a landlord, he was called to the Bar in 1798, one of the first Catholics to join the profession after they were permitted to do so in 1792. By the time of the Union of Britain and Ireland in 1800, most of the Penal Laws had been repealed, but Catholics could still not hold judicial or military office, sit in parliament or enter any but the most junior grade in the civil service. The Irish middle classes agitated but were not united, until the Catholic Association formed by O'Connell in 1823 brought mass action to bear on the British government. Local clergy helped organise a subscription of a penny a month from the people, which not only brought in a large income, but psychologically involved the peasantry in their own political movement. In the election of 1826 four Irish counties ejected MPs opposed to Catholic emancipation and elected new members who, though Protestant, supported it. Though he could not lawfully take his seat at Westminster, in 1829 O'Connell won a by-election in Co. Clare, helped by the small farmers who qualified to vote as 40 shilling freeholders. Voters victimised by their landlords were compensated by Catholic Association funds. Wellington and Peel, then Prime Minister and Home Secretary, realised reluctantly that a new situation had arisen. Despite division in the Commons and opposition from the House of Lords, the government pressed ahead, and in April 1829 the Catholic Emancipation Act became law. It was a turning point in history, and won for O'Connell the title of The Liberator.

O'Connell's home, a large but not grand house, weather slated against the storms, low dark rooms panelled in local oak, is set below austere mountain crags in woods of fir, beech and oak, its gardens fringed by pasture running into sand dunes spotted with wild orchids. Tucked away behind the mountains, the O'Connells played a prudent game, sidestepping the worst of the Irish defeats, holding on to their land. They prospered from smuggling. O'Connell's father, Morgan, was tried for his life for inciting his people to half-murder a customs officer who had caught him in the act of landing a contraband cargo. He was acquitted by a Protestant jury composed mainly of his customers. Young Daniel was taken under the wing of an uncle, Count O'Connell, a high-ranking officer in French service under the Bourbons who later became a colonel in a British regiment. He persuaded another uncle, Maurice, the second owner of Derrynane, known as Hunting Cap O'Connell, to adopt the boy as a protégé.

Hunting Cap was probably part feudal patriarch, part tough businessman. He was a member of the exclusive Royal Cork Yacht Club and a justice of the peace, but this did not interfere with the family business. Hunting Cap ostensibly exported hides, leather and beef, but together with Daniel's father he ran silk, rum, wines, lace, tea, brandy and sugar across from France. Matters were amicably arranged. When a Captain Butler swooped on an illicit cargo in 1782, Hunting Cap invited him to breakfast and then provided him with an escort back to his base at Waterville.

The count, for his part, smuggled recruits into France, and about 18 kinsmen of Derrynane served at one time in France, Spain and Austria. A moderate sea voyage away from Derrynane, the Continent would have seemed closer than London. It was not just the children of the well-to-do seeking education or employment who travelled to Europe. Early in the eighteenth century it was reported that 'when they have sown their Summer corn in the Spring, many [Kerry] families will take a vagary of going into Spain and there spend the summer in begging and wandering up and down in the northern side of the Kingdom'. A Ballinskelligs woman is said to have asked a neighbour for the loan of a mantle when she was going 'only to Spain'.

Privateers and pirates also sheltered in the local bays. The difference between the two was academic, their roles often interchangeable. Commissions written in pompous verbiage, known as letters of marque, were granted by governments, authorising private ships to attack ships of an enemy state or pirates, the enemy of all nations. The privateer might itself be an ex-pirate, a thief set to catch a thief. When Daniel O'Connell was carried as a boy to see the vessel of America's famous John Paul Jones at anchor off Derrynane, Jones was a privateer in Irish eyes but a pirate to the English, especially after he had attacked his home port in Cumberland.

After the death penalty was introduced in 1785 for smugglers who resisted arrest, it seems the O'Connells gave up the trade, though the smuggling of spirits was still commonplace at the end of the century. The Kerry landlords enforced the law when it suited. Hunting Cap not only supported the union with Britain but was one of the first to bring information to the government of Wolfe Tone's arrival in Bantry Bay. Mr White of Bantry, who beat him by 24 hours in getting the news to Cork, was awarded a peerage soon after.

We stayed two nights in Derrynane. A misty rain set in and grew thicker, the cloud lower. On a road a few hundred feet above the anchorage, cars crept by on full headlights in the middle of the day. The wind was brisk, stirring the heather, but its direction seemed favourable.

'A good wind for Valentia Island,' I called from the chart table. 'We can steer 295 magnetic the seven miles to Bolus Head, then swing round more to the north another three and a half to Puffin Island. After that, three more into the channel between Valentia and the mainland. They'll open the bridge for us in Portmagee and we can carry on to Knightstown.'

'Visibility is down to a few hundred yards,' Joan pointed out.

'Yes, but we have these several signposts and they're not far apart.' I turned to Pat for support. 'Madeline said there was a chance of them going to Knightstown this evening. You wouldn't want to miss them.'

'Well...'

Decision: indecision. 'Let's go,' I said.

We got the oilskins on, pulled in a reef in the mainsail, bounced for safety out between the rocks by gunning the engine and then bore away to fill the sails and get on course, plunging into painfully short seas, enclosed in our peculiar grey world. Now we were committed: in this mist it would not be easy to find and line up the rocks and beacons that would guide us back to Derrynane.

An hour passed. We kept a sharp lookout through the swirl for fishing boats bound into or out of Ballinskelligs Bay to starboard. It was Pat's very sharp eyes that first saw a darker shade directly on the bow. The image hardened into cliffs. Bolus Head. We swung to port to get good clearance. The tide had pushed us a touch sideways towards Ballinskelligs Bay, but there were no off-lying rocks here and our course at least ensured that we would not carry on past the head unaware that we had passed this first signpost. On then to Puffin Island, which grew out of the gloom like an outsized cathedral. It is well named, for scores of the 'parrots of the sea' attended our passage. Their stubby wings more attuned to swimming than flying, they bustled across the water in an attempt to get airborne, but their parents seemed to have neglected to give them flying lessons.

Skellig Michael lay a few miles away on our port side, but we could not see it. I had once gone out there on a calm day and climbed to the monks' stone-built huts on the summit. In about 1000 AD the name Michael – patron of high places – was attached to it, and from the early sixteenth century it is recorded as a main penitential station for the performance of public atone-ment. Indeed, I have noticed that Admiralty charts of the mid-nineteenth century mark several sites on Irish islands as 'penitential stations'. The annual pilgrimages to Skellig Michael were eventually stopped by the Church authorities, however. Possibly owing to changes in the Gregorian Calendar in 1782, Lent was held to begin later on Skellig than on the mainland, so you could marry there after the 'close season' for marriage had begun on land. Pilgrimage thus became an occasion for dancing, drinking and fun, and annual 'Skellig Lists' – humorous, satirical and defamatory doggerel – of couples who might marry there began to be published.

The privateer, John Paul Jones, almost wrecked his 42-gun flag-ship *Bonhomme Richard* on Skellig in August 1779. He wrote, 'At 8 pm Mizen Head lay astern, and with a fine breeze the squadron stood NNW along the ironbound coast of Kerry. By noon we were five miles SSW of Great Skellig.' At that point the wind died, and to avoid being set down on the rock he ordered his largest rowing boat to be launched to tow the ship clear. The tactic succeeded, but the oarsmen were all Irishmen who had been 'pressed' into his service and, finding the calm persisting, they cut the tow rope and pulled hard for Valentia and home.

Little Skellig is the second largest of the world's 23 gannet colonies, and every inch of the rock seemed whitened by tens of thousands of nesting gannets. As late as 1829 the island was rented for its gannets and their feathers, and guarded at breeding time by a boat crew of twelve men. Tomás Ó Criomhthain recalls in *The Islandman* of a night the Blasket islanders raided the colony. They had filled one boat with birds before the guard-boat arrived. Then the battle began, men 'hitting one another with oars and hatchets... till they bled one another like a slaughtered ox'. Two of the guards were killed and ten others were taken to hospital.

We made yet another change of course, and now the wind came almost astern. *Sarakiniko* pressed on, lifting to combers with white fingers of spray rolling up behind, sinking in the trough as they passed ahead, but always moving steadily along until we found shelter in the confines of Portmagee Channel. Joan came up, cups of tea wedged in the washing-up bowl, and we made our final peaceful run, teacups in hand, up to the bridge and the village pier.

THREE

North and East for Shannon

WE WERE NOT getting further around Ireland until a span of the road-bridge barring our path was opened, so Pat and I climbed a rusty ladder, sidestepped tangles of old fishing net, discarded oil drums and broken lobster pots, and pushed open the door of the Fisherman's Arms. We found ourselves joined at the counter by an elderly man who seemed to be familiar with the routine of the fellow who operated the bridge.

'So it will open at seven?' I asked.

He placed his empty glass on the bar top. 'Will ye listen to me. He got wet twice already today. There's another yacht coming through at seven so he'll open then – and of course,' he paused rather dramatically and I strained to hear, 'once that bridge is opened the cars have to stop. Are you following me?'

'I do believe I am,' I said.

The bridge did indeed open at seven, and we glided on for three miles through a human-scale agricultural landscape of gently sloping fields, sometimes touched into brightness by the wasteful gold of ragwort. The waters of the channel were scarcely wrinkled by the breeze. A heron floated indolently on the current. When our course bent to the north-west, Knightstown village and pier emerged before us. Had we gone to starboard the channel would have become the Cahirciveen river and taken us quietly up to the town's quay two miles away, but the *Sailing Directions'* description lacked allure. The river has lights 'which cannot be relied upon', and Pat and Joan thought the conclusion that 'A yacht might be left here unattended if local fishermen who are friendly can be contacted' somewhat enigmatic. Perhaps the writer should have met that genial crowd in the Fisherman's Arms, and in any case the town now plans to build facilities for visiting yachts.

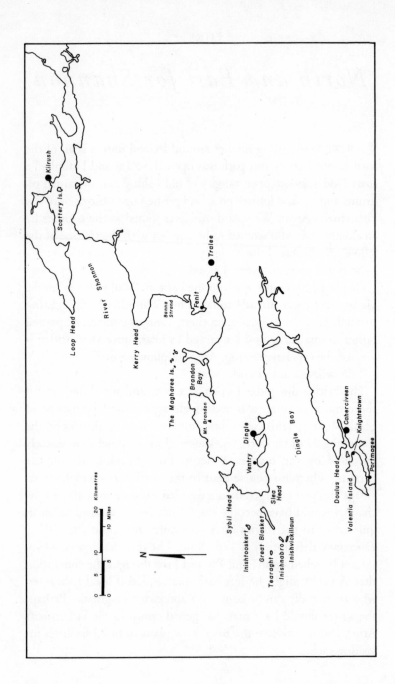

Dusk was closing over Knightstown, one of the most westerly villages in Europe, where the main street of Victorian and Edwardian houses runs to a waterfront clock tower which would not be out of place in Weymouth. Visually it seemed a step away from the Gaelic world which surrounds it, a place designed for the Knight of Kerry by a Scottish engineer, Alexander Nimmo. The FitzGerald family, Knights of Kerry, shared the island with Trinity College, Dublin, Trinity having obtained several townlands which had been confiscated in the sixteenth century. The Royal Hotel, which used to be 'Mrs Young's', got its grand step up from Prince Arthur of Connaught who visited the Knight in 1869. His Royal Highness was expected to land on Skellig Michael but, 'the sea being high and His Highness a bad sailor', he cancelled the trip and went to inspect Valentia's new telegraph station instead. Among the island's many famous guests, Lord Tennyson had been a visitor in 1848. He claimed that off Valentia he had seen the highest waves in Ireland and there is a tradition that here he composed the lines, 'Break, break, break on thy cold grey stones, O Sea.'

Alexander Nimmo should surely be better known wherever Ireland meets the sea. He was born in 1783, the son of a Fife watchmaker, and worked as a schoolmaster until the great engineer Telford assisted in his appointment as surveyor to a parliamentary commission for the reclamation of Irish boglands; Nimmo had earlier done vacation work establishing boundaries to Scottish counties. In Ireland he published many reports and maps and was asked by the Irish Fisheries Board to survey the country's harbours and piers. By 1822 he was engineer to the western districts. He built over 30 piers and harbours around our coasts, including the Wellesley Bridge and the docks of Limerick, and compiled charts of the coast and sailing directions for the Irish Sea and St George's Channel. He died in Dublin in 1832.

We nosed about, watching the red flicker on the dial of the echo-sounder, looking for shelter, secure holding ground, an easy row ashore and water where we would still float at low tide, four aims which usually come into conflict. Tonight it was easier, for the *Sailing Directions* suggested anchoring near the permanent moorings of the RNLI lifeboat, a spot 'well sheltered in winds from SE to SW'. We did so and gazed across at the comforting bulk of the Arun class *Margaret Frances Love*, the lifeboat which was first to reach the site of the Air India crash in 1985. They found the sea stained red. 'The crew,' Dick Robinson wrote in his *History of the Valentia Lifeboats,* 'were weeping when they eventually got back to Knightstown.'

The presence of RNLI vessels in harbours throughout Ireland illustrates a kind of co-operation which could be extended to other fields. The roots of the service go back to Sir William Hillary, veteran of the Napoleonic Wars, who was probably its founder. The dismally named 'Liverpool Institution for Recovering Drowned Persons' had been established in 1771, but Hillary adopted a more positive approach and in 1824 set up the National Institution for the Preservation of Life from Shipwreck – or the 'Shipwreck Institution' for short. Seven lifeboat stations were built on the Irish coast that year and two more in 1825, at Newcastle in Co. Down and Courtmacsherry in Cork. Another came to Arklow in 1826. Financial problems in England and the onset of the Irish Famine restricted further growth, and in 1861 the RNLI, as it had become, took several independent Irish stations into its fold. Ireland had 35 stations by 1911. When the new state was formed, the service remained attached to the RNLI: as the Institution relies on voluntary funding, Irish efforts could not meet the full costs involved. Today one lifeboat may cost well over £1m, and voluntary contributions are augmented by an annual grant to the RNLI from the Irish government. At present the facilities on the long Irish coastline are gradually being extended by the use of high-speed inflatables.

Joan called us down to a supper of smoked salmon followed by chops and new potatoes, our appetites quite unaffected by the slight swell. Rain began to whisper on the sprayhood and during the night the wind started a gentle keening. When I climbed on deck to tighten some loose rigging, the first streaks of dawn were rising behind Caherciveen. I blew out the paraffin-fed riding light and detached the lantern from the boom end. Chilled and damp – the rustle of donning oilskins would have woken Joan – I found the pleasure of burrowing back into a still warm sleeping-bag made the foray almost worthwhile.

Madeline and Aline, who had arrived late last evening at a local hotel, quickly spotted us next morning among the three or four visiting yachts. Once again we had a car to explore the shore.

On a windy headland high above the modern meteorological and radio station, we left the car and crunched along trackways winding through hillocks of slate, left behind after the closure of Valentia's renowned quarries. The ruins of the Squaring House lay near the quarry face. From here, the huge slabs were taken by horse wagon, and in later years by railway, down into Knightstown village to be cut into blocks for the London and other markets. From the Slate Yard behind the Royal Hotel, schooners with names like *Reaper*, *Gleaner* and *Sir Charles Napier* carried out cargoes which became the roofs of the old House of Commons, the National Gallery and the British Museum, shelving for London's Public Records Office and paving on Charing Cross, Waterloo, Blackfriars and many other railway stations in Britain. Valentia slate was even used in the construction of the San Salvador railway. It was rather heavy for roofing, being more flagstone than slate, but as it could be cut into large slabs and was very strong, it was also used for fish slabs, dairy shelving, fenders, fireplaces, wash-stands and billiard tables. A particularly fine billiard table, built entirely of slate, was bought by the Duke of Wellington and is still found at Stratfield Saye in England. So impressed was the Prince Consort by the piece that he ordered one for the new royal residence on the Isle of Wight, and had it enamelled to simulate white marble.

All around the island there are slate roofs, gutters, garden seats and paving stones, but competition from soft Welsh slabs and cheap Welsh and American roofing slates led to the eventual collapse of Valentia's slate industry in the 1880s, and it closed finally in 1911. It once gave a living to 500 people, many of whom emigrated when the quarry closed. In the west of Ireland you soon hear that 'the next parish is America', and it seemed like that in a Knightstown pub where a television screen large as a dining-table displayed the day's winds, rainfall and temperatures for each state of the Union. But for much of the nineteenth century, America was remote indeed. In 1838 a sailing ship had crossed the Atlantic in 36 days and, shortly after this, in gale force winds, a ship achieved a record 18-day crossing. The first scheduled passenger vessel under engine, the *Sirius*, crossed from Cork in twelve days in 1838 and the journey was cut to nine days 15 hours in 1842. Achieving faster communication across the Atlantic would have enormous significance. The search turned from the speed of seaborne transport to the possibility that a telegraph cable might carry messages under the sea.

Such a cable would need an entirely new kind of insulation to withstand the enormous pressure and friction to which it would be subject. After Dr Mont of the Indian Medical Service discovered gutta percha in 1843, a substance which was readily moulded when hot and hardened with remarkable durability when it cooled, a few miles of telegraph cable was covered in it and a successful transmission made to a ship off Folkestone. The following year the first telegraph message was sent to France. In the following years several short submarine cables were laid in Europe and by 1855 Howth was connected to Holyhead, but crossing 2,000 miles of ocean remained an immense challenge. Could an electrical impulse even travel this far? Charles Bright, the engineer responsible for telegraph services between London, Manchester and Liverpool, began experimenting in his Old Broad St offices in the quiet pre-dawn hours, and by connecting lines backwards and forwards achieved a continuous circuit of just that distance.

The logistical problems of crossing the Atlantic were still daunting. In mid-ocean lay some of the greatest submarine mountains on earth, some 1,000 miles long, 500 miles wide, reaching sea depths of over 30,000 feet. In the excellent museum at Valentia I saw some imaginative ideas for spanning the ocean. Cable might be suspended from balloons, said one; or from buoys, said another. A third felt that the cable would not have to settle on the ocean bed at all but would remain suspended at the level where the density of water became equal to that of the cable.

By 1854 Cyrus Field, Deputy Chairman of the New York and

Newfoundland Telegraph Company, was corresponding at length with the Knight of Kerry as to whether Valentia would be suitable as a cable terminus. Field came to England and set up the Atlantic Telegraph Company with Lord Kelvin and others, employing Bright as consultant. The engineer suggested that two specially adapted ships be used, one, the American frigate *Niagara,* to sail west from Valentia until her store of cable was exhausted, when she would contact the British battleship *Agamemnon* carrying further cable. The ends would be spliced in mid-Atlantic and the British ship would carry on to Heart's Content in Newfoundland.

On 5 August 1857 the shore end of the cable was set up at Valentia. The Knight of Kerry arranged a banquet and dance in John Driscoll's store in the Slate Yard. The Lord Lieutenant of Ireland, the Earl of Carlisle, came down from Dublin. There were long and fulsome speeches, but it was all a bit premature. Six days later, 350 miles from shore, the cable snapped in 12,000 feet of water at the edge of the Continental Shelf, where the sea floor falls to abysmal deeps. Further out in the Atlantic the *Agamemnon* suffered a great storm and was nearly lost.

A working cable was eventually laid in 1865, when the world's largest ship, the *Great Eastern*, was adapted to take the entire length across the Atlantic. People from all along the coast flocked to Valentia for the official opening of the new telegraph station, 'and a few yachts came from Cork and Bantry with less rustic visitors. Tents were soon improvised by the aid of sails, some cloths of canvas and oars and boathooks, inside which bucolic refreshment could be obtained. Mighty pots of potatoes seethed over peat fires outside, and the reek from within came forth strongly suggestive of whiskey and bacon... nor was music wanting. The fiddler and the piper had found out the island and the festive spot, and seated on a bank, played planxty and jig to a couple or two in the very limited circle formed in the soft earth by plastic feet or ponderous shoemasonry, around which, sitting and standing, was a dense crowd of spell-bound, delighted spectators.... The bright groupings of colour formed on the cliffs and on the waters by the red, scarlet, and green shawls of the women and girls, lighted up the scene wonderfully.'

Sir Robert Peel, son of the late Prime Minister, attended the ceremony, and from the station's instrument room the Knight of Kerry sent the first message by commercial telegraph across the sea to America: 'Glory to God in the highest, on earth peace, goodwill to men,' and called for three cheers. Valentia had become the Cape Canaveral of the nineteenth century.

Valentia's weather station is equally intriguing for the twentieth-century sailor. Inside a modern building set on a wind-blown outcrop at the furthest tip of the island, we found ourselves in an operations room where voices murmured into microphones, computer screens winked red and green, messages chattered from the fax machines and charts lined the walls: NW Europe, Western Approaches, Eastern Atlantic, vast reaches of water almost comprehended and tamed by symbols, colours and lines. Beyond the windows slopes of sheep-cropped grass fell towards the corrugated sea. This place of hushed efficiency is the most westerly weather station on the European mainland.

The station director, Gene O'Sullivan, placed his fingertip against the double-glazed window. 'You've come on a good day, but we get weather up here which is hard to exaggerate. A while ago we had a gale which smashed the outer pane, though this inner pane held; it vibrated, but it held.' He pointed towards the approach road winding up the hill. 'The relief man trying to walk up that morning was really using his bike as an anchor. An oil drum which came loose was sent bounding down the hill; just missed him.'

He led us into an older section of the station. 'Before the building was modernised in recent times, a gale damaged the roof. You should have seen the flood. Some of the staff had to sit on tables, yet they managed to keep things going. We can have Force 12 winds up here.'

'The highest on the scale,' Pat said admiringly. I think he was correct. When Admiral Beaufort, a native of Co. Meath, set up the Beaufort Scale for Winds, the idea was to give warships some idea of the sails to carry in different wind strengths. But when the wind reached 64 knots, about 70 miles an hour, all sail would be removed anyway, so there was no point in going any higher.

The director presented us with a souvenir straight from the fax's mouth, surmounted by an Irish harp and headed Meteorological Service: Central Analysis and Forecast Office. The message suggested friendly south or south-west winds for tomorrow. We would bring it back to Joan as evidence of our serious midmorning expedition while she had been relaxing with Madeline in the lovely gardens of Glenleam, former home of the Knights of Kerry.

I still had time to cross a field to the roofless ruin of the old Church of Ireland where the last Knights of Kerry lay in cracked and lichen-covered tombs. Peter FitzGerald, nineteenth Knight, held the title through the successful era of the slate quarry, the years of the landing of the transatlantic cable, the Fenian Rising and the setting up of the first Meteorological Office by the Royal Society in 1867. He helped install the new advanced storm warning signals invented by Admiral Fitzroy (of *Beagle* fame) and, by trying out whaling boats as lifeboats, built up such a competent crew that the area's first lifeboat was transferred to Valentia from the mainland in 1865. How he would have been impressed by the *Margaret Frances Love*, and the moment in the Royal Festival Hall, London, in 1991, when the Duke of Kent presented Paddy Gallagher, Honorary Secretary of the Lifeboat Committee, with the RNLI long-service badge. Sir Peter's successor, Maurice, lived until 1915. Poor health limited the spread of his interests, but he kept yachts at Valentia, especially the *Satanita* which he used for racing. It was the beginning of a new era, the twilight of the Ascendancy. The FitzGerald's cousin, Mary Ellen Spring-Rice, only daughter of Lord Mounteagle of Foynes, became an ardent Home Ruler and later a supporter of Sinn Féin, and crewed with Erskine Childers in July 1914 on the gun-running yacht *Asgard*. She stood at the bow as the *Asgard* approached Howth Harbour, wearing a red skirt as the agreed recognition signal for the waiting republican Volunteers.

IT WAS time to move north across Dingle Bay. I had visualised it sitting between the middle and forefinger when looking at my open right hand, with the Blasket Islands lying off the forefinger's tip. The sound between the Blaskets and mainland would be our door to the north Kerry coast and on to the Shannon estuary. We would first seek an anchorage tonight on the north shore of Dingle Bay by the long sandy beaches of Ventry village. From there we could plan the time of a favourable tide to take us through the boisterous sound.

The first *Sailing Directions of the Irish Cruising Club*, published in 1930, stopped short at Valentia. The west coast was considered an inhospitable place for the yachtsman. When J. M. Morris won the Royal Cruising Club Challenge Cup immediately after the Second World War for a northbound cruise in his 40-foot *Mary Jane*, he wrote in the *Club Journal*, 'I can well understand why Irish yachtsmen do not sail further north than Valentia. I have never seen any coast which so fills one with a sense of foreboding. The very names of these dread Blasket Islands, Inistearacht and Inistuaisceart, are enough to strike a chill in the heart of the mariner.' The latter island, he felt, 'looks as if it has a prehistoric reptile's armour clamped on the end of it'.

That was surely laying it on a bit. In any case, the modern yacht can more readily claw off when the wind sets on to an inhospitable coast and – if needs be – can get a push to windward from a reliable diesel engine.

We met Madeline and Aline on the pier, where Pat persuaded them that they should replace him today on *Sarakiniko* while he would drive around the bay and meet us on Ventry Beach. He waved the fax from Valentia Radio – Force 4, south-west – 'a soldier's wind' which even a landsman could handle. I heard the well-worn phrase, 'smooth as a millpond'. Pat was particularly anxious that Madeline, who had been put off by the short choppy waters of Lough Derg a year before, should have her morale restored.

When we hit the Atlantic swell outside the harbour I estimated our speed against the rocks at a miserable one knot. On a northerly course, a Force 4 south-westerly would have been delightful, but it was clear at once that we would have a head-wind instead. As we motored past the cliffs with implacable small waves breaking into fans on each side of the bow, Joan and I tried to cheer the passengers with unconvincing chatter about temporary wind shadows and the back-winding you may get near cliffs.

Notwithstanding the sea, the scene was glorious. Away to port lay the desolate mass of the Blaskets, uninhabited since 1953 but once the home of a thriving community and the inspiration of remarkable works of Gaelic literature: Peig Sayers's *Peig*, Tomás Ó Criomhthain's *The Islandman* and Maurice O'Sullivan's *Twenty Years a-Growing*. O'Sullivan wrote his book after he had left the island to become a policeman, but even in the English translation we can glimpse wit and poetry. 'It was a tender thought that struck me to write this book for the entertainment and laughter of the old women of the Blaskets... in order to send my voice into their ears again, the voice that always roused them.' Ó Criomhthain, describing 'famine and fortune in all my life's days till today... ploughing the sea with only our hope in God... when the swell would be rising to the green grass', concluded his autobiography in 1926. 'There are only five older than me alive in the Island. They have the pension. I have only two months to go till that date – a date I have no fancy for. In my eyes it is a warning that death is coming, though there are many people who would rather be old with the pension than young without it.' Wit, realism, sharp observation of nature and people, the island books have all these qualities and more.

I pointed over to the nearest of the islands, Inisvickillaune. 'Mr Haughey, the former Taoiseach, is the only inhabitant,' I said. 'He built a house there some years ago.' Someone groaned, 'He must be mad.' I forbore from reminding the crew of the reintroduction of the spectacular sea eagles there or that the island's 200 acres is now a unique reserve where the ancient Irish red deer is multiplying in hundreds after Mr Haughey acquired six from the Killarney mountains some years ago. It was not an afternoon for inconsequential chat.

I turned on the radio. We were tunefully informed that if we ever crossed the sea to Ireland we should not only see the moon rise over Claddagh but the sun go down on Galway Bay. The selection roused no enthusiasm.

I began to hope that Fungi the dolphin might arrive to divert the passengers. This remarkable creature has lived for some ten years or more at the mouth of Dingle Harbour, during which time he has become one of Ireland's tourist attractions. People have been known to travel hundreds of miles to toss about on the bay until he appears, and will talk of their meeting with the solitary mammal as if it were a religious conversion. Fungi has undoubtedly done his bit to add to the romantic aura of the region where the film *Ryan's Daughter* was produced. Whatever its status as a tourist destination, Dingle is a major fishing port, a role it has enjoyed since medieval times and earlier. Houses in the town bear the stone-carved motifs of the Spanish traders who worked out of here in the sixteenth century, though a slip known as the Spanish Quay sadly had to be destroyed when the harbour acquired deep water berths and a marina.

Sarakiniko was falling into the troughs now and began to pound, for her twin keels trap air which the hull expels rather explosively as it drops. It is perfectly harmless, though if you are standing below the shock reverberates through your ankles. I could achieve a smoother ride by sailing off some 45 degrees and keeping the engine on, but that would lengthen the journey. As we walloped across the bay, Pat's cheerful optimism was recalled with a particular emphasis. Eventually we saw him through the binoculars, waving us in towards a distant beach, and by the time we had reached it across the huge placid lagoon of Ventry Harbour, his family had ceased to add to Ireland's many shades of green.

We had reached a part of Irish-speaking Kerry, and after supper aboard found chat and banter ashore with some trainee teachers by the crossroads telephone-box. They were down from Limerick to improve the old tongue at a residential college. Apart from these girls, the inhabitants of this remaining part of the Gaelic world all seemed to be in their net-curtained bungalows watching the telly.

Few cars were using lights even at 10.45 pm. We were of course now ten degrees west of Greenwich and the sun set 40 minutes later than it did in London. Off to the west, jets bound for the

USA drew trails which shone like golden matchstick across the evening sky. An occasional car passed by but the silence soon returned, broken only by the whistling of oyster-catchers, the cries of gulls foraging in the shallows, and the braying of a donkey bemoaning his loneliness. Madeline and Aline returned to their car to resume their holiday, which would take them away from our future anchorages. We rowed back to *Sarakiniko* under a sky of stars and sat in the cockpit agreeing that urban man was losing the pleasure of long twilights and starlit darkness. With street lighting, flood lighting, domestic security lamps – artificial light of all kinds – expanding relentlessly, I have known a city child to be astonished at the sight of stars on a frosty night in the countryside.

We rose before 5.00 am to tea, a biscuit and the sound of distant cockcrows. Starting in eastern Europe a few hours ago, that rousing call had been flowing from farmyard to farmyard with the first light, and here on the western edge of Europe was reaching its finale for today. For us the Shannon estuary lay ahead, 50 miles north-east of the Blaskets. What a great river it is. A recently reopened waterway, funded to aid border counties by the Irish and British goverments and the International Fund for Ireland, now joins the lovely Erne lakelands in Northern Ireland to the Shannon, so boats can sail some 250 miles from Beleek in Co. Fermanagh south-west to Limerick. The Shannon estuary opens ten miles wide at the mouth, and if an ebb tide joins forces with the river current to push against the prevailing winds, the mariner will find turbulent seas to cope with.

Today, once through the Blasket Sound, we would run along the north Kerry coast under the massive cliffs that buttress Mount Brandon and seek an anchorage near Tralee Bay among the islands which the old charts call the Seven Hogs but on ours are marked as the Magharees. It would be about eight miles west along the coast to reach the entrance to the sound which, with its exposed position, uneven bottom and strong tides, can be a rough and unpredictable channel. It would carry us into unfamiliar waters. I had not sailed north of the Blaskets before.

We gazed back at the oval expanse of Ventry Strand as we ran out. They still race curraghs here but the event competes with sailing and rowing festivals in several places now. I wondered if it was a milder affair than that described by Maurice O'Sullivan, in for the day from the Great Blasket. 'The sun was sinking behind Mount Eagle in the north and the evening fine and warm; mirth and merriment, laughter and shouting here and there after the day; every man merry with drink, children with cheeks stained from ear to ear with eating sweets, tricksters hoarse with shouting, racers exhausted from all the sweat they had shed, tinkers at the roadside sound asleep after two days walking to the races... all of them making for home and talking of nothing but Tigue Diarmid and his crew.... "Musha, aren't we unfortunate," said Tomás, "that we can't stay among them and take a turn at the dance because of the long road we have to travel and, worst of all, three miles of sea to cross? Oh, isn't it heartbreaking entirely?" "And maybe the sea rough," said I.'

Across the shoulder of Mount Eagle, houses defined the precipitous line of a road running on to Slea Head overlooking the Blasket Sound, a Famine relief road, much of it blasted out of the mountainside with explosives. Along this reach of coast stands one of the greatest concentrations of ancient monuments in Ireland. Even from offshore one could distinguish stone beehive huts among the little farms, some probably still used for storing farm implements. Cave dwellings, souterrains, forts, churches, standing stones and crosses: in all there are said to be over 500 sites on this peninsula.

The number of beehive huts and Christian remains in the Dingle peninsula – at the end of the nineteenth century over 400 beehive huts were counted in the space of a few miles – helps to confirm Dr Peter Harbison's view that the islands along the west and north coasts were ideal stopping-off points for pilgrims on their way to Mount Brandon. Brandon is one of the three Irish mountains associated with pilgrimage, along with Slieve League which stands over Donegal Bay and Croagh Patrick above Clew Bay in Mayo.

In *Pilgrimage in Ireland*, Dr Harbison argues convincingly that the beehive huts at the western end of the peninsula were probably temporary shelters for seaborne pilgrims, waiting for a clearance of the mist which so often clouds the summit of the mountain. Pilgrim roads have been traced running up from Ventry Harbour, whose sheltered beach is ideal for landing curraghs. Dr Harbison is surely right to suggest that we tend to see too many things from a purely land-based perspective today. The monuments around the shrine of St Colmcille on the Donegal coast, for example, only make sense when they are understood as having been built by people who came to that valley by sea: a ring of hills cuts the glen off from the surrounding countryside. The Dingle peninsula is a further example of the sea's significance as a carrier of people and culture.

The sound seemed quiet, the tide behind us. Whorls of water gave way to lines of suds, the tidelines of indefinable channels. We closed on the island's White Strand, passing by the recess in the rocks which served as the island harbour. The village roads are vividly green now and run between stark gables and tumbled stone, though a few remain in good repair for people still come in summertime and there are plans to develop the island as a heritage park. We sailed past a huge flock of cormorants bobbing on the water. Over on the mainland spray from the ceaseless swell drifted like fog about the lower cliffs. Skirting the rocks which lay around Beginish, a small island in the middle of the sound, we wondered how the great Armada galleons could possibly have made their way between this island and Great Blasket half a mile away. For a thousand-ton ship the safe passage would be no more than 100 yards wide, and even then it had to escape the hazard of the Ballyclogher Rocks lying further out.

Yet ships of the Spanish Armada – originally 130 ships carrying 29,453 men – did find anchorage off the White Strand in September 1588. Limping up the North Sea and around the north of Scotland, using inadequate charts which smoothed out the rock-rimmed Irish headlands, the retreating Armada had directions for home which ordered them to keep NNE up to 61.5 degrees north, off the Shetlands. The ships were admonished to 'take great care lest you fall upon the island of Ireland', so at 61.5 north they were to run WSW 'until you are in the latitude of 58 degrees and then SW to Cape Finisterre'.

The altitude of the noonday sun, measured by a cross-staff or astrolabe, would readily have given the Spanish their latitude, but a longitude calculation remained a hazard at sea until the late eighteenth century; due to its cost, the practical chronometer did not come into general use until around 1810. Frequently it did not matter. Vessels coming across the Atlantic to England would 'run their easting down' and, if they kept to 50 degrees latitude in the later stages of the voyage, would find themselves eventually in the mouth of the English Channel. Rounding the west coast of Ireland, however, was a different matter.

The *San Juan Bautista*, flagship of the Squadron of Castille, took a sunsight on 31 August which put the ship at 58 degrees north. Believing that they were well out in the Atlantic, they began to work southwards, and on 9 September seemed to be at 54 degrees north – about level with Achill in Mayo – and, by their reckoning, some 700 miles out from Ireland. They were not – islands were spotted at dawn on the 11th. The ship attempted to beat west and north-west for the next few days but a heavy storm set in; the wind turned west and then, lamentably, north-west, driving the Spanish boats back. Dawn on 15 September revealed two big islands ahead. Astonished lookouts also saw ships, the flagship of Admiral de Recalde and another ship driving towards spouting rocks – the narrow channel between the Great Blasket and Beginish.

'We followed him, totally ignorant of this coast and despaired of escaping it.' But they got through in a space 'about as wide as the length of a ship' and the three vessels came to a relatively safe anchorage – exposed if the gale came to blow from the north-east but, in that event, they could up anchor and run for Spain.

Juan de Recalde had some knowledge of the area as, eight years before, he had commanded six Spanish ships which landed 600 Italian mercenaries in Smerwick Bay some seven miles away, a disastrous landing, for most of the foreign soldier had been killed by English troops. Now as they anchored at White Strand, de Recalde himself was ill and four or five of his crew were dying each day. It was vital to get water and food. A landing party of eight men crossed to the mainland but they were captured and hanged. A second party of 50 armed men narrowly escaped confrontation with a company of English troops who marched from the garrison at Dingle, which like most coastal areas was on the alert for ships of the Armada. De Recalde (who did eventually get his ship to Spain but died very soon afterwards) sent a boat to the island each day 'to refresh ourselves and take water' but they 'could do but little and with much labour'. We do not know from the Spanish diaries if the island was then inhabited and the weather may have made landing difficult. Neither was the ships' holding ground – sand lying on rock – particularly secure. The sailing masters worried about their cables chaffing on the sea-bed.

After nearly a week another gale sprang up 'out of a sky cloudless and with little rain' and de Recalde's anchor began to drag. His ship collided with the *San Juan Bautista*. In the midst of the chaos in the anchorage, another vessel was seen to seaward, the *Santa Maria de la Rosa*. Her sails in tatters except for the foresail, she ran in before the north-west gale, cast her sole remaining anchor, and seemed to lie facing the north-west wind in relative security while the north-flowing tide pressed on her stern. But when the tide turned, wind and tide combined to increase the strain on her anchor. She dragged across one of the other ships and – 'a most extraordinary and terrifying thing' – sank without warning, drowning all but one from the company of hundreds of men. An English record states that the survivor came ashore 'naked upon a board'.

There is a note of his interrogation. He appears to have been a young Genoese called Giovanni. It was he who told of the drowning of high-born Spaniards in the Armada debacle, such as the Prince of Asculo, the illegitimate son of King Philip II. Some historians believe this was a false tale offered as a gesture to please his captors, but the scholar Robin Flower records how local people would point out a stone near the schoolhouse at Dunquin and say that it marked the grave of 'the King of Spain's son'.

Giovanni told his inquisitors that when the ship's anchor dragged it had finally hooked on a reef and, in an effort to avoid collision with the pinnacle (known as the Stromboli Rock), his father had ordered the cable cut and attempted to raise sail so as to run to the ship on to the beach. He was at once accused of wrecking the vessel and killed by one of the ship's military officers. In fact, if Giovanni's account was true, running for shore may have been the only option they had left.

The *Santa Maria* went down in at least a hundred feet of water. She had sunk so fast, possible heeling over if she had been riddled with shot holes, that there was a chance she would be relatively intact. A search for her began in 1963 in an expedition led by Desmond Branigan of Dublin. In these restless waters it was a most dangerous job; one diver, Sydney Wignall, was almost swept away on the tide. Work continued and, after a month-long diving session in 1968, an anchor some ten metres long was found snagged on a rock. It had one fluke missing and its ring broken. Three more anchors were later found. Wignall and his team unearthed great piles of shot and ballast. By 1969 the searchers knew that they had found the *Santa Maria* when they discovered two pewter mugs inscribed 'Matute' – Francisco Matute was an infantry captain on the ship. They also discovered small guns and, under a large pewter plate, the legs, pelvis and ribs of a sailor, probably crushed by ballast as the ship went down. There were traces of charcoal from the galley fire just ahead of the likely position of the mainmast and piles of brush-wood which could have been kindling.

The Blasket artefacts are preserved in the Belfast Museum, which also holds finds from several other Armada discoveries along the Irish coast. The Armada is but the best known of hundreds of shipwrecks along our coasts, many of historic interest. It may be that one day there will be a joint Spanish-Irish initiative to explore the Armada wrecks further. Indeed, the task has a European dimension for many of the ships were foreign vessels, chartered or requisitioned by Spain, and the Genoese youth, Giovanni, was just one of the thousands who died with no personal interest in the conflict.

Presently the Blaskets lay well astern and we turned north-east. The wind remained light but the swell was high enough to cause a trawler some 300 yards away to disappear from sight periodically.

The whiskered face of a seal came up to gaze at us briefly. In the Blaskets, seals were once 'more prized than a pig.' Tomás Ó Criomhthain described hunting them in caves, the men with candles on their heads as the swell surged in. 'Every barrelful of seal meat was worth a barrel of pork. The skins fetched eight pounds. It's odd the way the world changes. Nobody would put a bit of seal meat in his mouth today.'

It was 9.30 am when Smerwick Harbour began to open up. We relaxed now that the tumble of the Blasket Sound lay astern, and when Pat shouted 'Net!' the line of floats was only a few yards from our side. A long net this one: we found the inshore end marked by a small red buoy uncomfortably close to the cliffs. Having slipped around this hazard, we almost ran into another monofilament half an hour later.

Away to starboard the slopes of Mount Brandon climbed into a lowering cloud base which hid any view of its 3,000-foot peak. We were looking into Brandon Creek. Out of here in May 1976 Tim Severin and his crew sailed a boat made of 49 ox-hides stitched together and lubricated with fat, the first step on their journey to recreate the possible transatlantic voyage of St Brendan the Navigator. They gambled their lives on the accuracy of their research into the curragh-building techniques of the early Irish navigators.

Early Irish literature abounds in stories of voyages embellished with marvels and miracles. The *Navigatio Sanctii Brendani* (the first version was probably composed over 200 years after his death) is really an Irish equivalent of the *Song of Roland*. It was widely studied in medieval Europe and may have influenced Columbus. Brendan certainly made voyages to establish monasteries, four in the west of Ireland, others in Brittany and Scotland; the isle of Barra in Scotland is named after him. It is said that he selected 14 monks for his greatest adventure and fasted for 40 days beforehand, surely not the ideal preparation for a slog across the north Atlantic. At any rate, Severin's Brendan Voyage rescued the early Irish seafaring achievement from the realm of speculation and doubt, and it is no longer possible to say that the journey could not have been done. However, the

Navigatio may not be the record of one trip but the main surviving account of a seagoing Christian culture which sent boat after boat on regular voyages with the mixed aims of communication, exploration and pilgrimage. Irish monks certainly made long voyages, and I am sure they loved the sea. The first page of our *Sailing Directions* bore lines from St Columba: 'What joy to sail the crested sea/And watch the waves beat white upon the Irish shore.'

On the bow of *Sarakiniko* Pat stood watching the shoreline away to port. 'It's Kerry Head on the south side of the Shannon,' he called. I followed the line of his finger and spotted a knob of grey.

'It could be one of the Magharees.' I squinted through the handbearing compass. 'No, I think you must be right; the islands are a bit more inshore.'

There are few things better than a good crew. We would be across the Shannon tomorrow, I thought, and in a few days a new crew would come on board. 'A shame you're both leaving,' I said.

'When do the new lads arrive?'

'In a day or so. Barry Singleton gets a flight from Heathrow to Shannon and Tony O'Gorman gets a lift up from Clonmel. They're both sailors. Barry has often crewed on *Sarakiniko*. Tony you know.'

'He keeps a small boat in Dungarvan, doesn't he? Can they stay long?'

'Barry less than a week; he has some court work to get back to. I hope Tony can stay all the way to Donegal. Anne can rejoin up there, I think.'

Joan came up. 'Who will cook?'

'Turn about. We'll keep it simple. The minimum time from tin to tum.'

We were approaching the heights of Brandon Head. Much of it is cliff, but set into a gully at the foot of the cliffs we noticed some neat little fields. Possibly we were looking at the Monks' Fields, for a settlement in this area dates from early Christian times. No track seemed to lead down to these remote acres overhung by a thousand feet of stone and scree. Nor could we spot any possible access by boat from the low cliffs underneath.

The wind had failed and we were under engine, creeping like a beetle under the mountain walls. Some writers describe a mysterious aura in the region. From our small boat my main impression was that mankind is a fragile thing. The mountain in itself may possess a curious physical force. Robert Fisk writes in his book *In Time of War*, 'There were so many crashes on Brandon that the Irish Army Air Corps conducted tests over the mountain later in the war at the request of the Allies because air crews suspected that the hillsides there contained some kind of magnetic force that distorted aircraft navigational equipment.'

Across Brandon Bay we came among the Magharees Islands, half a dozen of them, scattered confusingly in the approaches to a mainland inlet called Scraggane Bay. Free speech is a characteristic of life on *Sarakiniko,* so each tricky bit of pilotage will be accompanied by cries of 'You turned too soon' and 'You should keep on,' but eventually anchorage was achieved in Scraggane Bay near a solitary yacht from Wales. Its rather elderly owner, sailing single handed, had rigged his trysail on to his backstay. 'To keep her head into the wind,' he shouted, 'it should stop the rolling.'

Joan looked up, dismay on her face. 'Oh God! Another night on the floor.'

'The cabin sole,' I corrected.

'It makes no difference.'

As we bent over a cockpit lunch the Welshman went past, a flash of designer colours on a sailboard. He spun round half a mile away and bounced back to yell, 'I'm a sailboard freak. Going right across Brandon Bay tomorrow.' Five minutes later he crossed our stern again. 'Did you get the forecast?'

'Yes we did; not too bad.'

'I think he's lonely,' said Joan, 'and now he's gone back to his boat.'

Five minutes later the sailboard was on the way again. This time he spilled wind skilfully and came alongside waving a fax. 'Just got this from Bracknell. It may help you.'

We walked up a slipway past upended curraghs. Shining like

long black garden snails, these were the first we had seen. An affable man balancing on an oil drum to paint a trawler saw us examining them.

'Mainly the lads use them now to get in and out to the fishing boats.'

The oars, I noticed, were long and about two and a half inches broad throughout. 'No blades,' I said.

'No. Straight all the way. Blades would catch the wind.'

Behind the spongy hillocks, covered in seapink and campion, were some neat lawns and disciplined flower-beds in front of ranch-style homes. The man from the trawler came past on his bicycle and explained that the houses belonged to an American lawyer, a German and to an Irish family down from Dublin.

'Quieter in winter?' I asked.

'Ah yes. Too many houses, too few people.'

But the housebuilding goes on. The vans and battered cars of workmen were parked not far away, their owners whistling, radios blaring. Pat climbed a farm gate – like a good countryman, on the hinged end – and claimed he could see the coast of Clare to the north. Our road map showed a crossroads where Joan hoped for a shop selling ice-cream. We set off across a country-side of wide skies, fields in which cattle fed themselves in leisurely fashion, and many white bungalows. A remarkable stock of aban-doned motor-cars, tractors and agricultural junk peered from rank grass and wild flowers. There were not many trees but, as a substitute, telephone and electricity poles marched in every direc-tion supporting cat's cradles of wire. We discovered a general store behind which meadows ran down to the beach. This was a practical place and seemed to sell everything from rubber eels and brandy snaps to fishing lines and rice, with supplies stacked on timber shelves, hanging from the ceiling, or lying about in open cardboard boxes on the floor. A lady driving a beaten-up old banger halted outside for a chat with a friend passing by in a BMW, their windows open to each other.

'Sure, they're all fine, Jenny. One's in Germany, the other out in Saudi Arabia. Oh, they'll all be back next month.'

Back on board even Joan agreed that the swell had faded.

Sarakiniko tugged gently at her chain, yawing a little this way and that, running up on it and falling back like a horse restive to be off. Young men, massive shoulders bursting out of their T-shirts, walked curraghs to the water and started on training sprints for the coming regattas. The craft sped out towards the islands, black bananas which seemed scarcely to kiss the sea. An unladen curragh moves very fast and can change direction instantly, the last an essential attribute, for its seaworthiness depends on meeting big seas bows on and riding over them. 'It is astonishing what a sea they will venture to encounter, one where a ship's boat would immediately founder but these boats mount with every wave,' says a report on Co. Clare published in 1808. 'It is nothing uncommon for a man to put his foot through the skin when much worn; if he has nothing at hand to cram into the hole he must keep his leg there until he reaches the shore.'

Curraghs were perfectly adapted to their environment. On a coast with few harbours they could easily be carried ashore. In regions with few trees where timber was expensive, the frame, with the exception of the gunwale, could be made of hazel and sally rods tied with fishing cord. Sacking and tar completed the raw materials. Repairs to a tear from the rocks were a matter of hot tar, canvas and needle and thread.

Ten minutes got the mainsail up next morning, the rubber dinghy lashed down and the anchor and chain in. On a light wind we turned away from the crescent of beach and laid a course for Kerry Head. Fenit Harbour and its sheltered marina, to which we might have fled had a heavy northern swell come into Scraggane, now lay east of us under the early sun. Further in lay the town of Tralee, where a replica of one of the more famous Irish emigrant ships, the *Jeanie Johnson*, is at present being built. A three-masted barque originally designed to carry 200 passengers and a crew of 17, she took emigrants directly from Tralee to ports in the United States and Canada between 1847 and 1858, and never lost a passenger. At the turn of the century the replica ship will cross the Atlantic following the route of her namesake.

We crossed Tralee Bay and continued past Banna Strand, where Sir Roger Casement was put ashore from a German submarine in

1916. The submarine had been accompanied by the *Aud*, carrying arms for the intended rebellion, but ship and submarine were separated and the *Aud* was later captured by the Royal Navy; her crew scuttled the ship as it was being escorted to Cork. Casement had come to supervise the arms landing, though other accounts suggest that he meant to persuade the rebel leaders to call off the rising. The submarine commander did not get the impression that Casement intended to persuade his fellow revolutionaries to defer their rebellion, but concluded that he was simply pessimistic about its chances. After landing on Banna, Casement was very soon arrested, and later tried and executed for treason.

The commander of U 19 was Raymund Weisbach, who as tor-pedo officer on the submarine U 20 fired the missile that sank the *Lusitania*. 'I fired one,' he told Dr de Courcy Ireland in 1966, when he returned to Tralee for the anniversary of the ill-fated rising, though he agreed that two explosions had been heard. A modern theory suggests coal dust may have provoked the second. He presented de Courcy Ireland with the original track chart of U 19 and it is now among the fascinating exhibits in the National Maritime Museum at Dun Laoghaire. In May 1917 Weisbach was himself torpedoed by a British submarine based at Haulbowline in Cork. He had been given orders – surely drafted by a landlubber – to obtain the name and port of registry of any ship before attacking it. His craft was torpedoed when he surfaced in heavy weather to try to do so. Weisbach and six surviving crewmen were rescued by the British vessel which sank them, and the German officer had unstinted praise for the commander of the British submarine (later Admiral Raikes) who revived him with whisky and lent him his spare uniform. After the war Weisbach supported the Weimar Republic and, in the Second World War, failed to obtain any significant posting. Described to me by John de Courcy Ireland as a thoughtful and unassuming man, Weisbach, whose involvement with Ireland had been so tragic, died in 1971.

We swerved around lobster-pot buoys as we rounded Kerry Head, a rocky hammerhead reaching out into the Atlantic and guarding the mouth of the Shannon. The tide helped *Sarakiniko* up the great estuary for several hours, then it died and turned against us and we had to motor hard to keep the fields of Co. Clare slipping astern. An oil tanker appeared, moving lazily up-stream.

'The first real ship we've seen since we left the English Channel,' Joan remarked.

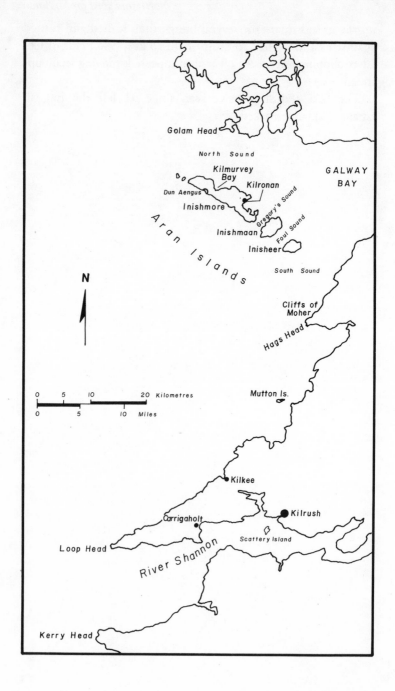

FOUR

To the Isles of Aran

THE DEMANDS OF farming and domestic life deprived me of Pat and Joan. Joan would rejoin in Donegal; Pat seemed to accept my injunction that he must take a break from harvesting to meet *Sarakiniko* at Bangor and sail down the Irish Sea.

'Madeline would see it as your duty.'

'I'll tell her you said so.'

There were few people about at mid-week. I sat in the cockpit reading, listening to *Sarakiniko's* fenders squeak against the pontoon, unable to decide whether I was lonely or relishing this short period of solitude. The deck was cluttered with cans of diesel and bags of groceries when Barry and Tony climbed aboard. They had not previously met, but I knew they would get on. They were a crew who knew that a good joke is often as valuable as a lifebelt, and anyhow it takes at least a week to get tired of another man's stories. Barry was a London barrister ensnared by the lure of the west. I myself had crewed for Tony – though only on land, when we hoisted his boat on a trailer to bring it to his inland home. It was not the best of voyages. Some miles later one of the wheels collapsed and the boat was shipwrecked on a Co. Waterford ditch.

Beyond the marina stood the remains of a small brick-built station house; a derelict curragh lay on the nearby railway platform, black bow curving up from a bed of nettles. This was the Kilrush terminus of the West Clare Railway, immortalised by Percy French.

Are you right there, Michael, are you right?

Do you think that we'll be home before the night?

We took so long in startin'

Sure you couldn't say for certain

But we might now, Michael, so we might.

'Didn't he sue the railway for bad timekeeping?' I asked the laid-back fellow manning the marina's fuel pump.

'No. They say 'twas the other way round: they sued him for the bad publicity.'

As he replaced the hose I asked what I owed.

'The office seems to be shut. You had 77 litres. Just tell them tomorrow.'

Kilrush, on the southern lip of the Clare coast, had long been a working harbour, while Kilkee on the Atlantic coast, a place still glorying in a magnificent beach of golden sand, was Limerick's favourite seaside resort. Eventually, however, Kilrush overcame the drawback of having a harbour that dried out at low tide by building a pier at the nearby hamlet of Cappa to take trippers who would arrive by paddle steamer from the city.

Kilrush prospered by sending cargoes to Limerick, especially boatloads of peat. James Paterson, a former lieutenant in the fleet of Royal Naval gunboats based on the Shannon, dispatched the first cargo of oats from Kilrush in 1807 and the first of butter in 1810. By 1813 he operated two packet boats into Limerick. Paterson's Corn Store, built in 1812, was demolished only in 1967, while his home, Bonny Doon, is still occupied. Colourful and graceful houses line the immensely wide main street which slopes gently to the harbour. Kilrush was a tidily planned estate town, conscientiously developed by the landlord family, the Vandeleurs.

We were now in one of the country's finest cruising grounds, a great river set not only with delightful towns and small villages but with creeks and quays innumerable. Mud in places, of course, glorious mud: Shannon folk had designed a special flat-bottomed boat, the gandolo, to slide over it.

When a man wandered down the pontoon and introduced himself as Adrian O'Connell, we welcomed someone who could help us match harbours to history. As our *Sailing Directions* noted, he had run a boatyard at Clifden in Co. Galway and was now based in Kilrush. He had noticed the Royal Cruising Club burgee at our masthead, and advice and reminiscences were soon flowing as he knew several of our members.

'Where do you go from here?'

'Probably to the Aran Islands,' I said, 'and then I think the Connemara mainland.'

I took out a sheaf of charts, and with a pencil he plotted a route between the islands of Clew Bay which would take us safely into Westport.

When I told him we had anchored at Derrynane, we discovered that Daniel O'Connell was Adrian's ancestor. He told us that Daniel's son, Maurice, had organised a regatta at Kilrush in 1832 and, elated by its success, had subsequently established the Western Yacht Club. By 1837 the club had no less than 460 members who between them owned nearly 200 yachts. The Kilrush regatta nonetheless kept a place for local fishing boats, turf boats and curraghs in its races.

With time and money to allow them make full use of a wonderful coast, members sailed north to Galway and in 1834 organised a regatta in the bay, the race for larger yachts being won by the Knight of Glin's 30-ton cutter *Reinvella*. It was a substantial vessel by latterday standards but there were larger; Crofton Vandeleur's Kilrush-based *Caroline* was all of 49 tons. The club's name was later altered to the Royal Western of Ireland Yacht Club. In the 1830s six members lived in Kilrush, another 23 in Limerick and many more in counties along the river: the O'Briens of Dromoland and Cratloe, Macnamaras of Doolin, the FitzGeralds of Glin, and the Wyndham-Quins of Adare, newly created Earls of Dunraven. Prosperous Limerick merchants such as the Barringtons and Russells were members. The O'Connell link ensured a station at Tralee in Kerry. Those seemed to have been relatively benign years, the Napoleonic Wars a fading memory, the Famine a horror still to come.

The crown of British yachting in the eighteenth century was the Royal Yacht Squadron in Cowes, whose members enjoyed the special privilege of flying the Royal Navy's White Ensign. Although other clubs had also been entitled to do so, the British Admiralty decided to restrict the White Ensign exclusively to the RYS when it began to suspect that members of several prestigious clubs were often trying their hand at a little smuggling on the side. Clubs were duly notified, but the Clerk at the Admiralty apparently forgot the Royal Western, whose members continued to receive warrants to wear the White. Eventually the Royal St George Yacht Club at Kingstown (as Dun Laoghaire was then called) spoiled the fun by asking to have the same right. Questions were raised in the British parliament, and in 1858 the Admiralty reasserted that only the RYS should wear the ensign on its yachts.

At its height, some 18 yachts were registered with the Royal Western in the Shannon estuary alone. The club, however, was devastated by the Famine, although of course its affluent members did not share directly in the sufferings of the ordinary people. By the 1870s the Royal Western's headquarters had moved to a terraced house on the Cobh waterfront, from where it continued to dominate west coast sailing until 1882, when the Royal Galway Yacht Club was formed.

It is remarkable that three challenges for the great yachting trophy, the America's Cup, were made by two men whose homes lay on either side of the Shannon estuary. A naval officer, Lieutenant William Henn of Paradise House near the tiny port of Kildysart on the north shore, competed in 1886 with a 102-ton cutter *Galatea*, built by J. Beavor Webb of Fermanagh. He was beaten in two straight races. Subsequently the Earl of Dunraven, who was introduced to yacht racing by John Jameson in Dublin Bay, challenged through the Royal Yacht Squadron in 1893 and 1895 with those huge cutters *Valkyrie II* and *III*. His failure to win the cup did not diminish his love of boats, for even at the age of 79 he was building *Sona*, one of the first diesel-powered yachts, and testing her on the Shannon in 1921.

We took a day off to motor out of the lock and visit Scattery Island, less than two miles offshore. Scattery is one of the most important sites of early Christian Ireland. St Senan founded a monastery there in the sixth century and remains of seven churches are still extant. The island's 120-foot-high round tower has been a sailor's seamark for many centuries. The Vikings sailed in and raided it, of course, and they must have been astonished and presumably delighted to find that the monks, for some reason, had built its doorway at ground level.

Regard for *Sarakiniko*'s topsides led me to anchor off rather than lie against the rough stone pier. The ruins of O'Kane's Castle peered above the shingle. Hundreds of people would once go out to Scattery to perform penance on their bare knees, but it has remained untouched since the last residents left in the 1960s. The derelict houses of the village remain surprisingly intact, even to a postbox set in one wall. Many island families were river pilots, guiding ships along the estuary to the docks at Limerick.

Beyond the village lay fields abundant in flowers, lanes spongy with moss and bracken, and hundreds of rabbits having a wild time. The land is of ecological interest, for no artificial fertiliser has ever been used here and Scattery is therefore one of the few remaining examples of semi-natural grasslands in Ireland. We wandered over carpets of wild flowers, marvelling at the fact that St Senan had had the will to refuse entry to this Eden not only to all ordinary women, but even to a sister saint, Cannara, who was brought here by an angel. The poet Thomas Moore – of the melodies – set that scene in song.

> Oh haste and leave the sacred isle
> Unholy barque, ere morning smile
> Upon thy deck though dark it be
> A female form I now do see.
> For I have sworn this sainted sod
> Shall ne'er by woman's feet be trod.
>
> Oh Father, send not hence my barque
> Through wintry winds o'er billows dark.
> I come with humble heart to share
> Thy morn and eve in daily prayer.
> Nor, my feet, Oh holy saint
> The brightness of thy sod do taint.
>
> The lady's prayer St Senan spurned.
> The wind blew fresh. The barque returned.
> The legend hints that had the maid
> Till unto morning's light delayed

And given the saint one rosy smile
She'd ne'er have left his lonely isle.

At the southern tip of Scattery we came to the military battery built between 1806 and 1815, part of a series of defences constructed on the Shannon to protect Limerick. Though over 60 miles from the open sea, the city had a prosperous trade in corn and provisions, and carried ships of up to 500 tons. Its merchants were rich, including many Catholics such as the Roches, who built a huge warehouse on the quays and owned ships employed in the West Indies trade. This protective battery had six 24-pounders and a bomb-proof barracks for 20 men defended by two howitzers. Similar batteries were built along the Thames estuary and, as none of these survive, one hopes Scattery's unique example of coastal artillery defences will be carefully preserved.

For many years the War Department blocked attempts to build a lighthouse on Scattery as they felt it would get in the way of their firing practice, but one was constructed eventually. The Mahon family became the lighthouse keepers until 1933, when they were withdrawn to the mainland, but they continue to cross to the island to tend the light, maintaining a family tradition which goes back to the 1840s.

SARAKINIKO, NO longer in the first flush of youth, did not have to follow the tradition once expected of new boats by sailing around Scattery 'sunwise' and taking on board pebbles or island water as a guarantee of safety at sea. We left Kilrush, however, on an afternoon of such poor visibility that no artificial aid would have been spurned, though our destination was only the pier of Carrigaholt, some nine miles towards Loop Head.

We had decided that the Aran Islands should be our next objective, but the desire to get there was tempered by the fact that we were facing into the unknown once we passed beyond the Loop, and the weather forecast was uncertain. I turned to the *Sailing Directions*, which informed me that 'The 45 miles of coast from Loop Head to Black Head at the entrance to Galway Bay has no safe anchorages and, being exposed to the full ocean swell, is best admired from a comfortable distance.'

Barry brought a folded chart to the cockpit. Yet again I wiped the mist off my glasses.

'However thick it gets, we should easily see Carrigaholt Castle; it's right above the new pier.'

'I was thinking about the old harbour up at the village,' Barry said, 'about half a mile further in. It dries out at low water, but we could get in on the rising tide.'

'It's simpler to anchor off the new pier and walk. The inner harbour seems very small and there could be fishing boats and mooring lines all over.'

Barry looked at the compass. 'The wind seems to have gone south-east.'

'I suppose we could be exposed in that case,' I admitted, but when Tony reminded us of our plan to leave for Aran at 5 am we decided to chance a rolly night by the pier.

The head of Carrigaholt pier did just about give us shelter. A few yards inshore the water remained placid; a few yards beyond rolled a gentle swell. We left *Sarakiniko* swinging on her chain, launched the dinghy, climbed the rusty ladder to the quay and walked to the village past rioting hedges of fuchsia. Talk flowed in the pub. Maurice Healy's description in *The Old Munster Circuit* of a Cork conversation seemed equally apt for Clare: 'One voice starts but is almost immediately joined by a second and third which descant about the first, adding to it, embellishing it and sometimes even contradicting it but never interfering with the story.'

I found myself boxed in a corner beside a man who may have been called Don O'Driscoll. While the sound system belted out country music, I listened with interest to his fishing lore, and it poured out when he heard we were sailors. 'On yer own boat; man, ye must be rich.' By his account the Shannon was the very Valhalla of sea angling. Apparently the river brings down such a variety of nutrients that a rich foodchain persists all year round. The lower links – shrimps, prawns, sprats and sand-eels – attract shoals of mackerel, herring and smelt. These draw in the bigger predators like pollock, cod and herring, whose abundance attracts dolphins and porpoises, tuna and blue shark and, if you like, the final predator, the European angler who lands at Shannon Airport.

'Catch and release is the big thing now,' my informant insisted. 'Lots of the lads around here don't even gaff the big ones; they lasso them. And after you land your fish you might hardly get time to take a picture before it's unhooked and back in the water. I tell you, last year they got 79 blue sharks up to 120 pounds with just three boats out of Kilrush.'

In 1991, Irish waters within the state's exclusive 200-mile fishing limits were declared a sanctuary for whales and dolphins – the first in Europe. We knew of the Shannon estuary's resident population of 30 or 40 bottlenose dolphins; indeed, we had seen several today when at least a dozen black fins broke the water near *Sarakiniko*. Occasionally one would leap from the sea and re-enter in a fan of white spray. I had seen several boats in Kilrush offering 'Whale and Dolphin Watching' trips, and their skippers did not expect many demands for money back.

The Irish Whale and Dolphin Group, which lobbied to have those species protected in Irish waters, distributes identification posters and information sheets to schools and societies, arranges sea watches to assess populations, breeding successes and local movements, records strandings and monitors threats to cetaceans, which range from surface drift net entanglement to contaminants. The Department of Zoology at University College, Cork, and the Ulster Museum co-ordinate national efforts to protect the wild mammals, while a study of a recent mass stranding of white-sided dolphins in Killala Bay in Co. Mayo was part funded by the National Parks and Wildlife Service.

There are two or three strandings every year around the coast, usually of dolphins but also of larger whales such as fin and minke and killer whales. In early 1995 some friends in Co. Waterford came on a large minke whale which had come up the River Suir and was stranded on a mudbank as the tide receded. Working in the dark they successfully refloated the whale some five hours later, and it swam away downstream. Booklets – 'Live Stranding Guidelines' – are now distributed about the best way to handle a beached whale or dolphin.

Times do change. There were two small whaling stations near Achill, Co. Mayo, up to the First World War. On the island of Inishkea South they caught an average of 60 whales a year, an annual yield of some 4,000 barrels of oil. Another station worked from Ardelly in Blacksod Bay. It has been estimated that between 1908 and 1920 whalers in Mayo and Donegal killed over 1,000 whales, a significant number, though a trifle compared to the 37,000 killed in the Arctic in 1930 alone and the reduction in the world blue whale population from 330,000 to 16,000 in ten years. These became fully protected in 1966.

Hunting for small whales was commonplace along the coast. Porpoises were exported from Galway and the east coast to Bristol fish merchants throughout the eighteenth century. On his *Tour of Ireland* in 1776, Arthur Young visited Donegal, where he wrote of Thomas Nesbitt of Kilmacredon who was involved in whaling in England and the West Indies. The reputed numbers of sperm whales off the Donegal coast from November to February each year induced him to start a fishery there, and in 1758 he bought a 140-ton vessel in England and hired harpooners to man it. Only one whale was caught in the next year and 1760 was equally disappointing, even for the several Greenland, Dutch and English vessels who worked off the Donegal coast. The whalers enthusiasm remained undaunted:

Equip your Boats with Sharp Harpoon and Lance.
Let's strive our Pullick Treasure to Advance.
So shall Returning Gold reward our Toil
When London Lamps shall glow with Irish Oil.

In May 1844 the *Northern Whig* wrote: 'Bantry Bay has been the scene of great excitement, high enjoyment and most valuable occupation for the people of the locality this week, in consequence of a very large shoal of whales – Grampus species – which entered that harbour on Monday and found their way to the romantic bay of Glengarriff on Tuesday – the evening of which day found all kinds of boats, weapons and missiles in requisition for the attack on the herd. An immense number were secured – a correspondent states 300, the value of which he computed at

£1,500,000. Nothing could exceed the spirit-stirring character of the whole scene, enhanced as it was by the beautiful weather and splendid scenery of the Bay.'

Quite how the weather and scenery enhanced that scene is not very clear.

This part of Co. Clare is shaped like a foot reaching its big toe towards the Atlantic. Carrigaholt shelters in a twist of the instep. In his analysis of early sea charts, the late Professor T. J. Westropp concluded that there was a long-held tendency to place Ireland too close to Spain. 'Even in the eighteenth century,' he wrote, 'there was a trace of this in that [a] village on the Shannon was by tradition called Carrigaholt-next-Spain.' It was to be our only landfall in Clare besides Kilrush, for the track to the Aran Islands would gradually draw us away from the coast.

Clare has long had a reputation as a bastion of nationalism. It returned Daniel O'Connell to Westminster in 1829. It was here that Parnell made a famous speech advocating the practice of boycotting in the land agitation of the late nineteenth century. In this century, Eamon de Valera was for over 40 years the Member for Clare in the Irish Dáil.

Traces of old unhappy days remain. In the Square at Kilrush I had seen Dutch backpackers stare in bemusement at a statue commemorating the Manchester Martyrs, Fenians who, attempting to free comrades from a prison van in 1867, killed a police sergeant and were subsequently hanged: 'Judicially murdered' the inscription declared. Carrigaholt carried a roadside plaque 'In memory of Lieut. Walsh, murdered by British troops, March 1918.' That the English never remember and the Irish never forget is an irritatingly self-evident cliché, but if one understands why statue and plaque were erected, one may not wish them removed.

We stood with mugs of tea at 4.30 next morning, groaning and complaining that there seemed to be no wind anyway, until Tony in his quiet efficient way began to drag the dinghy aboard and we had to get moving. The southern Shannon shore was visible in the oblique light as we motored down to Kilcredaun Point. The wind picked up. We shared the helm, an hour each. I returned to my bunk after breakfast, absorbed in a book while a sailing breeze moved sunbeams to and fro across the bulkheads, the boat a private joy carrying us towards the horizon. My pleasure in *Sarakiniko's* comforts was all the greater for Ridgeway and Blyth's *A Fighting Chance*, an account of rowing across 3,000 miles of implacable Atlantic in a 20-foot open cockleshell, *English Rose III*. We were bound for the place where they had landed after 92 days at sea, the Aran island of Inishmore.

Eventually the towering mass of Loop Head loomed above us. A lonely coast this. There had been very few dwellings visible once we passed beyond Kilclogher Head on the way to Loop. The cliffs and terraces lurched towards the sea, the rock folding in layers and whorls of stone. We had never seen stratification on such a scale. It was bone white in the sun, dark and metallic in the shade. No more the old red sandstone of Munster. We were drawing nearer the raw limestone of Connaught, which Cromwell's surveyor Ludlow called 'a savage land, yielding neither water enough to drown a man, nor a tree to hang him, nor soil enough to bury him'.

A south-west wind had been pinching the boat, but now as the lighthouse drew abeam we bore away north and the wind filled the sails. The new course should lead through Gregory Sound, which separates the big island of Inishmore from Inishmaan. The third island, Inisheer, lies closer still to the Clare mainland, the southern side of all three islands facing the full force of the Atlantic swell. 'Owing to the steep cliffs on both sides of Gregory Sound the sea can be very unpleasant in a high swell' warned the *Directions*, but the swell seemed moderate today and the sound was free of reefs. We might even carry the tide through and bear away to port for a sheltered anchorage on the north side of Inishmore.

The wind picked up more and the porpoises arrived, diving under the hull, pacing us on the beam, cutting ahead, usually in twos and threes, and leaping from the water so that we could see their beady eyes and grinning faces. They plunged in unison so close to the bow that water spattered on deck where Barry and Tony knelt with cameras. I clipped on the automatic steering and went below for my own camera, and in the saloon I could hear an occasional squeak communicated through the resonance of the hull. For about half an hour they surrounded the boat with a display of magnificent energy and enjoyment.

To starboard the coast was receding. We tried to make out Mutton Island and Spanish Point, where survivors from two Armada ships, driven back by gales when they could not clear the Blaskets, swam ashore to face execution by the High Sheriff of Clare on the orders of Sir Richard Bingham, Governor of Connaught. From a seaman's viewpoint this is a coast to put behind one. 'No secure shelter,' declared the *Directions*, 'save a fine weather anchorage inside Mutton Island.' But the author hastened to add: 'This area is rock strewn and offers no shelter in a heavy onshore swell and is also a lee shore in winds between north-west and south-west.' Further north the sandy beach of Lahinch, where the seas run in through Liscannor Bay, is ideal for surfing, but it offers 'no safe shelter' for the mariner. A drying pier, yes, but 'subject to such a scend in gales that craft in it will be broken up'.

John Holland was born in Liscannor in 1841. His family was closely involved in the Fenian movement, and when John Breslin and John Devoy began to raise funds to develop a form of 'underwater canoe' to attack British warships, Holland contributed a design that became known as 'the Fenian Ram'. Work on it began in 1879 in New York. Thirty-one foot six inches in length, it weighed 19 tons and was powered by a 15-horsepower petrol engine; an electric motor took over once it went underwater. Its development became such a drain on the Fenian Skirmishing Fund that Fenian leader O'Donovan Rossa called a halt to the project. Holland later broke with the Fenians, but his early model was resurrected in 1916 and put on show to raise funds for the victims of the Rising. He went on to design several submarines but it is perhaps ironic that he sold his final plans for a submarine to the British Admiralty.

'I think I can see the Cliffs of Moher,' Barry called. They lay on the horizon to the north-east, quite visible in the distance, a succession of snout-like headlands rising sheer above the sea in great bands of stratified flags. They are one of the wonders of Ireland, not because of their height – Slieve League in Donegal is three times higher – but because of the awesome five-mile reach of precipices overhanging the sea. I thought of Ridgeway and Blyth coming in near here and the wind strong from the west, building to a gale.

I had problems of my own to hand. 'There seem to be two islands ahead,' I said uncertainly, 'but not in the right place and fairly small: Inishmore is nine miles long.' Barry gazed silently through the binoculars for some moments.

'It could be cloud or haze.'

'No. It's land I'm sure.'

Tony clambered back from the bow. 'It's land, but I think it's not two islands. See the way Inishmore dips right down half-way along.' We followed his finger and made out a trace of the low ground connecting tall cliffs which stood out on either side. We were right on course. Presently Gregory Sound opened up and, in late afternoon, we carried the last of the tide past the end of Inishmore. A holiday crowd were fishing, casting lines from great tables of stratified rock, waving as we passed. The village of Kilronan lay a few miles away round the corner. Should we anchor there? The smaller islands of Inishmaan and Inisheer passed to starboard. Near the harbour entrance and our point of decision, we saw four crowded ferries. Two passed astern; two were just casting off. Further down the northern coast of the island was the inlet of Kilmurvey. 'It's only a few more miles,' I said, 'and we could walk from there up to Dun Aengus.' The prospect of finding a spot of our own seemed especially attractive on such a lovely evening. Barry pointed out that we were short of bread but was reminded that things of the spirit come first. We could make bread. We turned for the inlet, crept in past the rocks and anchored. On the skyline Dún Aengus stood out against the sunset.

These stark Gaelic-speaking islands have fascinated visitors for over a century. They provide a fertile habitat for all kinds of romanticism. In his classic *The Aran Islands*, published in 1901, Aran's most famous literary visitor, J.M. Synge, celebrated in rather dull prose a primitive place preserving its integrity against the assault of the modern world. That was a long time ago. He could not have anticipated the dilemma, quite separate from environmental considerations, of dignified people being compelled to hand over more and more of their identity to the tourist trade. No tourist is allowed to forget that Robert Flaherty made the film *Man of Aran* on Inishmore in 1934: it is shown several times a day to the summer visitors. The pressure of tourism is a worldwide problem now, made more complicated by the fact that thoughtful visitors wish the industry would moderate its growth while local businesses think otherwise. The fact that the Irish language survives here may provide the islanders with a curtain of privacy against the prying gaze of the thousands of visitors who pour into this small island each summer.

Synge could hardly have anticipated the airstrip either, nor the satellite dishes or the outboards clamped on curraghs, and surely not the figure in shorts standing on the empty beach next morning, balancing on one leg, instep of the other against his knee, arms held aloft. I called down to Tony.

'Perhaps he's trying to signal us,' he muttered from the depths of his flea-bag. Barry was equally uninterested. 'Irish semaphore maybe,' he grunted. I decided on an early pull ashore and found myself chatting to a New York banker who had been practising Tai Chi on the strand.

We made a foray to the village, a pleasant walk past stone-walled fields strewn with purple orchids, the smell of tar from the road reviving nostalgic memories of how roads used to be. Four men were shovelling limestone grit into the potholes. Tourists swayed past them on jaunting cars.

When Barry explained our bread shortage to the woman in the pub, she kindly left the bar and fetched a loaf from her own kitchen. Then she filled our water containers. I decided to push our luck further.

'Do you have showers, by any chance?'

'No, thank God, not a drop for days.'

I cannot say if we discovered the real Aran. Probably not. Nor do the boatloads of tourists dumped on the quay at Kilronan.

But I feel we became aware of its intangible dimensions. The stones of Inishmore press the past upon you. Scores of remains of the early Christian period survive on all three islands, and one foundation, St Enda's, was a landmark in the development of monasteries throughout Ireland. It is said that St Brendan visited Enda before setting out on his wondrous voyage. A stone inscribed with the legend 'Pray for Bran the Pilgrim' was found in 1822 at Temple Brecan on Inishmore. There are remains of round towers which may have been useful seamarks, and tradition suggests that the islands were on a coastal or inter-island pilgrimage route.

As we climbed towards Dún Aengus, the vista which opened up before us was so fantastic it had the quality of a dream. The land seemed made of tiers of fine lacework – terraces of stone walls fading into the sky, and built, you think, simply to fence fields already made of flagstone. Here soil was created by the basketful: a layer of seaweed and a layer of sand set into the warm limestone to make earth, the island itself a patchwork of thousands of such tiny fields. One walks carefully. Most of the flags are seamed with ankle-trapping rifts, out of which grow foxglove, saxifrage, maidenhair and little yellow and orange roses. On the ridge running down to the edge of the cliff, a single limestone flag may cover a whole acre. Caught by the light, this landscape of grey stone resembled a place glittering in flood, falling away from you until, at the end of its reach, the eye drops suddenly on to the purple-black sea.

The citadel above, possibly 3,000 years old, stands on a cliff edge 260 feet above the sea. It is one of the sights of the western world. A stone chevaux-de-frise covers the last 50 or 60 feet of ground before the fort. Attackers trapped in its upright shafts were at the mercy of the soldiers positioned on the walls of the *dún*, concentric drystone walls some 20 feet high and 15 feet thick, surrounding the inner enclosures. The walls terminate at the edge of the cliff, as though they had been chopped off. There would have been no escape for the defenders if the fortress were-taken.

From the cliffs of Aran, as the sun seems to fall through the surface of the ocean, one can easily understand how an imaginative people would see in the mists of the Atlantic the legendary Isle of the Blessed, the place that the ancient Irish called Hy Brasil, where souls may sojourn before going to heaven. In Low Latin, Hy Brasil apparently means 'of a reddish colour', and it is said that when Portuguese navigators discovered the country around the Amazon, forested with trees of a reddish hue, they called the land Brazil. The fabled land is depicted on tenth-century Anglo-Saxon maps and was shown for centuries thereafter as lying off the south-west coast of Ireland, roughly circular in shape with a strait through its centre. Bristol merchants financed several voyages in search of the island from 1480 onwards. In 1325 charts placed it south-west of Galway Bay. A Captain Nesbitt of Killybegs, Co. Down, claimed to have landed on Hy Brasil in September 1674 on a return voyage from France. A.G. Finlay's *Memoir of the North Atlantic Ocean* records Brazil Rock as having been 'seen' by a British ship in 1761 at latitude 51 degrees 10 minutes north, longitude 16 degrees 12 minutes west, which would put it some 250 miles west of Kerry. Hy Brasil remained on charts until 1865, though by then it was reduced to the status of a rock.

Professor T. J. Westropp, addressing the Royal Irish Academy in June 1912, spoke of seeing remarkable mirages in the west of Ireland. He had seen images of islands several times. 'One evening in 1872 as the sun went down,' he recalled, 'a dark island suddenly appeared far out to sea, but not on the horizon. It had two hills, one wooded, and between these from a low plain rose wisps and curls of smoke. My mother, brother Ralph, and several friends saw it at the same time.' He stated that in subsequent years he had seen such apparent islands off Clare in 1887 and off Mayo in 1910, and felt that it 'was not wonderful that the belief should have been so strongly held, affecting early map-makers and sending Columbus over the trackless deep'.

Could there have been a western island in remote times? An island which later sank into the ocean floor? After all, some 150 miles west and south-west of Ireland the Porcupine Bank and the Great Sole Bank lie in the comparative shallows of 150 and 100 fathoms. The similarity of the Irish tradition to the classical tale of a lost Atlantis is also obvious. Perhaps a race memory is preserved of a land which did protrude above the Atlantic in the remote past. I doubt if there is such a thing as a legend without some foundation in truth and history.

The legendary island inspired the nineteenth-century poet Gerald Griffin.

On the ocean that hollows the rocks where ye dwell
A shadowy land has appeared, as they tell.
Men thought it a region of sunshine and rest
And they called it Hy Brasil, the Isle of the Blessed.
From year unto year on the ocean's blue rim
The beautiful spectre showed lovely and dim.
The golden clouds curtained the deep where it lay
And looked like an Eden, away far away.

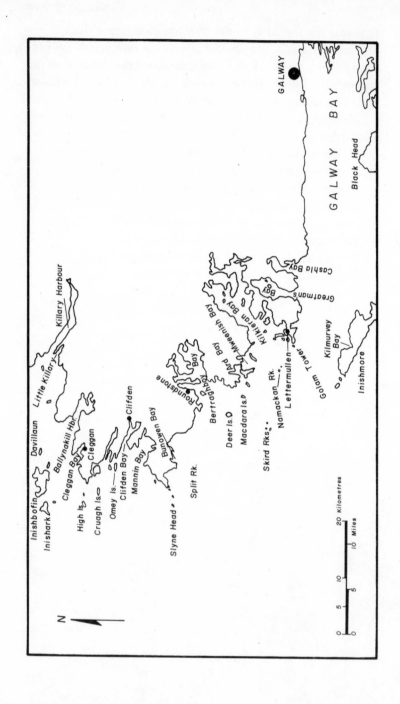

FIVE

Rocks, Reefs and Rollers

THE RAGGED COAST of Connemara was waiting. The barometer had dropped during the night and now the Shipping Forecast warned of south-east winds climbing to Force 6. The mainland eight miles away was only occasionally visible, and over the next few days we would have to steer through a long sprawl of reefs and islands and navigate around Slyne Head, a formidable point in bad weather.

Once we were safely around Slyne Head, we would run north to Inishbofin's sheltered harbour. The job this afternoon was to seek out a snug anchorage in the creeks along the way. Tomorrow perhaps we would reach Roundstone. It was best to put a reef in the mainsail and push on now, watching the weather hour by hour. Barry wound the winch and the sail went up, snaking and rattling in the freshening wind. I pulled on the reefing line until the lower five feet of sail lay bundled over the boom. The jib needed no immediate attention for, with roller reefing, the sail can be wound up or expanded from the cockpit. Purists may stick to tradition and enjoy changing jibs, dropping one sail down the forehatch, dragging the other up, and being hit by bucketfuls of cold water over the bow. Not any longer for the skipper and crew of *Sarakiniko*. 'You and I have fought the good fight,' I shouted to Barry.

'For long enough,' he grinned. 'Three cheers for roller reefing.'

Golam Tower was the secret of landfall. We had caught a glimpse of it earlier before the murk had closed in, but we knew it bore almost due north, and as the boat surged into the chop and got a mile offshore, we spotted it again. As a stern wind urged us away from Inishmore, small white horses were covering the sea. Away to starboard lay the huge rectangle of Galway Bay.

Galway might have become a transatlantic terminal, a rival to

Liverpool and Cork, but all efforts to establish a service from there seemed dogged by misfortune. When its line to Galway was completed, the Midland and Great Western Railway decided to finance a scheme for a mail and passenger service across the Atlantic and chartered a 900-ton steamer which sailed in January 1851 to Halifax, Nova Scotia, in ten days. However, she ran aground in fog on the return trip and, though passengers and crew were saved, she was a total loss. A John Lever of Manchester revived the scheme in 1858, with a company known as the Galway Line. His ship also suffered mishaps which culminated in its running out of coal on the return voyage so that the captain, like his enterprising counterpart in Jules Verne's *Around the World in Eighty Days*, had to order masts, bulwarks and part of the cargo to be used as fuel. The *Indian Empire* made it to Galway, but the trip from New York had taken 34 days. Nevertheless, in April 1859 the Post Office awarded the Galway Line a contract to carry the Newfoundland mails. The line planned to use four paddle steamers, which would be named after the provinces of Ireland, but the first, the *Connaught*, was lost by fire near Boston and the others suffered gale or collision damage. The last wooden paddle steamer to be built for Atlantic work was the *Adriatic*, displacing 3,700 tons. She crossed to St John's in less than six days – indeed once in five days six hours – but the lucrative trade being developed by Cunard killed the Galway Line, despite offers of free rail travel to emigrants. The last sailing under its blue flag with red cross and golden harp was in 1864. The *Adriatic* ended up as a storeship off the shores of Nigeria.

Galway Bay seemed strikingly empty today but presently Tony shaded his eyes against the sparkle on the water.

'Hookers! Three Galway hookers, I think.'

In a few moments we could see the black hulls more clearly, their bows bluff like a Dutch barge. The long curve to the hooker's low stern might be traced to the lines of open fishing boats, built for hauling nets aboard. We could see the gaff rig and the huge dark brown sails, which would once have been dressed with a mixture of tar and butter. The mast looked massive, the rigging a challenge to men's muscle. The traditional hooker was

ballasted with stone, which formed a platform on the bottom of
the boat on which the crew could light a fire.

These craft were the workhorses of the coast. Weaving through
narrow channels, often lying against crudely built piers, they were
given a decided tumblehome, or inward slope, to their upper topsides to minimise damage to the hull. The boats we saw may have
been racing; a revival of interest in classic boats is sweeping the
south and west of Ireland and several hookers have been built
recently. Though the hooker was highly seaworthy it had seemed
to be a dying breed until Johnny Healion restored the *Morning
Star* and showed her paces at regattas in Connaught in 1976,
while Ireland's foremost hooker skipper, Paddy Barry, sails an 86-
year-old vintage craft, *St Patrick*, in which he has won the Irish
Cruising Club's senior trophy, the Faulkner Cup, in 1987, 1990
and 1994. He has sailed his boat through arches of ice off the
coast of Greenland, across the Atlantic to Bermuda and along the
East River, Manhattan, where American sailors awarded him the
Blue Water Medal in 1990. In 1997 he took a replica of
Shackleton's ship's boat into the Southern Ocean on an expedition
to recreate the amazing rescue voyage the explorer had made in
1917.

During his attempt to cross the polar continent via the South
Pole, Shackleton's ship was crushed in the ice and sank, leaving
his crew marooned on Elephant Island, 600 miles south-east of
Cape Horn. With a southern winter approaching, Shackleton
and five companions set out in the 22-foot open whaler, *James
Caird*, to sail 850 miles across the Southern Ocean to get help in
South Georgia. Despite atrocious weather conditions out and
back, they returned to Elephant Island four months later and rescued the entire company of 22 men who had stayed behind.

There has always been keen Irish interest in that extraordinary
voyage. Half of the *James Caird*'s crew were Irish, as was
Shackleton, who was born in Kildare. Tim McCarthy, from
Cork, remained irrepressively hopeful all through the rescue
voyage, while Kerryman Tom Crean, Shackleton wrote, 'always
sang when he was steering... the song devoid of tune and monot-
onous as the chanting of a Buddhist monk'. His vocal efforts

were described by another crewman as 'noises... deduced as representing "The Wearing of the Green"'.

Sailors Paddy Barry, Jamie Young and Jarlath Cunnane, together with two mountaineers, sailed from Elephant Island early in 1997 in a replica of Shackleton's boat, the 23-foot *Tom Crean*, built by a team in Kilkenny under boatbuilder Michael Kennedy. Two Force 10 storms saw the little craft, which had been lying to a drogue, violently rolled through 360 degrees on at least three occasions. When another storm was forecast, a decision was taken to transfer to their 54-foot support vessel while 374 miles short of South Georgia, and the *Tom Crean* was then deliberately sunk. Their brave effort had failed, but the expedition increased the respect of all sailors for Shackleton's astonishing feat.

Not far inshore, at Kinvara, they hold a *Cruinniú na mBád* (Gathering of the Boats), adding realism to their racing by loading the vessels with traditional cargoes of turf. The biggest hookers, up to 44 feet overall, could carry a cargo of some ten tons. The smallest, the *pucán*, which purists might not call a hooker at all, was an open rather than a half-decked boat and carried a lug sail, which some say made it a close relation of the Egyptian felucca. Connemara film-maker Bob Quinn puts forward an interesting theory in his documentaries that the west coast of Ireland was much influenced by north Africa. And certainly Algerian pirates such as those who sacked Baltimore are said to have made charts of several coastal areas.

It is difficult not to take a road system for granted and forget how much depended on sailing vessels. Until the later nineteenth century there was little wheeled traffic ashore and most people who could afford it preferred to travel on horseback. As to carriage of goods, coal from Kilkenny's pits, for example, was loaded in coarse baskets on to horse-carts and drawn the 80 miles to Dublin, a journey which took about six days. Turf was the fuel of the west, and hundreds of boats carried it from Connemara down the coast to the Galway market. A great quantity of seaweed was also transported.

There were some 500 boats engaged in the herring industry along the Connemara coast, but despite their number a mere decade before the onset of the Famine, John Barrow wrote in *A Tour Round Ireland*: 'Perhaps there is no country in the world where fish is more abundant or of finer quality than in all the bays and banks of the west coast of Ireland... and not many countries where so little advantage is taken of such a supply. One of the greatest blessings would be a prompt and energetic prosecution of the fisheries, especially for the poor cottager and daily labourer whose families derive a bare existence by feeding on potatoes, moistened perhaps occasionally with a little milk.'

He answers a question I have often asked: why did maritime counties starve, their people driven to seek sustenance from raw limpets and edible seaweed, when fish filled the seas? The blame, Barrow declares, lay with the 'ancient and miserable fishing apparatus of boats and nets – the same now as centuries ago, the dogged habits of the fishermen, want of capital and a lack of means of getting catches moved inland. When a catch is uncertain regular customers cannot be expected so, when they have a great catch, there is little demand for it.'

The fisher-folk of Galway and Mayo were too poor to buy salt to preserve the herring catch. The Galway market was filled with unwanted fish, tons of it 'producing the most disgusting effluvia'. And suitable as the light curragh was for inshore waters when crewed by men of skill and courage, boats of about 50 tons were needed if nets were to be used in deep sea. Away to the north the island of Achill had four curraghs but only one fishing boat, probably of twelve or 15 tons, and gear was often sold prematurely to buy Indian meal as no one anticipated that the potato would fail for three successive years. The Society of Friends did much to supply loans for redeeming boats and nets, and provided boats, gear and warm clothing to Mayo fishermen, but famine relief could not make good a structure which was all but beyond repair, and so people starved within sight of the sea's bounty.

The freshening south-east wind drove us on towards a tangle of islets and reefs. We decided, once past Golam Head, to make smartly to starboard and go for the gap between Golam Island and another called Freaghillaunmore on its north side. Reefs lay all about; the chart looked as if someone had spattered ink over it. The best water here, according to the *Directions*, lay 'two-thirds south of the gap', but there were rocks less than seven feet below the surface at low tide. We crept in, uncomfortably close to pot buoys and dense ribbons of weed being tugged by the current. We moved along the shore past two fish farms, where a man in a launch was scattering food to wildly leaping fish. The wind gusted, piping up and down the rigging and smelling of rain, but *Sarakiniko* had won shelter in Lettermullen Bay. Traces of smoke blew horizontally from the chimneys of some distant cottages. Poor land, scattered with furze and rock, sloped into mottled hills, everywhere interlocked with the curves of water. Wavelets clattered against the hull as Barry and I stood for a while checking to ensure the anchor was holding.

An hour later blue sky appeared as though a curtain had been lifted, the wind dropped away and slanting sunlight lit the bay in shades of lemon and green. We set off for the shop at Lettermullen a few miles away along a tortuous bog road, walking past little stone-strewn fields and rocks embossed brilliantly with lichen, and on the way met a woman exercising a collie. 'I saw you from the cottage above coming in,' she told us. She had retired from a job in Croydon to care for an ailing mother and it seemed likely that she would remain here now. There was something admirably dogged in her determination to create a suburban style garden by these sandy coves and rugged rock spits.

When she told us how much further we had to go, we decided instead to return and settle for pasta and wine on the boat. We wanted to get out through the narrows while the tide was still rising next morning for, if we struck a reef, there would then be a chance of lifting off. First light found us cautiously twisting between a dozen buoys obstructing the fairway: a disabled engine now would have us on the rocks. When we were through, Tony clambered back from the bow.

'I saw rocks right under her a minute ago, but there seemed no point in worrying you.'

We spent the morning rock-hopping, six miles north-west to St Macdara's Island, another six north to Roundstone. We had to identify the reef – Eagle Rock's top-mark was supposed to look like 'a pork pie with a spike', Carricknamackan an 'upturned boat' – line it up with the rocks falling astern, and take compass bearings on those further ahead. Visibility was poor, about two miles. We sailed by Mason Island, with its sad remnants of gables and walls, bleak foundations of a dead community, and then past four huge fish farm netting pens afloat off Red Flag Island, a sign of new activity. Such farms seem an intrusion to some. Ecologists talk of damaging concentrations of waste on the sea floor, and it is widely claimed that the wild sea trout is endangered by parasites linked to intensive sea farming. I suspect a kind of aesthetic objection too, a feeling that King Salmon should not just be casually scooped into baskets. On the other hand, fish farming is a genuinely new industry which could help to lessen the west's dependence on a kind of tourism which sells a romantic myth while letting in Disneyland and the theme park.

We could see the waves exploding on the rocks to seaward, but further in the islands broke the swell. Uplifts of oily-looking water warned us of rocks set deep beneath the surface. As we turned north between St Macdara's and Deer Islands, the wind freshened rapidly, heeling the boat and sending spray lashing into the cockpit. We kept the chart open before us and referred to it constantly. Traditionally, boats passing St Macdara's Island would dip their sails three times in homage to the saint, a tradition repeated in Scattery, Inishglora and several other islands. On St Macdara's a church which probably dates from the sixth century is one of the oldest in Ireland, and on his feast day, 16 July, hookers used to fetch the pilgrims and lie off the sheltered side of the island during the pilgrimage mass. After mass there were picnics and a regatta. A writer in 1683 stated that the island was an inviolable sanctuary but admitted that the only ancient furniture in the church was a wooden statue of St Macdara, which Malachy O'Cadhla, Archbishop of Tuam, had buried 'for special weighty reasons'. The church looked magnificent, its high stone roof excellently restored. No other building distracts the eye across the beds of rock and windbeaten grass.

The mainland was on the bow now and, in visibility which had much improved, the great Connemara mountains, the Twelve Bens, stood shoulder to shoulder in tones of charcoal grey. The wind strengthened further, urging us up Roundstone Harbour. Just as we saw the pier half a mile ahead, the echo-sounder warned of only two feet of clearance for the keels. Roundstone Bar on a falling tide: would *Sarakiniko* make it? We clawed the sails down urgently in case she ran aground at speed. Under motor now, eyes on the flickering dial, we knew that each yard achieved was a yard less to row for shore if we hit the mud and had to anchor out here. The ebb pushed against a sharp wind. A solitary French yacht lay anchored ahead, gyrating in the gusts. We edged towards the pier and lowered the anchor some 200 yards off. It seemed to hold at first, but then we realised we could see more and more of the inner harbour. Clearly we were dragging. Barry stood at the bow, hauling in the chain. The anchor broke surface carrying an oilskin-clad mass tangled in seaweed. Barry looked at it in horror. Tony laughed, went forward with a knife and cut it away – the anchor had hooked a full set of oilskins stuffed with something that looked like an old cushion.

By the time we anchored again, the chop had grown to short breaking waves; this was not the time to try rowing a loaded dinghy to the pier. We shut the hatch on the weather and had a second breakfast, listening to that most satisfying sound, a hard wind when you are safely at anchor.

When the sea went down we rowed ashore amid the screaming gulls. It was time to provision now for the bleak coast that lay ahead. Roundstone's colourful, slated houses rose prettily from the little enclosed harbour. French and Dutch visitors strolled along the main street of the village; Dubliners chatted as people do who come back to a place year after year. Jaguars and Volvos crept along in search of parking space. Further up the village sunburnt men were pitching a small funfair, children joyfully getting in the way, the whole set-up 40 years out of date and all the better for that.

I wanted to phone Joan in London, but two German girls beat me to the phone-box, so I stood around, waiting for them to run out of coins. I heard them call out numbers and replace the receiver; in a moment Mother had called them back. Eventually I tired even of watching the play of sun and shadow on the Twelve Bens, coloured now as no harsh Mediterranean landscape is ever coloured, and went to seek out Barry and Tony, last observed with bags of groceries retiring into O'Dowd's Bar. Rather surprisingly, they had moved on to a craft complex on the edge of the village, and I found them wandering among shops and studios selling everything from lotions to leprechauns, shillelaghs and sheepskins. To my eyes it looked like a shopping centre where history, environment and culture were skilfully packaged and sold.

I had to keep such churlish reactions at bay and pull myself together. In this end-of-century Ireland, what were we really seeking: something of the last great peasantry of western Europe or something that would show a successful outcome to all the struggle and bloodshed over land, all the wars and risings, all the brutal toil? Did one not want the people of Connemara to count their blessings in cars and television sets, in rents from chalets and caravan parks? Was there really a dilemma to tease the conscience? The skilled men in the craftshop, stretching and moulding goatskins to make a *bodhrán* – a traditional single-sided drum – were in their own county with their own mountains around them. Until quite recent years, this land had barely supported a subsistence standard of living. Standards change.

Seen from afar there is a powerful romance about places such as the west of Ireland. It shimmers on the horizon, a vision of life not only without crowds or the rat race, but without malice or envy or crime. Thackeray came to Connemara in 1842 and called into Roundstone. Twenty years earlier there had been no village here, just a store and a small pier, until the Fisheries Board accepted Alexander Nimmo's plan for a harbour which was built by 1825. Nimmo himself had sufficient confidence in Roundstone's future to buy land around the harbour and offer it at low rents to those prepared to build two-storey houses, and several Scottish fishing families came here to live.

Thackeray has left us a description of his visit to the Sessions House: 'A room of some twelve feet square with a deal table and a couple of chairs for the accommodation of the magistrates and a Testament with a paper cross posted on it to be kissed by the witnesses and complainants who frequent the court.' He sat in on several cases. 'I had leisure to make moral reflections, sighing to think that cruelty and falsehood, selfishness and rapacity, dwelt not in crowds alone but flourish all the world over... just as much at home in a hot house in Thavie's Inn as on a lone mountain or rocky seacoast in Ireland, where never a tree will grow.' Pretty trite observations, perhaps, but a corrective to easy nostalgia for a myth of lost innocence.

Jobs remain few in Connemara. The stony handkerchief-sized fields cannot sustain a living. The sea is always treacherous. Those born here have tended to be realistic and escaped to the cities at the first opportunity. But depopulation and decline on the Celtic fringes could be coming to an end. In Scotland the population of the Western Isles is stabilising, the emigrants replaced by newcomers from the British mainland. A year ago we had visited a Hebridean island which has long been our source of smoked salmon, which our family receive by mail order. Half expecting to find a smoke house with peat smoke permeating the ancient thatch, we came instead to an immaculately tiled interior, stainless-steel smoking ovens and a business worked from a computer database. The husband and wife proprietors had migrated from Surrey. 'It's fine if you can stand six hours daylight in mid-winter,' they said. Their greatest problem was that 'Brussels is trying to stop the sending of fish by post. That would finish us.' At the moment, that threat seems to be dormant.

Now there is another option drawing what the Irish call 'blow-ins' to the western edges: information technology. Radio and television started a process by which technology is at last making it possible to combine the romantic pleasures of remoteness with the economic and cultural advantages of the city. Physical access to islands is easier. On those we visited we found a great sense of relief that a helicopter can be called up in cases of serious accident or dangerous illness. The fear of isolation is passing. But the biggest change is in communication. Personal computers, fax machines and the electronic super-highway offer the opportunity to plug remote places into instant contact with the urban world of business and information. It is becoming possible to earn a living from a 'telecottage' in Galway or Mayo as an accountant, translator, copywriter or secretary, working for companies with offices anywhere in the world. The time difference between the west of Ireland and America is enabling some Irish people to work through the Irish forenoon and transmit completed data to New York in time for the start of its daily business.

Lack of schooling and the cost of educating dwindling classes have been further reasons for the decline of the Celtic fringes. No longer perhaps. One of the world's first computer universities is being established on the Scottish island of Lewis, linking some of the most isolated people in the world with the most modern education available anywhere. The coming century will be one in which no man has to be an island.

WE HAD our next island to reach now, Inishbofin, some 30 miles from Roundstone. For the first 15 miles out to Slyne Head the chart looked as though a cat and a fly, each with muddy feet, had walked over it, the one marking islands, the other rocks. In reasonable visibility we could readily find Deer Island again and sail north of it. 'Deer Pass is free of danger,' I read, 'but the sound between Croaghmore and Croaghbeg is very narrow and often lobster pots are set in it.' Quite. And after passing Deer Island we had rocks with names like Wild Bellows, 'always marked by a breaker', and Sunk Bellows, 'a most dangerous rock which often breaks intermittently and, being a considerable distance offshore, the clearing marks for it are hard to identify'. Beyond would be the black beacon towers on the last islet of the two-mile chain ending in Slyne Head. 'With its strong tides and long projection from the shore, this is a formidable headland and should be given a berth of two miles or more in bad weather.'

After some deplorable language, the anchor came up next morning much tangled in plastic sheeting, confirming a suspicion that years of dumping had given Roundstone Harbour many patches of foul anchoring ground. In a fresh south-east wind and glorious sunshine, I ticked off the islands as we passed, sometimes snaking a way through the lobster buoys, always watching patches of seaweed in case they might conceal a rock. More tea then to calm the nerves. Is that Sunk Bellows? It's got to be. Therefore Wild Bellows is one and a half miles off on the port bow. Inshore lay bay after bay against which rocks and islets were difficult to distinguish. A small depth-charge exploded not far off. Wild Bellows? I squinted through the handbearing compass. It was lying exactly due south. Ten minutes later Tony spotted one of the towers on Slyne Head so we altered course. As the wind came astern we began to roll uncomfortably, but the tension had eased.

'You must get the names right,' I said to Tony, pointing at the chart. 'Mullanncarrickscolta.'

He peered more closely at the chart. 'It says "breakers".'

I could see them, spray flying like the mane on a white horse.

By 12.15 the two towers on Slyne Head bore due north. Dark clouds grew even darker over the mountains but out here all was sunshine. If only the boat would stop this infernal rolling. 'We'll get a better ride when we can turn north,' I called to the crew, who were bravely attempting a second breakfast in the saloon, 'but we'll keep out a while longer and get past the Barrett Shoal, the bit marked "great rippling".'

Soon we swung north. We had turned another corner of Ireland. The swirls and eddies which hinted at the reception this place offered in bad weather began to die away. The chain of rocks and islands reaching out to Slyne Head seemed like giant stepping stones, the origins of their names lost for ever. Many were Anglicised versions of the original Irish, which often gave a simple and useful topographic description. Mullanncarrickscolta was probably *Mullach an carraig scoilte*, the top of the broken rock, and it was listed as 'Split Rock' also on the chart. But how did that inlet come to be called Cromwell Sound and another Eagle Sound? Why Crab Rock and Duck Island? One of the loneliest was Chapel Island. How did they ever build a chapel, for someone did, just up from Church Bay. To get there you have to find your way through rock-strewn channels far out from an already inhospitable coast.

Presently the indented shores of Mannin Bay and Clifden Bay opened up. Near Mannin an aircraft wing is carved in limestone to show where Alcock and Brown completed their pioneering Atlantic flight in 1919. When *Sarakiniko's* motion eased, I went below to the shelter of the saloon and opened the chart fully. An old chart this, based on a survey by Commander G.A. Bedford, his three lieutenants and 'T. Horner, Mate' in 1847-48, the Famine years. It carried on its margin a profile of the coast as it is seen from fixed points offshore and running right up to Achill Head, even including Croagh Patrick in distant Mayo – what a pity our clinical modern charts omit these useful silhouettes. The chart has the appeal of a nineteenth-century engraving; in the bottom margin a tiny gaff-rigged boat was depicted running in a heavy sea towards a schooner beating out from the coast under topsails.

The swell died, sun streamed into the companionway, and thick cheddar sandwiches with white wine helped to make the afternoon more peacable still. Omey Island stood to the north-east, its magnificent hard strand stretching for about a mile and a half along the shoreline. Omey was once a kind of Epsom for Connemara, its beach used for horse-racing, running, cycling and curragh racing, a place for the gathering of gentry, clergy, shop-keepers and farmers, with the sand dunes as the grandstand.

The boat swung easily. Barry slept in the cockpit. It was Tony who first saw the dark cloud expand and climb towards the sun, skirts of grey rain hanging under it. This one was not going to clear away inland and drench Roundstone. 'Get some sail off quick!' Tony's face creased in concentration as he took a grip on the jib reefing line, heaving until the forestay revolved, winding in two-thirds of the sail. We had just minutes before the squall hit. Wind and rain ripped across the water with an unpleasant hiss and tore into us, burying *Sarakiniko* in darkness. Even above the noise of the wind I could hear the rain hammering the water. Visibility was down to 300 yards, less when one's spectacles were two circles of steamy uselessness. The boat was coming up fast on the cliffs of High Island, but fortunately I had got a compass bearing on the sound before the squall hit. Already the seaward horizon was growing light, and five minutes later the rain stopped as if a tap had been turned off, the wind all but vanished, and the boat was left slopping in a confused sea.

But if that was the mother of squalls more of the family were lined up behind. As we cleared High Island the cliffs were lost once more in swirling clouds and another downpour seemed to turn the surface of the sea to steam. It felt like being in a barrel at the foot of a waterfall. Then, like a glimpse of the promised land, we saw the sun shining a few miles ahead on the harbour entrance to Inishbofin.

Our brief view of High Island had shown some ruins, possibly of the abbey, possibly a beehive hut. The penitential stations here may have been the later stages of a maritime pilgrimage which carried on to Croagh Patrick. If the case for seaborne pilgrimages up and down these coasts is strengthened by local devotion to seagoing men like Brendan and Columcille, then another such was St Colman, who became the saint of Inishbofin. Of Connaught origin, as a monk on Lindisfarne he championed the Celtic method of fixing a date for Easter. When the Whitby Synod of 664 AD settled that question in the Roman way and condemned the Celtic custom, Colman left Lindisfarne with all his Irish and some 30 English monks and came via Iona to settle at Bofin, where he established a Columban monastery in 665 AD.

A century ago Bofin had a population of about 1,000; today the permanent population has stabilised at around 200. Bofin, Inishturk and Clare Island to the north lie in the approaches to Clew Bay, and the island's fine natural harbour was the sea base of the notorious Grace O'Malley, the pirate queen whose galleys ranged over these waters ruthlessly. After her death in 1603 Bofin and Inishark fell into the hands of the Earl of Clanricard. Half a century later, when Cromwell had secured control of all Irish counties save those west of the Shannon, the earl opposed the parliamentary forces and with authority from the Duke of Ormonde sought aid from France. In 1651 the Duke of Lorraine sent two frigates with arms and money. One was used to defend Galway; the other arrived at Bofin. When Galway fell, Bofin became the last stronghold holding out against Cromwell's advance, but it, too, was forced to surrender in February 1653.

The ruins of the Cromwellian barracks stood out against the skyline as we entered the harbour, keeping a close watch on the alignment of the white seamark towers which guided us past the reefs and Bishop's Rock. We swung to starboard towards the harsh bulk of a modern pier half a mile away, where several yachts and fishing craft rocked at moorings. Heads bent against another squall, we anchored among them, thudded ashore in the dinghy and hoisted ourselves on to Bofin.

The squeal of a derrick drew us to a battered vessel grounded against the old stone pier beyond the village. Drums of oil and a big septic tank were being offloaded; sacks of potatoes and nets of cabbages followed. Presumably there was some good reason for importing such basics to a reasonably fertile island. The vessel, still named *Mail Boat*, still gaff rigged with brown mainsail and tattered jib, had obviously served Bofin for many years, and its efficient-looking crew would probably run it for many to come. As we moved off a cottage door opened and a boy called to his younger brother: *'Tar isteach'* (Come in). When I realised I understood the words without consciously translating them, they stirred a sense of kinship in me.

Bofin was one of Ireland's main fishing stations in the nineteenth century. Boats would come from as far away as Kinsale to fish the Bofin Bank running north-west to Achill Head, a fishing ground which was 'remarkable' for herring, cod and ling. Up to 10,000 people might assemble on the island at the height of the season, many coming off larger vessels – like hookers and others – which could outfish the islanders' rowing boats. Curraghs, incidentally, did not appear in Bofin until around the mid-nineteenth century. Records suggest they came from Kerry, though the boat was new to that county then and had probably originated in Clare.

Despite huge shoals of fish, Bofin was ill-organised. For want of salt and curing facilities, the catch had to be taken to the merchants in Westport over 30 miles away or sold off to larger vessels. 'Contention frequently happens during the Herring fishery, especially at Bofin island, which is considered a kind of neutral ground where each party meets in strong force and dreadful conflicts ensue,' an 1837 report informs us. The local coastguard officer reported instances of fishermen cutting competing boats' nets, and declared that the fishermen were indolent and 'the use of ardent spirits does prevail to an injurious extent'. Earlier, a report alleged in 1822 that there was so much distress among the poor 'that they used for food fish-heads which were unsound from lying long on the beach'.

Such poverty was commonplace in the west of Ireland. The Congested Districts Board was established in 1891 to aid communities which lacked a sufficient supply of arable land, and worked to amalgamate smallholdings, improve livestock and farming methods, and of course offered help to the fishing industry. We explored the ruins of one of the two fish-curing stations it established on Bofin. The pier was built by the board in 1897 as a result of a report by Alexander Nimmo, and though many of the steps leading down to the harbour floor were now silted over, the pier was still used. Much was done to bring in larger vessels, like the Isle of Man 'nobbie', a two-masted decked boat some 35 feet long, and a Scottish boat called a 'zulu'. This type had been developed around 1880 in the Moray Firth, and the odd name may have resulted from a memory of the recent Zulu Wars. As a result of these improvements, drift-net fishing arrived in Inishbofin. Buyers came from England, Germany was a substantial market, and the industry prospered up until the 1920s. But the Cleggan disaster of 1927, when nine Bofin fishermen and 16 from mainland Rossadillisk were drowned, quite demoralised the island community. Bad weather had been forecast, but no one on Bofin had a radio. More men might have been saved had they cut their nets and rowed for home, but nets were expensive. The drowning was a blow from which Bofin never fully recovered.

We were tempted to immerse ourselves in the company of a lively group of French and Germans sitting outside the pub, but got diverted by a sagging marquee around the corner where a notice proclaimed that Sydney Bernard Smith would give Bofin a one-man show, 'House Party at Baldrigga' and 'How to Roast a

Strasburg Goose'. When we looked more closely, however, we saw that tonight's show was cancelled 'in sympathy with the family of the missing man'.

'It's a drowning,' explained a Dubliner at the gate of his rented cottage. 'The island is upset. A chap went fishing off the rocks on the north side and he hasn't come back. Twenty people have been up there searching the cliffs.'

'We saw a helicopter.'

'No, I think that was just the Fisheries Patrol.'

More yachts had anchored now and another was running into harbour. I met a girl in oilskins who told us she was crewing on the Kilrush to Sligo Race. Inishbofin was their stopover.

The wind began to increase and, after a meal on board, Barry and I readily gave Tony shore leave. He joined a session in the pub which in retrospect we should not have missed: an American played the fiddle and a Swede pumped away at the uileann pipes, traditional Irish pipes inflated with the elbow. He clattered on to the boat after midnight, soaked to the skin.

'I got held up coming back. I met the Bofin football team at the pier. They came in on a trawler after a game at Clifden.'

'On a trawler?'

'Yes. And the tide was ebbing so it grounded about 30 feet out. When I came along they were arguing the toss: some were trying to pull the trawler closer with a grapnel, others were arguing they could reach it in our dinghy. One was shouting, "Couldn't that bugger coming from the pub lend a hand?"'

Barry stirred in his sleeping-bag. 'Naturally, Tony, you did.'

'Actually, they revved up the engine again and somehow they got the trawler alongside. But then they remembered they had left the goalkeeper out on the mooring, waiting in a curragh. God knows why. They meant to moor the trawler out there again, I think, and use the curragh to come ashore. So now I had to go off to get him. They guided me with a spotlight but when I reached the curragh it looked empty. Just when I got alongside, this guy rose up out of nowhere. He said he had been lying down because the spotlight was dazzling him.' Tony finished towelling his head. 'He even seemed to be sober.'

In the morning we rowed across to the medieval harbour, its semi-circle of weed-covered walls revealed by the ebb of the tide. We beached on shingle which once, no doubt, received the bows of galleys, and climbing up from the beach entered a cut-stone doorway into the ruins of Cromwell's barracks. After Bofin's surrender the Commonwealth Council ordered that 'no Irish shall keep any boats upon any part of the coast of Iar-Connaught, the county of Mayo, or adjacent islands, also to exclude all ill-affected Irish out of the Island'.

It is said that some 50 Catholic clergy were shipped to Aran and Bofin to await transportation to the West Indies under the old 1585 statute which declared Roman Catholic priests to be guilty of treason. In July 1657, and in later years, money was made available 'for the building of cabins and making of Prisons for the said Popish priests' on Boffin. Ten years later, the exiled Archbishop of Tuam reported that priests were not as badly treated as earlier, but noted that on Bofin they had to live on herbs and water. Indeed, the following year priests awaiting transportation from Co. Wexford petitioned the Council not to be sent to Bofin because of their age. Then came the Restoration and, in 1662, when the Duke of Ormonde arrived in Ireland as viceroy, all priests in Ireland were released. Bofin remained fortified against French privateers, however, all through the late seventeenth and early eighteenth centuries.

Gulls and angry oyster-catchers chattered and swooped in the rising gale as we stared at the rough masonry of guardrooms and kitchens and wondered where they found fuel for the several massive fireplaces in this grim place. The pits hidden in nettle beds may have been cellars or prisons. It was time to warm body and spirit with a brisk walk across the island.

Worn-out old boats and specimens of one of the world's great concentration of beat-up motor-cars stood outside the bungalows along the road. On islands where there is no licence, no driving test and maybe no insurance, the mainland is scoured for vehicles which should have long gone for scrap but which are recycled to shatter the island peace. Those which have truly expired rest half buried in the ditches. We climbed over stone walls and made our

way around a bog down to a track by the sea. As we passed by
some hens and chickens, who were having a lovely free-range day,
a formidable-looking lady advanced towards us. With straight
iron-grey fringe under a tam-o-shanter, baggy shorts, wellingtons,
and a plastic pipe as a walking stick, she was flanked by two red-
tongued dogs.

'Knocking the stones off me walls!'

'No. Not a single stone; we were reared on farms.'

'Oh, ye'll be tourists. I know. And putting yerselves in danger
too.'

Eventually Barry, who has calmed the ire of many a judicial
bench, mollified the indignant voice a little by admiring her
hens.

'Yes, they get the pickings in the seaweed, but 'tis I have to give
them two meals a day. Two meals.'

'And the sheep. All yours too?'

'Ah, just a few, and they need the looking after.' She waved the
plastic tube at one of the dogs. 'Yesterday his feet were cut to bits
on the stones. I went down the rocks meself, but the sheep kept
on, and I said, "If the sea gets you divils it won't get me."'

'Any news of the missing man?' I asked.

'No. They searched. He's gone.' She waved towards two men
out in a curragh. 'Those two saw him just across there yesterday.
He must have slipped on the weed. He'll come ashore in 14 days,
or maybe 21.'

'Was he a visitor?'

'Oh, a local man, and we had two local men go last year too.
They were fishing and the tide rose. They tried the narrow
channel, but the water runs fast there.'

The dogs got restless. One began to bark, counterpointing the
shrill voice, and we made to move. 'If ye use the strand by the
Stag Rocks ye'll go down to yer necks in one place.'

'We'll be very careful.'

'Do that.'

We made our way back to the village by way of the fourteenth-
century church, said to be built on the site of St Colman's seventh
century monastery. It stood in a rushy valley which fell down to a

beach of white sand. Offshore lay an island and behind it the Connemara mountains. A stream trickled through the rushes. A curlew flighted overhead. Suddenly I heard the rasp of a corn-crake and the years fell away. It was a call which had lured me through a Co. Waterford hayfield as a young boy, trying to catch sight of this bird.

The old graveyard was a wilderness of bramble, but I could still see that some of the oldest graves were heaped with round white pebbles. Cist graves of about 2,000 BC nearly always contained round white stones; the cairn of the great Bronze Age tumulus at Newgrange in Meath, dating from around 1,500 BC, was originally covered in white quartz which must have been brought there from a great distance. It is said that boatmen on the west coast would remove any white stones from their boat's ballast, and when a priest on Clare Island wanted some brought over from the mainland for a new church, he could find no fisherman to carry it for him. A practice which may go back 4,000 years still links white stones with death.

Before we left the graveyard I noticed a bullaun stone at the east end of the ruined church. They are found in many places, such as at the start of the pilgrims' road to Mount Brandon, on the Blaskets and the Magharees, and on the islands of Inisheer and Inishmurray. Bullaun may mean 'little pool', and there may have been a belief in the healing properties of the water collected in the hollows of the stone. Perhaps pilgrims applied the water to any afflictions on their bodies. No one knows.

The bullaun on Inishbofin has been used in tests of strength; apparently few men are able to lift it. As we had seen specimens of the island males, communing in monosyllables at the counter of Day's Bar, we did not aspire to do so.

SIX

By Erris and Eagle

WE HAD TO leave Inishbofin and Barry had to leave us. London and work were calling. Anne, who had left *Sarakiniko* at Glandore in Co. Cork, hoped to rejoin us at Westport in the south-east corner of Clew Bay.

Today we would sail to Clare Island, 18 miles to the north-east. What then? We had planned to weave through the scores of grassy islands in Clew Bay and sail to the pier at Westport, but as Tony and I worked the dividers across the chart and examined the lines Adrian O'Connell had drawn through the maze, it was also apparent that if we headed directly north-west from Clare Island we could put the formidable cliffs of Achill behind us all the sooner. Better weather was forecast, but we could not be sure how long it would last. We looked at each other. Skip Westport?

'If we go right in there we would not lay Achill if this wind turns into a westerly.'

I glanced at our burgee flapping gently on its stick at the mast-head. 'Wind's about south. If it stays there tomorrow it's just right for Achill Head.'

Tony opened our road map of Ireland. 'Anne could join us round the north Mayo coast; perhaps at Killala.'

'Quite a bit extra for her, coming from so far south.'

But Anne would not arrive for three more days, and this fact persuaded us to press on. We passed a message on to Clonmel from the doorless telephone-box near the pier, saw Barry on to the ferry, and got *Sarakiniko* ready for sea. Canvas was already hoisted on the seven yachts in the Kilrush to Sligo Race. The forecast for Irish coastal waters was a south-east wind up to Force 4 becoming north or north-west, and, 24 hours hence it should be fresh from the west or south-west. It seemed to support our decision to get on around Achill. At any rate it eased our

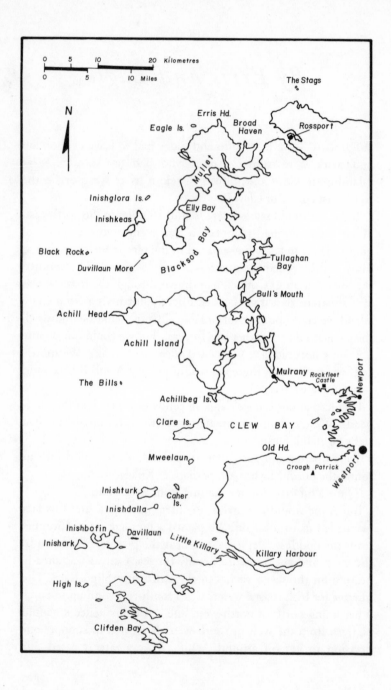

consciences about putting more mileage on Anne's journey.

We moved out past the Bishop's Rock, standing well above the swell. There is no evidence either that Cromwellians tied a bishop here and allowed the rising tide to drown him or that Grace O'Malley sealed the harbour entrance with a chain boom, but both stories are still told. I feel sure, however, that O'Malley must have used Inishbofin as the main base in her rule of the islands.

As we began to clear the east corner of Bofin, we could see more of these: Inishturk, some eight miles off and, away beyond it, Caher Island. Tony had met an Inishturk man in the pub who said about 60 people still lived on the island. It was once occupied by a son of Grace O'Malley, Owen, for it was here that he and his followers were massacred on the orders of Richard Bingham, Governor of Connaught, a harsh man unsparing in his efforts to impose Elizabethan control over Mayo and the islands. Dim in the east lay the entrance to Killary Harbour, Ireland's only fiord, an eight mile tongue cutting into the wild bogs and barren mountains, a safe anchorage used 80 years ago by the British Navy's Atlantic fleet. A shoal near Killary's entrance is marked O'Malley's Breaker on the chart. Tradition claims that Grace O'Malley, chased in here by a fast Scottish galley, lured it to destruction across this shoal. The imprint of Grace O'Malley is found all along this stretch of coastline.

The south side of Clare Island grew clearer as we sailed northeast. From a distance, its wide green slopes seemed covered by swathes of recently mown hay. But it was not hay. The darker lines were rushes growing in the hollows of old 'lazy beds', earthen ridges which ensured that potatoes, and sometimes oats and barley, could be grown on the rain-drenched hillside. 'Strange they should be called lazy beds,' Tony said as we gazed across to the island, sobered by the thought of all that human labour. On our mid-nineteenth-century chart, hundreds of little dots showed dwellings concentrated in about 13 villages; 50 years later, when the Congested Districts Board bought out the island's owners, the 4,000 acres were occupied by only 95 tenants.

The board's inspector declared that 'nature did little for the island and mankind has robbed it of all it could'. People seemed only to know that they had certain grazing rights over certain parts of land. There were no fences. Cattle and sheep roamed at will, and when a crop was in the ground it had to be guarded by the tenants' families. When the Congested Districts Board took on the management of the island, it built 50 miles of fencing, homes, cattle sheds and drains. From the sea we saw a massive drystone wall which strode across the island, assertive as the Great Wall of China. The five-mile wall had been built at a cost of £1,500 to separate pasture from tillage.

As we turned into the harbour we saw the high tower-house, O'Malley Castle, sitting on a green peninsula near the modern pier. There is no firm evidence that Grace O'Malley ever lived in this castle, though she probably did. We anchored among some fishing boats moored off the shingle beach. We were sheltered from the prevailing westerlies, but the bay would not be a comfortable or even a safe place if rough weather gusted in from any point south of south-west. An O'Malley fleet of galleys would have been safer in the splendid natural shelter of Inishbofin.

Clare Island was a strategic point governing the entrance to Clew Bay, however. From here a local ruler could control shipping to the mainland, exacting dues or pursuing piracy, smuggling and shipwreck with impunity. The broken signal towers standing on every other Irish headland were not only built in fear of comparatively modern French invasion. Many, such as the ruined towers still remaining on the bluff point at the north-west corner of the island, are much older.

In his works on the earliest European charts, Professor Westropp found that in the fifteenth century European traders seemed equally, if not more, aware of the Irish islands than of mainland settlements. They would sail from Dingle on to Aran, to Inishbofin and to Achill Sound, the islands acting as buoys to mark the way and keep ships from wandering out into the dreaded unchartered sea. Islands like the Skelligs, the Blaskets, the Arans and Inishbofin appear on charts which were little more than diagrams, maps which omitted even the Shannon estuary, Galway Bay and the great sea loughs.

All along the coast, a host of individual small ports traded with

The skipper on the bridge as Sarakiniko *sets about her circumnavigation* (Tony O'Connor)

Joan takes the helm while Pat watches the Magharees retreating astern

Kinsale, Sarakiniko's *port of arrival* (Michael Diggin)

Glandore Harbour (Miles Clarke)

Mizen Head lighthouse, now home to the 'Mizen Vision' (Michael Diggin)

North Harbour, Cape Clear (Miles Clarke)

*Left: Dún Aengus,
standing on the edge of
the cliffs on the Aran
Island of Inishmore
(Michael Diggin)*

*Below: Roundstone
Harbour with the Twelve
Pins in the Background
(Michael Diggin)*

Grace O'Malley Castle, Clew Bay

Achill Island and on to Erris Head — a rock-strewn coastline for the sailor (Michael Diggin)

Once the workhorse of the coast, the Galway hooker is currently enjoying a revival (Michael Diggin)

*above: The medieval
galley, or birlinn, has
been described as the
shuttle in the loom
between Ireland and the
Western Isles of Scotland
(Giles Clarke)*

*right: A rare picture of
one-man curragh, a
boat now almost extinct
(Giles Clarke)*

Rathlin Island's Harbour

Ireland's Eye, from Howth Harbour

The lighthouse on Hook Head, the second oldest light tower in Europe

western Europe. One survey listed 70 such harbours. The *Calendar of State Papers for Ireland, 1601-03* assesses particular ones: Ardglass in Co. Down, 'A crib for small boats'; Dundrum 'for small boats and barks'. Dundalk was 'a shole bay', Malahide 'a bar haven'. With shipping putting in and out of so many coves and bays, the English authorities found it difficult to impose their control along the coast. They complained that the rebels, the Scots and the French traded together extensively. Into Strangford Lough came Scottish barques 'with munitions, cloth, wine and aqua vitae', and at Lough Foyle 'some of the Scottish galleys trading with these parts bring victuals and other necessaries to the rebels'. English 'rebels' – the descendants of the Anglo-Normans, lords who had fallen away from their allegiance and adopted Gaelic ways – were distinguished from Irish 'enemies' – the more numerous Gaelic lords, about 60 in all, who still maintained their native customs.

Romantic exaggerations about the life and times of Grace O'Malley, clan chief and sea raider, have hardened into legend. She was born in about 1530. A survivor of the Spanish Armada, Captain Cuellar, in all probability a deeply embittered man, wrote that in nearby Sligo at this time, 'the chief inclination of these people is to be robbers and to plunder each other, so that no day passes without a call to arms. For the people in one village becoming aware that there are cattle or other effects in another, immediately come armed in the night and... kill one another. The English, getting to know who has robbed most cattle, then carry away the plunder.'

O'Malley came of age in a warring world, an era of shifting alliances and ready betrayals. Her family had been chiefs of the western islands for 200 years. They saw the Irish parliament declare King Henry VIII King of Ireland in 1541, yet English power was weak beyond the area around Dublin called the Pale. Many Anglo-Norman families who had won huge tracts of land in Ireland in earlier centuries had abandoned their allegiance to the Crown. Notwithstanding some punitive expeditions, Henry hoped for 'good and discrete persuasions' to win them back and convert the Gaelic lords into loyal subjects. He had some success:

Burke of Connaught became Earl of Clanricard; O'Brien, Earl of Thomond; O'Neill of Ulster, Earl of Tyrone. By the time of Henry's death 40 of the main Gaelic and Anglo-Norman chiefs had come to terms. But agreements were made to be broken. Munster later rebelled. Ulster simmered, brooding on treachery.

The daughter of Owen O'Malley began a life of violence and plunder when, at 16, she married Donal O'Flaherty, chief of the 'ferocious O'Flahertys'. They prospered by harassing ships trading into Galway Bay and, when he died in about 1566, she continued to dominate the coast. An account of how nine of her galleys chased two Spanish cargo ships, one being boarded and captured and the other fleeing but being wrecked on Achill Island, may be typical of her adventures. Queen Elizabeth's Deputy for Ireland, Sir Henry Sydney, described her as 'a notorious woman in all the coasts of Ireland'.

She increased her power by a further marriage to Sir Richard Burke, among whose coastal castles was Rockfleet on Clew Bay, sited at the boggy end of a mile-long inlet. I recall once gazing out from its upper windows and thinking how easily an enemy ship would be spotted while still well down the bay. Grace lived at Rockfleet, and after about a year she had her followers eject her husband from his properties. An expedition financed by the traders of Galway attacked the castle in 1574, but when O'Malley refused to surrender, their ships retreated after a two-week siege. The English crown now sent the naval pinnace, *Handmaid*, to patrol Irish waters. Rockfleet, behind the islands and shallows, became O'Malley's base and refuge.

Warships which could keep the sea for weeks were now being built with broadside guns, and it may be that Grace suspected the days of galley power were passing, for the planking of what were really only armed transports was too thin to stand up to round-shot and their scantlings too light to mount effective guns. The galley, or birlinn, has been called the shuttle in the loom of the maritime kingdoms of the Western Isles of Scotland and the west of Ireland. It is said that the Lords of the Scottish Isles could at one time muster up to 200 boats which would pour out of the Sound of Mull like bees from a hive. Until recently little was known of their hull forms and rig, but a remarkable practical experiment in nautical archaeology flowered on a May day in 1991 when a 16-oar swan-bowed galley, *Aileach*, carrying a square sail depicting an image of Grace O'Malley, departed from Westport on a voyage to Stornoway in Scotland. This first sea-going galley for 300 years was built in Donegal by the firm of James MacDonald and Sons of Moville. The project was planned by two friends: Ranald Clanranald, active Highland chief and direct descendant of Somerled, the twelfth century Lord of the Isles, and Wallace Clark, who could trace a simlar descent

The galley built in Donegal was 40 feet long and drew only two feet of water. It was taken by road down to the O'Malley heartland from where the six-week voyage began, the crew seeking a sheltered anchorage each night. They rounded Achill Head into Blacksod Bay and, using the Belmullet canal, entered the great expanse of Broadhaven. From here they sailed around the northern coast and eventually reached Stornoway in the Hebrides. The voyage proved that such a vessel could make offshore passages and, with a good man at the helm, run before the wind safely or lie-to in winds of Force 7 in a 20-foot swell.

It is likely that Grace O'Malley also used very large skin-covered curraghs, for Connaught may even then have suffered a shortage of timber. Samuel Pepys put into his scrapbook, now preserved in the Pepys Library in Cambridge, two drawings by 'Captain Thomas Phillips, one of His Majesty's former engineers', made as late as 1685. They show a skin-covered 'portable vessel of wicker, ordinarily used by the wild Irish', with a single mast on which one square sail is hoisted almost to the masthead. There are curved struts for a canopy-type shelter in the stern and an aggressive spread of bull's horns decorates the bow. A second drawing illustrates 'the method of working up' the boat. It shows the frame being covered in dozens of vertically stitched skins as it rests on a beach upon four rollers. The boat may have been 30 or 40 feet long.

By 1576, with her fleet outgunned at sea, Grace O'Malley was meeting the Queen's deputy, Sidney, and offering to augment his forces. 'There came to me,' he reported to the Queen, 'a most famous feminine sea captain called Granye Imallye and offered her services unto me wheresoever I would command her with three galleys and 200 fighting men in Scotland or Ireland.' The offer was refused, possibly for lack of funds.

In the following year, Grace O'Malley fell foul of the Earl of Desmond and was imprisoned in Limerick and then in Dublin. Her prospects of circumventing English power diminished further when Sidney was replaced by the autocratic Sir Richard Bingham, who wrote in 1585 that for 40 years O'Malley 'has been the nurse of all rebellions in the west'. In 1589 she sailed to Scotland with seven galleys to bring mercenaries back to assist in a Burke rebellion. She raided the Aran Islands the following year. When she was eventually captured, she appealed directly to Queen Elizabeth, quickly received an 'interrogation as to her means and intentions' and was allowed to sail to London, where she successfully petitioned Elizabeth for funds and a licence to harass the Queen's enemies.

This tactical switching of sides did not greatly help, for the O'Malley rent rolls were unpaid and her impositions on trading ships and fishermen were effectively prohibited by Bingham, whose dispatches urged the government to build and send galleys to clear the coasts of O'Malley and other rebels who 'live by robbing poor fishermen and others that pass in small vessels'.

Her agreement with Queen Elizabeth allowed Grace to retain some of her lands in return for keeping down piracy. Clare Island remained in her hands. Yet shortly after returning from London she raided Bunowen, near Slyne Head, and burned the house of her son Murrough, probably because he had helped Bingham. In 1596, at the age of 66, it is reported that she raided the island of Barra in Scotland.

Her rumbustious life ended in 1600. By this time Bingham could report that his ships had freed the coasts of Irish pirates and 'cleared the Shannon of the traitors' galleys wherein they begin to abound being now grown very perfect seamen'. A year after her death, her son commanded a 30-oar galley with some 100 men aboard, in a skirmish with an English warship, *Tramontaney*, off south Donegal. The English captain recorded that he forced this huge galley, 'manned with people called the Flahertys', to 'run onshore among the rocks.'

His 132-ton ship, with a crew of 70 and 21 guns, was the largest of several vessels patrolling northern waters in that year. They were there to deter Hebridean galleys from fetching Scottish help to O'Neill in Ulster, who some months before had been decisively beaten at the Battle of Kinsale. *Tramontaney's* chart of the seas around the northern half of Ireland is now in Trinity College, Dublin, and shows Donegal Bay with greater accuracy than any previous work.

We beached the dinghy under the O'Malley castle and asked the way to the old thirteenth-century Cistercian abbey. It lay on a gentle slope above the sea. The O'Malley coat of arms is inscribed over the main arch and bears the inscription: *Terra Maris Potens O'Maille* – O'Malley Powerful on Land and Sea. We could just discern paintings of a deer and a hound and an animal like a dragon on the plastered ceiling. When writer and photographer Thomas Mason came here 60 years ago he could also make out faces and a harp. Have these been since lost? Restoration work is under way now. There are, after all, only two other examples of medieval fresco paintings in Ireland, at Holy Cross Abbey in Tipperary and at Knockmoy Abbey, Co. Galway.

Some say Grace O'Malley is buried here. No doubt the fine altar tomb we saw was erected for someone of great importance, so the tradition may be true. Mr Mason had been shown a skull which was kept in a recess in the wall and was told it was the skull of the pirate queen. But they also told him of the day an islander was cutting seaweed on a rock and, happening to look up, found he had been drawn out to sea, moored to a whale.

NORTH OF Clare Island lies Achill, Ireland's largest inhabited island. A bridge across the sound joins it to the mainland, while at its westernmost point at Achill Head a series of 2,000 foot cliffs falls directly to the ocean. Many a small boat would like to avoid the seas and weather which can be encountered there and instead run up the sound which opens invitingly only five miles north of Clare Island and gives access to Blacksod Bay and its many snug anchorages, but there is a problem.

'How high is our masthead?' Tony asked.

'Forty-two foot six from the deck.'

'And another four feet from the water.'

'Maybe. Why?'

He shut the *Sailing Directions*. 'The swing bridge at Achill will open on request, but we'd have an argument with a 10,000 volt cable overhead. It goes across 43 feet above high water level.'

'Achill would have a memorable day.'

A pity, I reflected. If those cables were set higher, seagoing yachts could use the sound to take them around this awkward elbow of Ireland. The sound has vigorous tides and tortuous channels, but would not be difficult for a boat under engine. The nineteenth-century writer William Maxwell commented that 'It needs skills and strict attention to the tides, but the Sound could be cleared in an hour with the same wind that would occupy a whole day if Achill Head was doubled.' He added that small boats and hookers had often foundered when deeply laden. Squalls of great violence often fall off the cliffs, 'but night and drunkenness have also been more fatal than all besides'.

We planned an early morning start to have a good run north around Erris Head and then into shelter in Broadhaven. In a few days a road-weary Anne would arrive at Killala pier looking for *Sarakiniko*'s masthead burgee fluttering above the trawlers. We had to be there. Broadhaven tonight. Killala tomorrow. We had a day in hand.

Coastal sailing is a matter of tides and arithmetic. The six-hour flow of a favourable tide can drastically affect progress. Add a two-knot tide to a sailing speed of five knots (which we optimistically use as our average) and you cover seven nautical miles in an hour. When the tide is against you, you cover a miserable three. Tides run hardest round headlands and, as one cannot avoid an adverse tide on any longish passage, it is best to set a departure time which will win a favourable tide near a headland. Achill Head was 14 miles away, but if we were to have the tide in our favour at Eagle Island and Erris Head some 25 miles further on, we would have to put up with some foul tide still running as we cleared Achill. We hoped it would be slackening off. The result of the morning's sums and measurements was that we would not hoist sails to a gentle wind, but motor fairly briskly towards an appointment with the eddies and tumble of Achill's spectacular corner where, the normally prosaic Admiralty *Pilot* declared, 'the cliffs descend into the sea in stupendous precipices'.

We motored out of the harbour and continued past six huge fish-farm netting pens which lay off the north-east coast of the island, bright pink buoys and blue netting standing out garishly against the muted colours of the hills, holding thousands of salmon captive. In the last century islandmen hunted basking sharks, which they called 'sunfish' because of the hours they spent on the surface of the water, feeding on plankton. A bank called Sunfish Bank runs for some 30 miles offshore. Fishermen set out from Inishbofin and Achill in open boats, six men taking perhaps three hours to catch one fish using a harpoon and often being towed by the struggling victim until it could be drawn to the surface and lanced. The shark was then lashed to the boat, a man climbed on to the body, opened the fish up and quickly sought the liver, for if the fish filled with water it could drag the boat under: they reached over 30 feet in length and weighed six or seven tons.

When paraffin arrived the demand for shark oil fell off, but around 1945 shark fishing began again, at first to protect the salmon fishery rather than for commercial gain. Later it was realised that there was a demand for shark meat and liver oil, and an export trade to the Far East developed in oil and fins. At its peak fishing off Achill secured 1,080 sharks in one season. Today they are rarely seen.

The wind freshened but the rough seas usually expected off the head were quiet today. We ran between an islet and the strangely named Priest Rocks which seemed to grow and diminish in the backwash from the cliffs, keeping the engine running in neutral. Just as well, for once or twice false winds bouncing off the rock walls threw the sails aback and, with some tide still against us, we could not risk a loss of steerage-way. Then the prospect ahead opened up. I moved the tiller and, for the first time, put a touch of east into our north-making course. From now on *Sarakiniko*'s track would turn more and more towards the sunrise each morning.

The Iniskea group of islands gave us shelter from the ocean swell as we ran up the Mullet peninsula, one of the loneliest spots in Ireland, its sandy claw reaching down to the Duvillaun group of reefs and islands, and the whole enclosing Blacksod Bay and making it a fine natural harbour. Long before the First World War a group of optimists hoped to establish a transatlantic liner terminal at the end of the Mullet's sandy finger, but nothing came of it. Belmullet, at the head of the bay, suffered from poor communications, the nearest railhead lying at Ballina, 40 miles away across the hills.

A century ago a canal was built along the channel through the narrow spit of land which divides Blacksod Bay from Broad-haven. If yachts could use it now, they could move in relative shelter all the way between Achill and the north coast of Mayo, rather than round the headlands on the coast as we were doing. Indeed, if access was also provided through Achill Sound, boats could make an interesting and sheltered passage all the way from Clew Bay. The Lord of the Isles galley had used the Belmullet canal, then recently reopened after years of disuse, on its voyage from Westport to Stornaway, but had had to creep under a modern road bridge and make maximum use of high tides to achieve the 400 yards into the Broadhaven channels. 'You're the first big boat through it,' local people told them. Local tradition holds that Grace O'Malley's galleys had also used the cut through the inlet.

Black Rock lighthouse appeared out to the west. The Irish Lights service vessels called it and the Eagle Island light, some 17 miles further on, their 'Cape Horns'. The deep-water 100 fathom line comes to within a mere 20 miles of the coast here, and in bad weather shoaling water, pushed up by the rapid rise in the sea-bed, generates notorious seas.

I had been scared about this corner, leading on to Erris Head. Conor O'Brien, after sailing around the world, recorded a day off Erris in his 26-ton *Kelpie*. 'If this was not the biggest sea I ever met it must have been mighty near it. The spray of the breakers was going over Eagle Island and that is 160 feet high. Three years ago I saw in the Indian Ocean a sea which I classed as phenomenal and my impression was that it would have looked big among the common stuff of this day but nothing bigger than one phenomenal sea. I think both waves exceeded thirty feet but only momentarily since, being caused by the superimposition of two sets of waves, they were quite unstable.' After 'feeling like being kicked down several sets of stairs', he achieved shelter at Blacksod, but with six feet of the boat's bulwarks broken out and her keel strained and leaking.

The seas here have taken many ships. William Maxwell gives us an account of seeing a pirate cutter in her element, 'standing in from the west under a press of canvas between Black Rock and the island of Duvillaun', but while the audacious cutter outwitted the law, she would soon have to reckon with gales off this northwestern corner.

'Nothing could be more beautiful than the approach of the smuggler,' Maxwell wrote. 'A private signal fluttered from the masthead and a Union Jack was flying from the peak while, occasionally, a sheet of broken foam sparkled around her bows as she held her onward course gallantly. In a few minutes after her having been first discovered, boats were pulling from the shore in all directions while the cutter closed the land fast. When abreast of the Ridge Point she suddenly rounded-to, handed her gaff topsail, hauled up the main tack and waited for the boats.' The narrator's friend said he could not go aboard 'being... alas, a poor esquire of this county and one of the King's justices of the peace... yet will not my old friend Jack Matthews forget me. But you shall board the *Jane* and witness a bustling business. See, you are just in time for the gig is on the water.'

So he embarked and reached the ship. 'It was indeed a bustling scene. A hundred boats were collected around the smuggler who had already "broken bulk" and was discharging the cargo with a rapid and yet orderly and businesslike system that was surprising. I was immediately recognised by Captain Matthews and politely invited to his cabin. Aware of the hurry consequent upon this

dangerous traffic, and on the plea of his presence being requisite
on deck, I would have declined but the gallant Captain remarked
with great indifference that he left the delivery of his cargo to the
agents and purchasers and could not spend an hour or two more
to his satisfaction that in entertaining in his poor way the
kinsman of his respected friend and, calling for the steward, he
stepped forward to order some refreshments.'

The captain's guest on this cheerful day observed 'no confusion
on the delivery of the tobacco to its respective proprietors, who
had already engaged certain proportions of the cargo, which they
received on the production of small tickets specifying the quantity and description of the goods. The business having been
previously arranged on shore facilitated the dangerous trade.
Matthews had been legally denounced for many daring and
successful contests with the Revenue but I could not but admire
his thorough indifference to possible consequences. He knew
that several men-of-war were at that moment cruising on the
station and that they had been appraised that he had sailed from
Flushing and that this coast was the spot selected by the owners
to effect a landing, yet he laughed and drank as gaily as I should
in a clubhouse.' The cabin, the guest noted, was arranged with
'muskets, pistols and blunderbusses secured in arms racks and
with cutlasses and tomahawks suspended from the bulkheads'.
Thus did the second hour slip away, 'and when I regained the
deck the hurry of the business was over. The contraband cargo
had been replaced by stone ballast, for, by previous arrangement,
each boat brought a quantity of shingle from the beach and
hence the smuggler was already in trim and ready to stand out to
sea.'

This vessel was apparently well known and had a formidable ar-
mament. 'Sixteen heavy carronades were extended along the deck
with two long brass guns of a smaller calibre... but the most
striking object was her ferocious-looking but magnificent crew.
They seemed not only formed for "the battle and the breeze" but
well justified their wild commander's boast that he could thresh
any cruiser of his own size and land his cargo six hours afterwards. To judge from the cases stowed away in the gig my cousin

had not been forgotten and the outlaw waved as we pulled away.' It was the *Jane*'s final landing. She sank in a gale off north-west Ireland on her next voyage. Nobody survived. Her consort, the *Blue-eyed Maid*, was struggling near by and could not help.

It has long been neccesary to maintain a good weather eye at this north-western outpost of the Atlantic. Had we time and tide we could have nosed in to a snug anchorage behind the tail of the Mullet, where I would have sought out Ted Sweeney, whose job it had been to file hourly weather reports from Blacksod Point during the war. Information had been disseminated internationally by merchant ships in the North Atlantic until the war began. After that, weather reports became a close secret. Much of Europe was a blank, as was the Atlantic except for occasional information from aircraft. However, the transmission of weather information from neutral Ireland to Dunstable, near London, continued.

As the tide of war turned, reports from the old coastguard station on Blacksod Point became essential to the planning of the Allied invasion of Europe. The station was manned by Ted Sweeney with help from his wife, Maureen, who also ran the local post office. The Normandy landings required a low tide at dawn, a full moon and clear skies, and reasonably good weather. June 5, 1944, was appointed D-Day.

The weather remained good through late May as a succession of depressions from Newfoundland steered clear of England and France. But in the early hours of 3 June, the chief forecaster for the Allied operations, Group Captain J. Stagg, began to have doubts about the good weather continuing. His memoirs record a message from a colleague: 'Petterson told us that Blacksod Point in west Ireland had just reported a Force 6 wind and a rapidly falling barometer.' Though the report upset the Allies' plans, Stagg was glad to have had his fears confirmed sooner rather than later. 'On hearing this I think I would have reached over and shaken his hand if he had been on the other side of the conference table instead of about a hundred miles away at the end of a telephone line.'

'I was sending an hourly report, day and night,' Ted Sweeney recalled years afterwards. 'It had to be phoned in to London. We got a query back. They asked for a check: "Please check and repeat the whole report." I went to the office and checked the report and repeated it once again. I just wondered what was wrong. I thought I had made some error or something like that. They sent a second message to me about an hour later to please check and repeat again. I thought this was a bit strange so I checked and repeated again.'

When his report indicated that a cold front had crossed the north-west coast of Ireland, London warned the Allied commanders that the front would be over the English Channel at the planned invasion time. Operation Overlord was delayed for 24 hours. The heavy rain and Force 7 winds which subsequently arrived on 5 June would have been disastrous for the invasion force.

It was only much later that Sweeney found out the significance of his forecasts. 'Months afterwards, perhaps even a few years, I was told by one of the Met office crowd that the reason they took heed of that report from Blacksod was that it was the first indication they got of a major change in the weather.'

The tide had fallen off and would soon start to run north in our favour. The North and South Inishkea islands were on the bow as we skirted a large rock off Duvillaun Island, and when we had gone past it we dutifully followed the *Directions* and held the rock mid-way between two points known as the Ears of Achill eight miles astern on Achill Head. The bearing took us clear of reefs hidden off the Inishkeas islands.

The tide changed. We could see a lobster-pot buoy pulling its line north as we turned the glasses on the little pier of Inishkea South. This had a successful community when William Maxwell wrote in 1832 how 'frequent and valuable wreck furnish the inhabitants with many articles of domestic utility... and immense quantities of sea fowl feathers are annually collected'. The feathers came from seabirds so unfearful of man they were caught with a noose or knocked on the head with sticks. The feathers went to stuff mattresses and the eggs were eaten. It was true that in winter, 'the sick must die without relief and the sinner pass to his account without the consolation of religion', but Maxwell noted that the island whiskey was some of the finest. 'Perhaps because the distiller could carry on his business in a leisurely way in this remote place where a Revenue officer would be marooned.'

Remoteness could not save it from the potato blight. A grain ship bound up the coast in 1845 was surrounded by eleven island curraghs whose crews snatched enough food to survive the winter. Inishkea was finally abandoned in around 1930 after ten of its men were lost when the curragh fleet, striving to row against a fierce winter storm from the west, was blown on to the breakers of the Mullet only two miles away.

More islands filled the middle distance. Off Inishglora we met the seals. They lay draped over the grey rocks as the boat ran between them and the reef that runs out from the mainland. Cormorants stood silhouetted on the outcrops of rock, drying their outstretched wings. As the swell heaved through the reef in tumbles of white froth, whiskered faces surfaced around us, staring and snorting. Then they would dive, smooth grey lumps, and re-emerge to glare at us again. We had met only an occasional one so far. Perhaps this was a token of the northern waters ahead.

In his book *Islands of Ireland*, Thomas Mason described a pet seal on one of the Aran Islands which disappeared for a few days and then arrived home bearing a harpoon which was identified from its inscription as belonging to a man in Kerry, 100 miles away. Research now establishes that seals travel up to 60 miles a day between habitats. The Sea Mammal Research Unit in Cambridge recently fitted tiny radio transmitters to 15 seals and found that one called Sammy swam 3,000 miles in three months, not at random but in a reasonably direct course between the points he regularly used for coming ashore in north Rona, Fair Isle, the Shetlands and the Faeroes. 'The last signal we got,' the ecologists reported, 'indicated that he was some 120 miles north-east of the Faeroes heading north.'

This research into 'foraging ecology' may help in settling disputes between fishermen and conservationists. And in looking at demands that the seal population along our coasts should regularly be culled, perhaps someone will also note the old Irish belief that seals are humans under an enchanted spell.

The wind shifted into the north-west and the evening grew grey and chilly. We could just hold a course now around Annagh Head, and then the eye of Eagle Island lighthouse emerged, winking three times every ten seconds some three miles further on. We sailed between Eagle Island and the cliffs of the mainland which, in a couple of miles, rose to Erris Head. The lighthouse on Eagle was rebuilt in 1895 after a December sea had cascaded over the old building, smashing the lantern glass and invading the keepers' dwellings. Remarkably, nobody was drowned. A distress flag was seen next day and, as soon as was practicable, wives and children were moved to the mainland. One-hundred-and-sixty-foot-high walls were constructed round the dwellings and store-rooms, and the 210-foot-high light peers cautiously above them. Made safe from the sea, who could anticipate that, on 20 August 1940, the glass and roof would be machine-gunned by a German fighter plane which was attacking a ship off the coast.

This was the sea where Conor O'Brien had so nearly come to grief. 'I shouldn't have taken his book,' I said to Tony. Even in this good weather there was an uneasy swell. Erris Head itself looked strange, the cliffs and the slopes above them black and bare. It was both a relief and an anti-climax to shape a course for the recesses of Broadhaven.

The sea seemed alive with birds: families of guillemots in line ahead managing to look like strings of fishing-net floats, herring-gulls swirling about the ledges, soaring shags, gannets with yellowish heads and tapering wing-tips. They rose slightly in the air when they spotted a fish, half closed their wings, and came swooping down like harpoons. Air sacs under their feathers fill out as they dive to cushion the impact when they hit the water and help bring them quickly to the surface again.

Tony had his eyes on Benwee Head, the summit that marks the far side of Broadhaven Bay. He pointed now. 'Look. The Stags of Broadhaven.'

These great stacks about a mile and a half off the coast are somehow reminiscent of the shell-shaped roofs of the Sydney Opera House. They would be our gateway to the north tomorrow. We looked towards Donegal, some 50 miles away but visible in good weather. They say that from the top of Slieve League, the highest maritime cliffs in Europe, one can in clear weather see one-third of Ireland.

The semicircle of Broadhaven, sheltered in westerlies, is wide open to any seas rolling in from the north. We went in search of a snug inlets four miles down the bay, past the pier at Ballyglass. Tony lowered the anchor after our usual sniffing round like an animal choosing the right patch to settle down.

A slight mist set in. The barometer had fallen. We did not go ashore but ate a vast quantity of the best lasagna ever after I had emerged, gasping but successful, from a head-first search for a bottle of wine in the dark hole beneath the awkward inner end of my bunk. Stores were running low but we had ample emergency supplies of chocolate, whiskey and peanuts, and there were several anonymous tins which had lost their labels in the damp bilges. Tony shook them carefully, holding them up to his ear, and claimed that he could tell which was soup.

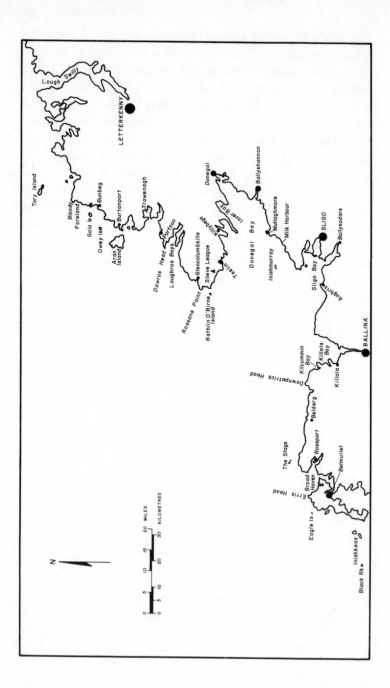

SEVEN

North-east for Tory

IN THE EARLY morning Broadhaven was shrouded in cold wet mist which left a sheen of droplets on our sweaters. We went ashore to the telephone-box to tell Anne that we would soon be in Killala. There wasn't a soul about, except two donkeys who nuzzled at the door of the telephone kiosk. Their long, upturned toecaps made them look as if they were shod in seven-inch slippers, and they followed us on these sadly neglected hooves as we went to look at the new RNLI boathouse. Blue trawlers lay against the pier, their magenta-red lobster buoys stacked on deck like party balloons. A yacht was chocked-up on the shoreline, anti-fouling half done, masking tape fluttering in the breeze. Tony peered at the name on its stern: *Tóg bog é.*

'What does it mean? It sounds rather rude.'

'It means "Take it Easy".'

Across the inlet the countryside rose in a stone-walled dome. White houses, scattered in the Irish way, lay about the crest, surrounded by triangular fields which spread downwards like a fan, each field widening progressively as the pattern reached the bottom of the hill. It was a striking and possibly a very old type of settlement, but there was nobody around to talk about field systems so we set about getting the anchor up. Presently the 800-foot cliffs of Benwee Head closed off Broadhaven, and as the mist returned, we dragged on our oilskins once more.

This is the region to which the traveller Caesar Otway came in 1840. Sea eagles were common then and Otway deplored them as pests. His was the general view, and by 1916 they had been virtually wiped out in Britain. After an elaborate programme using birds from Norway, ornithologists re-established the sea eagle in Scotland, while in Ireland Charles Haughey re-introduced the birds to the Blasket Islands. If sea eagles do come back to these lonely places, such a turn of events would surely puzzle nineteenth-century observers. Arthur Young wrote that 'in Mayo the eagles do great mischief, carry away lambs, poultry and will watch salmon jumping and seize them even out of the water'. They were so common that 'men with guns are sent out to kill and frighten them'. But I expect that we shall forgive much if we can see the fourth largest eagle in the world once more.

'The 24 mile stretch from Broadhaven to Killala is most in-hospitable and should be given a good berth; there is no safe anchorage, no shelter from the usual swell and fierce gusts off the cliffs,' ran the commentary in our *Sailing Directions*. The radio signals guiding our navigation system seemed to be upset by high ground – the longitude reading already placed us near Killala – and without it we would have to rely on dead reckoning. Visibility was now deteriorating. Rather than stand out to sea and estimate our distance so as to tack in for the entrance to Killala, it seemed wiser to probe from one headland to the next, relying on precise compass courses to take us past the dangers on the way.

Sarakiniko's navigation system would soon be replaced. Joan, who would rejoin at Lough Swilly, was to bring a GPS unit (Global Positioning System) with her. This modern wonder, smaller than a mobile phone, locks on to satellites to give a latitude and longitude reading exact to two places of decimals. I wished I had it now.

The wind was fresh, not strong, and we could just fill the sails on our present course; indeed, as the curtain of drizzle turned to rain, it seemed to go light and might yet fail us altogether. In the tumble of disturbed water thrown back by the cliffs, their tops bandaged in low cloud, it was difficult to spot the occasional buoy, and this was no place to wrap a line around our screw. The engine had not so far let us down, but I wondered how long it would sustain such faithfulness.

I still nursed a nagging mistrust of boat engines. In my early sailing years I would often try to raise crew morale by com-menting that an unreliable engine was the best sailing instructor of all, but I had enough eventful trips behind me now. We motor-sailed under the seven towering Stags of Broadhaven, one of the sights of the Irish coast, but we were too wet and preoccupied to bother much about them. We took turn about as the rain became a downpour so dense that the shore a mile away vanished from sight. The sea was beaten into pock-marked rolls of pewter. While one of us steered and kept lookout for an hour, the other did mental arithmetic on time and tide or bent over the chart table to recheck compass bearings, cursing the water dripping from our oilskins. We went forward regularly to check a darker patch in the murk. Was that Pig Island, a 200-foot-tall rock with an arch through it, or some other rock, or the next headland? It was important not to divert from the compass course to check. Lay a course and stick to it and you don't get lost. Visibility was a few hundred yards, then briefly a mile or so, enough to show shoulders of mountains lifting one behind another or long streaks of foam drifting back from the rocks.

Hands wrinkled all over like prunes, we spooned chicken soup from our mugs and ate the last of the bread. 'It's easing off,' said Tony, looking at the leaden sky, and he was right. Presently one could identify Downpatrick Head, for it is one of the most remarkable shapes on the Irish coast, a sandwich of layered rock running out from the shore, rising gradually until at its highest point it drops sheer to the waves. It was six or seven miles away. Just inshore of us a great waterfall arched down the side of the mountain and stained the sea brown with eroded soil. Then the cliff landscapes began to fall astern, giving way to slopes where the moor merged into farmlands. A weak sun arrived to pick out a pyramid-like structure on the nearby bluffs, smaller than but reminiscent of the famous pyramid at the Paris Louvre.

This was the Céide Fields Centre, where hundreds of acres of neolithic stone-walled enclosures which had been hidden under the bog had recently been excavated. The fields of a farming people who lived in harmony with hunters and fishermen, there are no defensive works in the 5,000-year-old site. The fields cover an area of some 24 square miles and run longitudinally with the slope of the land. It is suggested that the Céide settlement, with its tombs and house enclosures, was probably planned by an organised society walling off thousands of acres for cattle. That would make it, not a world of pioneers cutting fields from the forest, but one more like the heroic society of the Iron Age, depicted in epics like the *Cattle Raid of Cooley*. We thought the layout of the fields we had seen around Broadhaven offered a reflection of a similar culture.

Close up, Downpatrick Head revealed itself as a series of pillars or drums, most still attached to the cliffs. Gulls, guillemots and razorbills argued over territorial rights in the headland's slatey shelves. We passed near to one great drum, Doonbrista. Over 100 feet high, its grassy top was level with St Patrick's Chapel on the mainland a few hundred feet across the chasm. The many layered, many coloured pillar seemed quite unclimbable; indeed it looked narrower at the base than at the top. It had been farmland some 500 years ago, and when the land-bridge suddenly collapsed, twelve people were left marooned, quite beyond any means of rescue.

We approached the wide bay of Killala, passing the beach and little harbour at Kilcummin Bay where three frigates flying false English colours anchored on 22 August 1798. When Bishop Stock of Killala sent his two sons and the harbour surveyor down to pay their respects, they were at once imprisoned aboard. That evening over 1,000 men under General Humbert came ashore. A French soldier climbed to the top of the Bishop's Palace and re-placed the Union Jack with a green flag with a harp in the centre.

Two years after his fleet had fled Bantry Bay, Wolfe Tone, leader of the United Irishmen, had again secured French aid for a rebellion. Now it arrived too late; the uprising had been all but crushed in the rest of the country. The French and poorly armed Irish novices took Ballina and Castlebar, where the precipitate British retreat becoming known as the 'Castlebar Races,' but all to no avail. Some 4,000 troops and guns were ferried from Dublin on the canal to Tullamore, and then to the killing ground at Ballinamuck in Co. Longford where the armies of Lord Cornwallis and General Lake defeated the rebels on 8 September. French prisoners were returned to France, the Irish hanged. A month later Tone was captured as he sailed towards Lough Swilly in Donegal on board another French squadron. He defeated the hangman by committing suicide in prison.

At the end of another century, a changed Ireland now holds an annual ecumenical service with a 'Bishop Stock' address in Killala Cathedral and the town hosts an international Humbert Summer School on the theme of reconciliation.

The French frigates had had an experienced pilot, a man named Murphy from Drogheda, who made his career in France and later became one of the chief pilots of the naval base at Brest. I had not expected to sail into Killala originally, and had only a small-scale chart. It is a dangerous shallow bay and the town lies hidden behind a sandbar down in its south-west corner. We had to follow a mile-long channel running between shoals carrying only two metres of water, and squeeze through a gap between sand dunes and the shore to gain entry to a large lagoon. The lagoon dries out at low water, but at high tide boats can follow a staked channel 15 metres wide which leads finally to the pier. Three pairs of beacons have to be identified and lined up, one pair for each change of course. One mistake and you run aground.

Perhaps we should not have expected the twelfth-century round tower to be a distinctive shore mark; certainly it did not stand out as we started our run, an ominous ground swell already building up at the harbour's mouth. We steered too close to shoals and hastily turned away for deeper water. There were factory chimneys a few miles ahead but no round tower as yet. Eyes on the echo-sounder we kept on towards the coast and then spotted a buoy. South past it and we saw the green Killala Buoy. 'It has been moved,' declared the *Directions*, 'so leave it to starboard and then identify the white beacons on Rinnaun Point.'

'I can see only one beacon!'

Tony was on the bow, gripping the forestay. 'They're right in line: the two look like one.'

Our depth dropped to ten feet. Water was breaking to one side, looking disconcertingly sandy as we approached the dunes. *Sarakiniko* was closing on a beach, but over to port the next two beacons were moving into line, so, a few hundred yards off the shingle, we swung to port and ran along the shore.

'Are we far enough?'

'I think so.'

I looked at the shallows to each side, murmuring like the hissing of snakes.

'We'll be sheltered here for the night, especially when the tide drops.'

We anchored quickly, slapped the dinghy into the water, and the tide, still flooding strongly through the gut to the lagoon beyond, carried us swiftly to the third set of beacons and the channel to the pier. The pub had closed for suppers but the lady at the counter realised we were off a boat and had some excuse for being late, so she offered to heat up some roast chicken. It tasted as chicken used do years ago. 'It's my 80-year-old father,' she smiled, 'he keeps them running around in the old style.'

It was dark as we chugged back down the inlet, Tony waving the torch to show me the line of stakes. If we hit soft mud out here on a falling tide, we would be sitting on inflated rubber all night. A wan yellow gleam appeared to seaward – *Sarakiniko*'s riding light – and Tony's swift grab held us to the stern as she strained in the fierce ebb. We motored up on the rising tide in the morning and secured our lines at the root of the pier, out of the way of some half-dozen small trawlers. All was safe and ship-shape now, but nothing gets quite so filthy in a short time as a cruising yacht, so we brought out dust-pans to deal with fluff and dust and dirt, swished the wooden cockpit gratings in the water and searched for a skip for our rubbish, ignoring the tactless boys fishing from the pier who wanted to know what we had been doing to get so dirty. Later, in a big store near the quay where farmers and builders bought rolls of barbed-wire and nails by the sackful, we replenished the jerry-cans with diesel. At last we could sit with beers watching the tide recede, until eventually a car announced the end of a long journey from Tipperary with a cheerful hooting.

Tony's brother, Dáithí, followed Anne down the rusty ladder, and talk flowed as tea-cups were filled and thick slices of barm brack buttered. I suggested to Dáithí that he should join

Sarakiniko's crew for the run to Donegal. The car could remain parked for a few days at Killala and he could bus and hitch-hike back to it. Teatime merged with drinking time, but certain quantities of gin later the fun subsided when the BBC warned of south-westerlies up to Force 7 with moderate or poor visibility. We waited for the Irish Coastal Waters forecast, more accurate because it deals with smaller areas, and heard some deceptively casual talk of a trough of low pressure with winds Force 5 to 6, occasionally 7 north of Slyne Head. 'I might as well take to the road,' said the elder O'Gorman. For a non-sailor, it was a sensible decision.

'I haven't seen the sea since Glandore,' Anne mused as we stood on the pier waving Dáithí goodbye. *Sarakiniko* too was out of the sea. She lay in a kind of trough she had dug in the mud at the foot of the pier.

'We should have a fine sail tomorrow,' I had declared to Anne as we bent over scampi and the inevitable chips in the pub. It had been an interesting place, the walls lined with stills from *The Day of the French* showing troopers plunging through musket smoke in Killala's narrow streets. All through a night of uneasy dreams about gourmet living in a French-speaking Mayo I had been half aware of a humming of wind and knew now that I should have set the alarm for the 0555 forecast. The wind had hardened, and it was a 60-mile run to our next planned anchorage at Aranmore Island, and just over half-way there we would close on Slieve League as it bulges out from the coast.

Sarakiniko jerked herself on to an even keel and bumped and strained against her quayside lines, then she was free, rocking easily and triumphantly. Presently the tide would ebb and she would take the ground again, closing our window of opportunity. We should have to leave at once in any case if we were to reach Aranmore in daylight. The south side of the island is a maze of reefs, and even in the approach channel to the sound the depth at low tide is a mere foot or so a mile offshore. In poor visibility it is just not on. We could run up outside the island, round its north side and come down to find an anchorage along a fairly rock-free coast, but naturally this would add extra miles to our journey. We

discussed the problem at breakfast, and the reluctance of my conclusion that we should spend the day in harbour was cushioned
by the simple consolation you get from others' agreement.

It may sound an ambiguous compliment to suggest that Killala
is the right size because you can easily walk out of it into countryside, but that is one of the great attractions of most Irish towns. It
is full of neat pastel houses and small faded shops, their fronts
lettered in Gaelic script. A young German had been left in charge
of the Tourist Office this morning; a student I guessed, and I
expect he had only recently hit town. When I asked if he had any
information about the invasion he seemed astonished.

'I do not know this thing.'

'The French,' I added helpfully.

'French?'

To restore his equilibrium I bought a postcard I didn't want
and picked up a brochure about local walks written – I intend no
pun – in a rather pedestrian style: 'The countryside is rich in
pasture lands with fields divided by stone walls.' We left behind
the net-curtained terraces where washing blew horizontally in the
back gardens, and tramped out the road towards the dome of
Nephin Mountain gracing the south-western sky. A surprising
amount of traffic forced us to walk in file. I suggested it could be
commuter traffic to the big Asahi synthetic fibres plant outside
the town, grey sheds spreadeagled across the hill, chimneys rival-
ling Killala's round tower, a crammed parking lot and a
factory golfcourse. Some 340 people worked there at the time.

'Starting work in a Japanese factory at ten in the morning,'
cried Anne. 'You're having us on.'

'They said in the pub there's a teamwork system,' Tony called
from behind. '"See, Think, Plan, Do."'

'It doesn't sound in the Irish tradition, whatever it is.'

Perhaps it wasn't, but some workers here are emigrants home
from England, and down the road at Ballina a Ruhr subsidiary,
Shamrock Forge, manufactures tools under German management. 'A bit bossy,' the man in the newsagent's had informed us.
'The shortest distance between two points may be a straight line
for them, but it's a zig-zag round here.' Maybe, but we were

seeing bits of the answer to the crisis of Ireland's west coast. And some of the enduring economic difficulties: several months after our visit to Killala, the Asahi plant closed.

Later, when the tide flooded, trawlers bustled up to the pier with fish and I watched crate after crate of salmon being heaved off the boats into refrigerated vans. Buyers were busy scribbling dockets. '£44? No, Jim, £64 is nearer the mark.' As another trawler nosed up to the quay a collie, barking wildly, sprang off its bow and, ignoring the nets and fish boxes and offers of other canine company, hurried to lift a leg against a bollard. 'Fourteen hours at sea,' the owner shouted from the wheelhouse window, 'and he always waits!' Lines were taken ashore and there was a rumble of talk about tomorrow, Ballina Heritage Day. 'Maybe you'll be rowing, Kevin?' When Kevin came to confer with the man at the van, I guessed the weight of his largest fish at twelve pounds. He grinned at me and pointed. The scales showed seventeen and a half.

A boat becomes slightly claustrophobic when it's aground under a wall. We were thankful to wake to a bright morning with the wind in the south-west. This would be fair on our quarter for the northward run. The forecast was of south-westerlies Force 5, up to 7 at times. Well, they had said that yesterday and the afternoon had been tantalisingly fair. Impatient to be away, I grounded *Sarakiniko* on a mudbank as soon as she left the pier. We contained ourselves with another cup of coffee as the frothy water rose around us, and when she lifted again we crept through the channels to the open bay.

The wind seemed anxious to come from astern, a point which no sailor with a modern yacht particularly likes. It was fine for the old square riggers, but without a sideways slant to your sails from a wind coming across the quarter, the modern yacht will roll and roll, and if it yaws a little off course the wind can get to the back of the sail and slam boom and mainsail violently across the boat. An unintended gybe can mean a very sore head, or in rough weather such a mishap could smash the standing rigging which supports the mast.

Our rolling was aggravated by swell as the boat cleared the

shelter of the bay. Books shuffled back and forth in their fiddled shelf. The saucepans rattled in the galley. We lowered the mainsail and unrolled some more jib, and finally began to make progress. The weather was still clear, though one could only guess at the position of Sligo and Donegal towns away in the east. Between them rose a shape which looked like Table Mountain. It was Ben Bulben – 'Bare Ben Bulben' – under which Yeats lies in Drumcliff churchyard.

The sky grew dark but the rain held off. Little black-and-white guillemots kept diving ahead of the boat, drilling through the water as cleanly as a bullet. Slieve League and the off-lying island of Rathlin O'Birne grew on the bow. We concentrated on the steering, bracing ourselves against the rolling, and took turns resting below, wedged in a bunk, reading or listening to the radio, and wishing we had the time to explore every detail of the coast. Just to the east lay Sligo, Donegal town and the thriving fishing port of Killybegs with its great modern trawlers. It may prosper even more in the future. Drilling with modern technology in relatively shallow seas like the Rockall Trough only 75 miles away could yield results which would make the town a service base for oil and gas industries. But if we were to encompass the whole coast of Ireland, we would have to make sacrifices. Regretting the need to keep moving on, we wondered constantly if and when the weather would break, and whether fate would let us reach our next harbour.

Dim to the east, only a mile long and three miles offshore, we could just discern Inishmurray. Even this we must leave unexplored. Here in 807 AD was probably the first Viking attack on an Irish monastery. Great nine-foot-thick walls surround two ruined churches. There are beehive huts and slabs and altars, and large quantities of less Christian 'cursing stones' which an islander, wishing vengeance, would turn ritually during a nine-day session of fasting. Here there was an extremely unusual example, for Ireland, of a Latin inscription on an early Christian gravestone, which says: 'Muredach sleeps here.' The precious relic is now preserved in Dublin.

Tony had read that the long low shape of the island had

induced a British naval vessel to discharge a torpedo at it one night during World War I, rudely waking the small population. It was also famed for its poteen, 'Old Ireland,' but that happy time was long ago. The last 50 inhabitants left in October 1947.

Anne counts the success of a cruise by the number of days of spray and boisterous sea, and the day did not disappoint her. *Sarakiniko* was coming up fast on Slieve League now. Up there were more Christian remains, amongst them 26 penitential stations which were popular up to around 1800 when it ceased to be a place of pilgrimage. In the swirl of mist today a walker would be hard put to find them. The narrows between the cliffs and the island of Rathlin produced false winds which flogged the jib, snatched at the forestay and shook the mast, but our speed and the tide carried us through. Now the sea began to build. *Sarakiniko* rode the waves, surging forward with a crest for as long as she could hold it, then falling back into the trough until caught up in the next. Aranmore was on the horizon, perhaps 15 miles off, but the afternoon was growing late and the sea seemed to be collecting its strength. The waves came rolling up astern, growing steeper and steeper until an individual roller could no longer support its own mass and a small crest toppled forward and come sliding down the wavefront, a self-generating roll of foam. I slid below to check distances and felt a surge of affection for this boat, its solidity, neatness and precision. There was Anne, off watch at last, lying warm in the forepeak bunk, and outside, Tony, safety harness clipped on, feet braced against the motion, eyes on the compass. We could carry on into the dusk and clear Aranmore, but it had been a long day.

'Want any tea or anything?' Anne called.

'No, thanks. I should stay where you are for the time being. I'm thinking of an alternative anchorage for the night instead of flogging on to Aranmore. OK by you?'

'Yes, fine.'

There was an alternative, just one in fact. I mistrusted the latitude flashed by our misbehaving Decca system, but about a mile abeam I had seen an islet under the cliffs, just discernible on the edge of visibility. As the chart displayed only one islet we appeared to be coming past the treacherous shoals in Loughros Bay: 'Not been known ever to have been entered by a yacht,' according to the *Directions*.

I had read of the Spanish Armada transport, *Duquesa Santa Ana*, in Loughros Bay. The General-in-Chief of the Armada land forces, who had lost his own ship in Blacksod, transferred with his company to the *Duquesa Santa Ana* and they set sail for Scotland. They rounded Erris and a squall drove them in here. An Irishman on board reported: '...there fell a great storm which brake in sunder all their cables and struck them upon ground.' The captain, de Leiva, rallied the survivors and they dug in on an island in Kiltoris Lough: a gun mounted there was found in 1968. Elsewhere along the coast Spaniards had been slaughtered by the Irish, but in remote Donegal the MacSweeney clan offered them shelter. The refugees marched to Killybegs and transferred to yet another Spanish ship, the *Gerona*. Carrying about 1,300 men, the *Gerona* managed to reach Antrim before a gale drove it on to a reef near Dunluce. There were only five survivors. Trawling the sea-bed at the site of the shipwreck, Belgian archaeologist Robert Stenuit recovered guns, navigational equipment, hundreds of gold and silver coins and a great hoard of jewellery which forms one of the most remarkable exhibits in the Belfast Museum.

So much for Loughros. Past it lay Dawros Bay, 'only a temporary anchorage in calm conditions', so that was no good either. But get across the bay and around Dawros Head and we could turn and run east a few miles into Church Pool, a sheltered spot behind a sandy island. I put the parallel rulers away, called a new compass course to Tony, 070 degrees magnetic, and added optimistically, 'Whiskey and supper at anchor within the hour.' Nervously I watched the breaking shoals to starboard, and then came that lift of elation which makes sailing such an obsession when, 20 minutes later, a white tower emerged from the gloom: the beacon on Dawros Head. We slid into flat poppling water, found a firm anchorage in the sand, and later we sat, whiskey warming us from within, as the lights of Portnoo swung lazily across the portholes and the rather doleful wind funnelled gently up and down in the rigging.

THE DEEPLY indented coast of Donegal curves north-east in a sequence of inlets and islands running for 70 miles from Slieve League to Malin Head. Bloody Foreland lies half-way along, and out from it Tory Island. Aranmore, south-west of the Foreland, is the largest of the offshore islands and the gateway to the Rosses, a flat, rock-strewn heathland which breaks into 30 or 40 islets scattered along the coast. In the morning we rumbled off under engine, the wind light, leaving a wake of spun glass in the water behind. Presently the breeze came up, and after an hour's sailing *Sarakiniko* was approaching the archipelago of islands and reefs guarding Aranmore. The swell lifted over concealed rocks like muscles bulging and broke every so often with a sound like wheezy breathing. The island shapes changed as we moved along and we took constant bearings to check where we were, hunting with the binoculars for marks and beacons.

We anchored and went ashore on the sheltered side of Aranmore. The island village was a line of houses running along the beach, backed by woody dells and tangled hedgerows full of wild flowers. Coming in from the sea to such a lush corner, we could understand the decision of the white Arctic owl which, a notice in a shop declared, had been sighted in June 1993 and had remained in the island since. In the village pub a determined monologist was telling a visitor the facts of island life.

'You should be here in winter. You're lucky if you see the daylight; it's the windiest, wettest place on God's earth. No one to talk to, only the wife, and she stopped listening long ago.'

I stuck to the *Donegal Democrat* and read of the many people who had already visited this summer: anglers, ornithologists, divers, amateur radio operators and children from St Ciaran's special school in Dublin. The paper also reminded its readers of the second and third generation islanders back from Britain, the USA and Australia, and there were 200 young people attending the Irish College. The vibrancy of the island community was evident when they brought out the Aranmore pipe band behind banners in Irish and Russian to welcome 30 children from Chernobyl, gave them a lighthouse tour, a barbecue and a party, and raised £512 for the children's fund.

Gola, part of a family of islands about 14 miles away, was our overnight destination. The serpentine channels between the dozens of tiny islands, rocks and skerries required accurate compass courses or the continual aligning of beacon against rock, rock against headland. None of us had actually seen the Rosses (in Irish 'the promontories') until this afternoon, when they arranged themselves around the boat like an archipelago in still life, shafts of sunlight picking out red cliffs and white slivers of deserted beaches. The pyramid of Mount Errigal dominated the mainland to the east. Fishermen hauling lobster pots waved as we passed. The sea can seem a much friendlier place than land. Out here a boat moves in a kind of solitude, and there is inordinate pleasure in the little passing company you find.

We crossed Owey Sound. A few years ago, the late Miles Clark saw a rare type of curragh being used here. It was so small that it was propelled by one man kneeling with a paddle in the bow.

We motored cautiously into the horseshoe bay on the south side of Gola. 'None of the approaches are simple for a stranger,' the *Directions* warned, but two little islands offshore reduced the swell.

'Like a flooded crater in here,' I said, looking without enthusiasm at the cliffs encircling us.

Tony lowered the anchor slowly. 'If the wind changes we might swing a bit too close to the cliffs.'

'Yes,' I agreed, 'but it seemed a bit deep for anchoring in the middle, and there's more swell there anyway.'

'I'll put the kettle on,' Anne called from the galley, knowing that on *Sarakiniko* decisions about anchoring tends to become discursive. We had lost the cheerful sunlight and, when the dinghy was launched to collect more data for our debate, we found that the swell would make a landing on the low cliffs a hit or miss affair. We decided to move on to the east side of Gola. All this required of us was that we not hit Leanancoyle Rock lurking near by. Tony had the book.

'Could you read it again?' I asked.

'Keep 50 or 80 metres out going along the north side of Gola Island and continue, keeping the north-west point of Allage

Island only just outside or inside the north of Gola so as to pass north of Leanancoyle Rock. Got it?'

'Well, I suppose so.' Tony sprang forward to act as lookout when I put the motor in gear, but all went well. We anchored off Gola's deserted pier and came ashore. We followed a grassy track to the island village, which had a surprising number of two-storey dwellings, all of them deserted, their doors swinging in the wind, net curtains still hanging on the windows. The rasp of a chainsaw led us to two men and two boys who were sawing a telegraph pole into four-foot lengths. They were camping out in one of the abandoned houses. We asked them about the plaque bearing the names of two fishermen of Gola who had crewed on the yacht *Asgard* in 1914, running guns into Howth for the rebels.

'It's just been put up,' said one. 'The *Asgard* herself came in a few weeks ago. You know, the training ship.'

'We passed her off the Cork coast.'

'It was a great party here, I tell you.'

'Did you live here once?'

'Yes, till I was 14.' He swung a thumb towards the mainland. 'I come over now and again. The father stayed on, you know, stayed alone. He was over 80 then, but he was all right.'

I pointed. 'Was that a school?'

'Yes. The numbers kept falling.'

'No church?'

'No. They always went across to Bunbeg on Sunday.'

I looked at the tangle of walled enclosures and the rusty farm machines. 'There was a fair bit of arable land.'

'They grew what they needed. But it's not worth it now. All these sheep belong to one man and they'll run everywhere, so without new fencing...'

'And the houses still belong to people on the mainland?'

'Oh, they would. I saw you coming around,' he swung the conversation, 'and I said to the lads: "They know the rocks."'

Dusk was falling. A point of light blinked across the sea.

'Is that Tory?'

'Tory it is, eight miles out from the Foreland.'

'Well, we are getting around Ireland,' said Anne.

'We must try to get out there,' Tony said. 'People will ask.'

I agreed. 'Only wimps miss out Tory.'

After midnight I climbed on deck to quieten a slapping halyard. Tory's light flickered against the clouds every few seconds. Tomorrow would bring north-westerlies and in the following 24 hours they would grow 'fresh to strong'. The island's harbour would shelter us from the wind.

Across the sound the Donegal mainland seemed illuminated like a large coastal town. It was a remarkable sight. A landscape at night always seems more populous, but even in daylight Bunbeg appeared to have an unusual number of bungalows superimposed on the wilderness. Too often now one has to focus selectively when admiring Ireland's landscape and shut out pock-marks of bungaloid growth, houses that have come out of a builder's catalogue and been put together from materials antipathetic to the countryside. Did the planning authorities just let anything go? It looked as if they did.

Over the stern I could see a particularly vivid cluster of light, Donegal's International Airport at Carrickfin. So it is advertised, but perhaps it is not very international yet – you can fly to Glasgow, and approval for connections to Dublin was soon to be achieved under something called the Essential Air Services programme sponsored by the European Union. Good links with Dublin are necessary for Donegal, though Derry, a city rising like a phoenix, will probably always be the natural capital of north-west Ireland.

It was emigration from nineteenth-century Donegal which gave Derry its Catholic population. It is difficult now to grasp the extent of the poverty which uprooted people from the country-side a mere 150 years ago. Lord George Hill's *Facts from Gweedore*, a village up the road from Bunbeg, records that in a parish of 4,000 people in 1837, one owned a cart, one a plough and there were 27 geese and three turkeys. Between them the population owned 28 mattresses of chaff and two of feather and grew no vegetables except potatoes and cabbage. If abundant shoals of fish arrived the cost of salt soared. 'So great was the difficulty of getting even a coffin made that, to secure the services of a carpenter, many gave him an annual retaining fee of sheaves of oats on the express condition of making them coffins when they died.'

Such extreme poverty stood in contrast to the many prosperous areas of Ireland in the south and east, a point often forgotten. Fishing communities on the west coast were often victimised by the crews of wherries sailing around from relatively well-to-do coastal towns like Rush, Balbriggan and Skerries, who cut nets and intimidated the local curraghs. Lord Hill, who had bought 23,000 acres around Gweedore, did an almost unheard of thing by learning Irish the better to tackle local problems. He greatly improved the district by redividing, draining and fencing land, offering premiums for the best crops, building a corn store, houses and a shop at Bunbeg. When this humane man died in 1879 conditions deteriorated again.

'It's breaking white each side ahead,' said Anne next morning, peering over the sprayhood. 'That gap seems very small.' The exit through Gola's North Sound demanded precise handling, but despite the lively wind she guided *Sarakiniko* safely through the tumble.

Records show that in June and July the Irish coast experiences, on average, two gales in each month. The weather was still good, a morning of fresh westerly wind and a substantial but acceptable swell, but a vague unease which had dogged me for some time was not reduced when the Admiralty *Pilot* noted for Tory Island that 'It should be borne in mind that the weather in this area is particularly liable to sudden change and a vessel should be prepared to leave at short notice.'

Presently we were off Bloody Foreland. 'It doesn't live up to its name,' Anne said, gazing at the gentle slopes. 'There's nothing bloody about it.'

It does sound like the site of a great battle, but the name just comes from the reddish tint in the rocks.

Tory crouched out to sea, its back pushed up protectively against the cold north, its southern side sloping towards the mainland. To the west the light still flashed at the end of Tory's long low tail. The island grew clearer: cliffs, stone walls, a scoop of harbour and then the spread of white houses at the little village of West Town. We nosed for shelter towards the small pier, concentrating on a vacated mooring buoy until a churning of screws warned us of the departing mainland ferry coming astern from the steps. *Sarakiniko* achieved a rapid turn within her own length, Tony reached with the boathook and we had chain aboard, rusty but heavy, and time to wave to the only other visiting yacht, *Erquy*, skippered, as we found, by Cormac MacHenry, Honorary Secretary of the Irish Cruising Club.

Treeless Tory was notorious for its inaccessibility. When Thomas Mason came here in the early 1930s, wooden ploughs, shod with iron salvaged from wrecks and drawn by donkeys harnessed with straw ropes, opened the thin earth for the potato and corn crops. Harvesting was by scythe, threshing by flail and winnowing on a circular sheepskin riddle. Some carts had wheels but in the main they used 'slide carts' with iron-shod runners on the rear. Fish could be plentiful – even the ducks were fed on limpets – and the limpet shells were burned to provide lime. Wreck was a regular windfall and hearths were tiled with iron ships' plates. Shipwreck even produced food. 'A cargo came in recently,' said one fisherman to Mason, 'and it lasted a year. Ah, there was no want on the island then.' He could speak English, though many islanders could not.

Older people claimed that Tory's most notorious shipwreck, when the gunboat HMS *Wasp* went down in 1884, was induced by a cursing stone. The boat had been sent with soldiers and police to collect rents and rates, which the islanders refused to pay, but was lost on the western reefs and all but six people drowned. The stone was kept in the ancient graveyard near the foreshore and disappeared when heavy seas swept the graveyard away. Nonetheless, Tory has never since been required to pay rates.

When Diarmuid Ó Péicín, a Jesuit priest returned from missionary work in Africa, ended up as the island's pastor in 1979, he found on Tory a dispirited population which had dropped from some 300 to 200 people in ten years. They had a low expectation of the future – the island was awash with rumours that soon all the families would be forced to migrate to the mainland. Tory had no piped water – women and children walked daily to the well with buckets – no doctor, nurse or dentist, no sewage system or rubbish collection, no motor vehicles, save some tractors travelling on disintegrating roads, and many houses were boarded up or derelict. The island's decrepit generator produced about one hour of electricity a day. Even peat often had to be imported and donkeys were still used to pull wooden ploughs. The size of fishing boats was limited by the absence of an adequate harbour: in heavy gales, vessels had to be hauled high ashore.

Fr Ó Péicín enlisted the help of a journalist on the *Donegal Democrat*, Gerry Moriarty, who unearthed a report prepared by the County Council in 1978. The report, he wrote, 'suggested Tory's population of 200 should be rehoused on the mainland and the island used as a holiday home for American tourists, or a high-security prison, or a quarantine centre, or a firing range for the Army. The proposals revealed a breathtakingly negative mindset that was pretty prevalent at the time. Remember, this was a period when the death of the Blaskets and other islands was still being lamented. Yet Tory, an astonishingly beautiful island of great lore, of craftspeople, boatbuilders, musicians and artists, was being ignored.'

The evacuation process went ahead. Fifty-two people were moved in November 1981. The departure of 16 children halved the school roll. 'The disingenuous justification,' wrote the journalist, 'was that the families applied for the housing and that there had been no duress. What they failed to acknowledge was that the council and central government had refused to provide facilities... which might have given the islanders a reasonable choice in the matter.'

Ó Péicín 'railed against all this, galvanising some of the islanders, firing off heated missives to Church and State figures, confronting them directly, insisting on reasonable conditions for Tory'. When the County Council stated that it was willing to install piped water but unable to meet the full cost, the priest organised squadrons of volunteers who helped the council complete the work in ten weeks. The island had no transport service for schoolchildren and old people, so he acquired the chassis of a battery-operated milk float and had it adapted, fitted with cushioned seats and shipped to the island. Morale began to recover. A drama group was formed and a summer festival organised with the participation of the folk group Clannad from mainland Gweedore. Hundreds of visitors arrived. A Tory Week in Dublin publicised the island painters, fishermen who had been encouraged by English artist Derek Hill in the late 1960s and had developed a school of primitive painting which attracted wide attention. We heard of a recent exhibition in Milwaukee.

Fr Ó Péicín's time as a curate was abruptly terminated by his bishop in 1984, but now he had time to travel in Europe and America. Winifred Ewing MEP, campaigner for the Scottish Highlands and offshore islands, helped him in Strasbourg. Dr Ian Paisley, Ulster Unionist MP and an MEP since 1970, expressed his admiration for the work on Tory, and hoped that he and Fr Ó Péicín would soon meet on Rathlin off the Antrim coast. *The Irish Times* declared that a handshake between the voluble Protestant and the Papist priest would be the ecumenical gesture of the decade. In Washington the priest secured the support of the late Tip O'Neill, Speaker of the House of Representatives, who had a farm in Donegal. Ó Péicín arranged a meeting of island people at Cape Clear, Co. Cork, the first step in forming the Irish Islands Trust.

We knew nothing of all this as we lifted the rubber dinghy up on the slipway and walked ashore between white cottages facing one another across the single street of West Town. Traces of the old open drains defined the edge of the road. A few cats sat by the roughly mortared stump of the ancient round tower dominating the village centre, ostentatiously ignoring the seagulls walking up and down. The surface scraw has long gone from the flat plateau behind the village; tufted bare earth or flagstones of naked rock rise to the eastern cliffs. Even on areas reserved for grazing, the soil is thin. Bathed in a luminous clarity, the island landscape of scattered houses, stony tracks and grey stone walls had a kind of eerie quality. Until the silence was broken. 'She's back!' a smiling woman called to us from a cottage half-door. She pointed to a hen scratching at a clump of heather which hid several chicks.

'She disappeared a month ago and now brings all these back to the house; eleven of them.'

'I'm surprised a hawk or the rats didn't get them,' said Anne.

'No rats,' was the reply. 'Columcille cleared them all out long ago.'

The neighbourly woman seemed astonished that we did not know Mrs Robinson, then President of Ireland, had visited the island in recent months. Later, in the austere social centre that doubles as a bar, I found a faded copy of the *Donegal Democrat* and got the full run-down. Patsy Dan Mac Rúraí, King of Tory – *Rí Thóraigh*, a title which has been given to the island's leader by long custom – had greeted the presidential helicopter for the opening of a three-day festival. Pictures showed all, including the new hotel where Patsy Dan – the only elected king in Europe? – presided over lunch

Chris Murphy, a Belfast ornithologist, had explained to Mrs Robinson that Tory has unique bird life: the peregrine falcon, the snowy owl, lapwings and snow buntings; and apparently the corncrake, Ireland's most endangered species, is well on the way back in Tory. Perhaps the island is too. There is now a cabinet minister whose portfolio includes specific responsibility for the Irish islands, some £4 million has been allocated for a new harbour and a ferry service runs from mainland Bunbeg.

Of course, one could set government expenditure against a small island's population and feel that there were more vital calls on limited resources, but the nub seems to be that people on remote island are carriers of a particular heritage, preserving a cultural and spiritual way of life which is vital to mainland society if it, too, is to retain its identity. So we argued as we walked across Tory, and as to St Columcille's interdict against rodents in 500 AD, I fear we quite forgot to enquire further. Tradition suggests he believed that the islanders, who were reluctant to give him ground on which to build a church, badly needed his ministrations. I recalled that the pilgrims to Glencolumcille, which we had sailed past a few days before, once used clay from under a stone known as St Columcille's Bed to be scattered as a specific against rats. Similarly on Tory, clay from a ruined church used be distributed by the head of a local family who claimed descent from the original supporters of St Columcille. The saint is also said to have applied pest control in Inishmurray in Donegal Bay, and no rodents were ever seen on holy Inishglora off Mayo. Yet many a rat from sinking ships must have struck out hopefully for these shores. Do race memories of plague account for these local traditions?

On a narrow causeway at the eastern end of the island we found traces of fortifications and a small natural harbour nestling under 200-foot-high cliffs and tors. A snug place in most winds, it must have been a fortified haven of sea rovers from century to century; a hoard of Elizabethan silver coins was found here in 1931. It is said that this was the site of the O'Donnells' last stand against the English Crown, but the Admiralty chart names it as Doon Balor, Balor's Fort. He was the one-eyed god of the Fomorians, legendary early people who landed along the west coast.

Like Cyclops, Balor of the Evil Eye – the God of Darkness – could kill with a single glance. It fell to his grandson, Lugh, God of Light, to slay him. Lugh carried a Sword of Light and wore the Milky Way as his silver chain; the rainbow was his sling. His legend is of European dimensions: Lugh gave his name to the pagan Celtic feast of Lughnasa and to places such as Lyon, Leyden and Loudun. But it was in communities like Tory, beyond the echo of Roman trumpets, that such myths survived with least erosion. The one that appealed to me, as we made ready for the onward voyage, was that Lugh's ship, *Wave Sweeper*, could read a mariner's thoughts, and navigated without instruction.

EIGHT

Inlets of the North

TONY WAS STANDING in the companionway, holding out a cup of coffee. I had been watching the other yacht slip its mooring, bound for Lough Swilly as we were. I got the impression that Cormac MacHenry had a good nose for a change in the weather. Now they were away, mainsail already set, jib unrolling to a fresh westerly.

I reached for the coffee. 'Thanks a lot.' I took a gulp 'It's a great pity you have to leave at Lough Swilly, and Anne too. How will you get home?'

'Taxi to Letterkenny, I expect, and then buses to Dublin and on. When is Joan arriving?'

'In a few days.'

'And then you go round the top: Malin Head?'

'Yes, and on to Rathlin.'

Tory and Rathlin Islands; they each lie off the tips of Ireland's shoulders, with Malin Head between them some 50 miles from each. I watched the diminishing form of *Erquy*, hull occasionally half hidden in the swell.

'According to the books, the Atlantic eases up once Malin Head is behind one. Joan doesn't like swell.'

Tony said glanced at the shore. 'Their boats are all hauled up. That must mean bad weather.'

'I wonder. They mostly look as if they've been waiting there for a paint-brush for weeks.'

A few moments later *Sarakiniko*'s engine was ticking over sweetly as Tony dropped the mooring chain and we went astern past weed-covered rocks until we could turn and unroll the jib. Anne came into the cockpit, fastening her sailing jacket.

'A good wind,' she said cheerfully, watching flurries run across the water. Six miles away the mainland basked green in morning sunshine. I pointed an arm east.

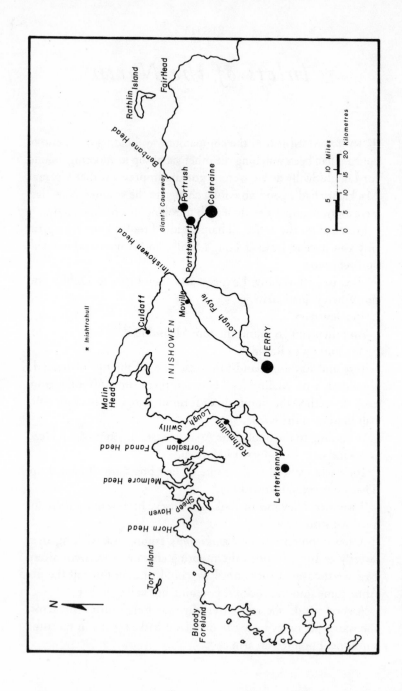

'We go close to Horn Head, eight miles on. You'll find it's much more impressive than Bloody Foreland.'

The breeze was dead astern – a gybing course – so it seemed more relaxing to leave the mainsail unhoisted and run directly downwind under the white balloon of the jib. *Erquy*, with mainsail up, had turned inshore to fetch the wind a little on one quarter; now she was gybing to fetch it on the other. She would reach Lough Swilly before us, but today it seemed better to travel than arrive. Bow to the morning sun, stern rising and falling rhythmically, *Sarakiniko* began running down a highway of dazzling silver rollers which reached before us to the very horizon, while a million white horses played to port and starboard. On each side of our bubbling wake, Bloody Foreland and Tory were sinking fast astern and the headlands of Horn and Melmore and even Fanad at Swilly's entrance began to sprawl out ahead like the paws of a recumbent lion.

More of Ireland's great sea loughs lay beyond Horn Head: Sheephaven and Mulroy Bay, which turns and twists inland for ten miles and offers perhaps the best anchorages on the north coast. Two uncharted rocks were discovered there some years ago by a British naval officer, Commander Gilliland. He suggested to the Admiralty that they be named after him and his vessel – Gilliland and Seagull respectively. The suggestion was accepted and charts were amended, but the Irish government, understandably, protested that this was national territory over which the British government had no jurisdiction. The politics of Northern Ireland extend some way out to sea.

Running some 30 miles into the heart of the historic province of Ulster are the inlets of Lough Swilly and Lough Foyle. Waterways like these shaped Irish history. Analysing the lengthy Elizabethan wars of the seventeenth century, when two civilisations grappled and the older one went down, Cyril Falls, in his detailed study *Elizabeth's Irish Wars*, concluded that the greatest Irish weakness lay in their lack of artillery. 'A gun or two was captured,' he writes, 'and the Spaniards supplied a number in the last phase; otherwise the Irish forces never possessed any.' This meant that no castle held by the English need ever fall unless betrayed, surprised or starved out, whereas practically no castle could be maintained by the Irish if the English could reach the scene with cannon of adequate weight.

England's problem was access. Maintaining a supply system in a country where it might be necessary not only to penetrate woods harassed by an elusive enemy, but to lay down hurdles to bring vehicles over sodden ground, was a formidable task. So the sea, Falls wrote, was almost always used when artillery had to be moved any considerable distance. 'Sea power served the English well... they made constant use of the indentations of the coast and of the navigable rivers to bring seaborne supplies deep into the country. Lough Foyle, Belfast Lough, Carlingford Lough, Waterford Harbour and the Barrow, Cork Harbour and the Bandon, Bantry Bay, Kenmare River, Dingle Bay, the Shannon and Fergus and Galway Bay provided shipping with channels penetrating far within the coast and enabled land forces to reach their supplies by relatively short marches accompanied by relatively little transport.'

A trap waits for you off this coast, the Limeburner Rock, an isolated reef carrying little more than ten feet of water at times, and lurking some three miles out to sea. We were well inshore when Tony picked out its guardian buoy, a feather of white above the swell. As he replaced the binoculars the VHF burst into garbled speech: 'Inshore yacht – nets!' I threw my weight against the tiller. The jib snatched and flapped as we swung off course and lost the wind. Anne grabbed the winch handle, dropped it into its socket and spun it to draw in and flatten the sail. White floats lay along the slope of the swell just yards away. Running lazily downwind under the jib is all very well while the way ahead remains clear, but a hoisted mainsail would have given us the manoeuvrability to tack into the wind and get away from the danger. Fortunately the engine responded at once and we surged away from the hazard.

'We're heading for the Limeburner,' Tony called.

'Yes, I can see the buoy. The fishing boat seems to be approaching. Can you call them up and ask them how far out this bloody net goes?'

The tide against us put a convex curve in the long line of net, forcing us a bit west of north. Tony emerged again.

'They say about two miles.'

'Do they, damn it.'

The fishing boat had turned and ran parallel to us on the far side of the net. 'And,' Tony added, 'we're to keep on north until we can clear around their bow.'

On the quay at Killala I had fallen to talking to a retired officer of the Irish Fisheries Patrol.

'Surely the length of net is specified?' I asked him.

He explained with naval precision that it was 800 feet maximum on the south and south-west coasts and 1,600 feet in the north and north-west, the maximum width being six feet and the season running during daylight hours from June to mid-August. And then he added, 'We once found a net 14 miles long; a record, probably. Now we have high-speed reels but the crews used have to haul them in by hand before.'

'Are there many patrol boats?'

'In my time there were seven for the whole coast and two aircraft. The aircraft are well equipped, especially with radar. Some time ago I was on a flight that picked up 92 contacts on our radar between Dunmore East and Kinsale.'

'And you have to identify them.'

'Yes, you have to descend to 200 feet – and that itself takes time – and then get the photographs and call up a patrol vessel.'

'Who gets the fish?'

'They should all be accounted for and taken ashore.' He looked me in the eye. 'And some might have got eaten.'

'You don't say so!'

'There were occasional departmental enquiries,' he laughed. 'We had a civil servant who took it very seriously. I can remember a meeting where he was assured that a salmon could sometimes die of consumption.'

The crews of patrol boats may often come from small shore-based communities themselves, but there is none of the embarrassment of helping to confiscate the nets and catch of a cousin or schoolfriend when the offender is a foreigner. That year, he told me, the Service had boarded 250 vessels in Irish waters and detained 27: twelve Spanish, ten British and five Irish. Seven cases had reached the courts and fines were usually heavy. European Union plans for continuous satellite-based monitoring of fishing trawlers will soon make it easier to check the movement of boats throughout prescribed sea areas like the Irish Box.

Though the lighthouse on Fanad Head marks the western entrance to Lough Swilly, the gateway is dominated by Dunaff Head four miles to the east. The 25-mile-long inlet is one of Europe's finest big ship anchorages. Five miles up where the waters grow narrower, Fort Dunree was the first of the defences guarding it. After the French scare a barracks was added to its tower and cannon, and over the years Dunree and the neighbouring Fort Lenan grew redoubts, moated ramparts, ammunition stores, underwater torpedo tubes, machine-gun posts, howitzers and heavy artillery. There are six derelict forts and batteries along these shores. They never saw action; Napoleon went to Egypt instead.

But here, as at Berehaven in Kerry 400 coastal miles behind us, convoys assembled during the First World War. For a time, indeed, the entire British Grand Fleet retreated to the safety of Swilly when fear of submarines and mines forced it to abandon its base at Scapa Flow in Scotland. When Ireland achieved partial independence under the Anglo-Irish Treaty in 1921, Britain ensured that the Irish bases remained in her hands. Churchill, inveighing against their transfer in 1938, described them as 'the sentinel towers of the western approaches'. But on 3 October the Irish moved in above the lough where, almost 140 years to the day, Tone had been captured from the frigate *La Hoche* and arrived in irons as a prisoner of the British Navy. There was one feature of the handover ceremony which symbolised a less painful consequence of the agonised embrace between Britain and Ireland. Sergeant King of the Royal Artillery, who struck the Union Jack was a brother-in-law of Quartermaster-Sergeant McLaughlin, the Irish soldier who raised the tricolour. The British troops left without much ceremony that afternoon, travelling in a bus across the partition line to the city of Londonderry

20 miles away, where the Union Jack seemed in no danger of coming down.

The barometer had dropped. The tricolour was stiff as a board on the mast above Fort Dunree. Under full sail and in easy water *Sarakiniko* threshed south between gently sloping farmlands. A substantial house peered between tufted trees in the distant parkland. 'Arcadian,' Anne commented. I agreed. It was beautiful as a dream. We reflected on the sharp contrast of trees and fertile arable fields after our weeks on the west coast. I also felt that the scale of these inland waters was not unlike the Solent, but it was another half-hour before we saw yachts under sail, even though it was a Saturday afternoon in July. Several appeared then, racing out from the club at Fahan a few miles ahead. As we lowered some sail to cut speed for the buoyed channel into Fahan, *Erquy* came out, Cormac MacHenry shouting that we might moor by the pier at Rathmullan over the way. We turned and followed cautiously across the muddy shallows.

At Rathmullan the lough curves and lies open to the south-westerlies for another ten miles. The pontoon seemed exposed, and swayed in the rising wind. Moored runabouts and launches nodded to each other in the chop as willing hands took our lines and we secured alongside. *Erquy* was tying up ahead of us. Presently Cormac MacHenry came along the spray-washed gratings.

'I'm doubling up my lines. It's forecast to reach Force 9.'

Fifty-mile-an-hour winds. I looked around at a solid ironwork pier, a sweeping beach, and the town's Victorian hotel, and felt a surge of relief that we were not on Tory.

We found ourselves liking Rathmullan a lot. It is the gift of Ireland to make one happy; certainly the country itself seems to be running better in the general pursuit of happiness than any other I know. Every passer-by in the street presented a relaxed affable air. And though there may have been coaches, cars and mini-buses crowding into the village resort from other towns, Rathmullan was no one's mere playground. Its roofs were dignified with slate, its streets had saved their attractive nineteenth-century shop-fronts, and the town had not been wrecked by planners. Within minutes of our meeting Jim Deeny, whose family had run the Pier Hotel for over a century and who had established the amenity of the pontoon, he was warning us that tonight's gale might exceed expectations.

'Even if you booked a bedroom from us,' he grinned, 'I'd tell you to stick to the boat tonight to look after her, but I'll be down to see you in the morning.'

Some drinks later and laden with eggs, onions and cheese for Anne's promised super-omelette, Tony and I slipped between a line of cars on our way back to the boat. One called out: 'You off the yacht?'

'Yes.'

'Martin Blake. Hop in. I'll run you back. Just been talking to Jim Deeny. My brother has a good mooring below the pier. He's away at the minute, so move down there tomorrow if you're here for a few days.'

'Well, yes,' I said, 'I'll be waiting for my wife.'

'No problem at all; just put something in the Lifeboat box. It's a big black buoy for trawlers,' he added, 'with a chain waiting to rupture you.'

I looked at Tony. 'My crew is leaving me in two days.'

'Well, the chain could be his last job.'

The wind had increased already and we walked down the rocking pontoon like ungainly spacemen. By dusk a fresh gale was singing in the rigging, slapping the sides of *Sarakiniko* with angry wavelets, making her snatch and rear viciously as she fought the short rippling crests. The wind direction had shifted a little, coming straight down the lough, and beating on to the head of the pontoon, which was anchored at right angles to the pier. On each lift the bow snubbed at the doubled mooring lines. It was a long night. Anne probably suffered most, not just from the incessant rubbing of a fender a few feet from her ear, but from being hoisted and dropped inside the low cubbyhole of the forepeak with the insistent regularity of a steam hammer. I went on deck at first light. Cold gusts tore across the deck. Some small launches seemed to be trying to leap onto the pontoon. I read-justed the rags which we had wrapped around the two bow-lines to prevent their chafing on our metal cleat, and decided to secure a third one.

When hope of sleep is abandoned it often comes. Morning sun was flooding the cabin when I woke. The wind, though sounding as violent as ever, had shifted slightly to the north, giving the pontoon a mite of shelter. Later on it became quite comfortable to sit in the cockpit protected by the sprayhood, watched by one inquisitive driver after another as they took their cars slowly to the pier end, turned and crept slowly back again. I expect there was little else to do on a Sunday when the wind was lifting cat's paws of sand off the beach.

They might have gone down to the Heritage Centre and read of the Flight of the Earls. At Kinsale, our port of arrival in Ireland, occurred the battle which was Ireland's Culloden and led to the extinction of the old order. We had now reached the anchorage from which, on 14 September 1607, O'Neill and O'Donnell's successor, his son-in-law Rory, together with their families – 97 people in all – took away into the night the last hopes of a Gaelic Ireland.

For O'Neill, Earl of Tyrone, the trauma of that day must have been heightened by the absence of his five-year-old son, Conn, for he was in fosterage and the whereabouts of his foster family – probably migrating with their flocks – could not be readily discovered. But the exiles felt time was pressing, the Queen's deputy, Chichester, reported to the Privy Council, and they cleared westwards and set course for Spain. On 30 September, near northern Spain, the ship was blown off course by gales and forced to run for the English Channel, reaching an anchorage near Le Havre. The French King, unwilling to offend the English Crown, would not permit the Irish party to travel through France to Spain, and sent them instead to the Spanish Netherlands. Several children stayed there, at Louvain, as did some priests and clerical students. A depleted party finally arrived in Rome where, with little to do and in an unfamiliar climate, O'Neill languished and died. The others reached Spain. Many joined the Irish regiment of the Spanish army. O'Donnell's son was to become a Spanish admiral and die in a battle against French forces in the Thirty Years War.

After the earls' departure, sporadic revolt continued for a time. A kinsman, Shane MacManus Óg O'Donnell, retreated to the islands with 100 men and five vessels, pursued by Sir Henry Folliot, Governor of Ballyshannon. The chase extended from Aranmore Island to Tory. 'The weather growing foul and night drawing on,' the first English attempt to land on Tory failed, but finally the castle at Doon Balor – which we had seen a few days before – was taken by treachery; the defenders were cut down after being promised their lives if they surrendered. Shane escaped because of 'the continual foul weather and contrary winds', but Folliot added that he was 'deprived of his mother and two children and his boat, which I think he regards more than them all'.

The earls' lifesize effigies, splendid in seventeenth-century costume, face the visitor at the entrance to the Heritage Centre where a large map depicts their long journey from Rathmullan to Rome. From there O'Neill had never ceased writing to the Spanish King, beseeching him for help, but Philip had now more pressing things on his mind, and the exiles got no further aid from Europe. Perhaps it is solace to their ghosts that this elegant memorial to their lives and times has been set up with the help of European Union funds.

The wind dropped while we pored over panels and maps and studied the development of Ulster's planned towns in the aftermath of the earls' flight, when the fateful colonisation of Ulster with English and Scottish settlers began. Unlike the Marian and Elizabethan plantations, and though twice almost exterminated, the colony took deep roots and continued to grow. We examined a scale model of Londonderry, the city developed by London's merchant guilds, and the diary of a local RUC officer in 1912 which recorded: 'Twelve battleships in the Lough today under Admiral Sir Charles Beresford.'

When we emerged, riders were cantering on the long sandy beach and the lough had flattened to an expanse of restful water. *Erquy* had left, bound for Rathlin Island. We moved *Sarakiniko* to the mooring offered by Martin Blake where, shoulder to shoulder and uttering some short words, Tony and I dragged the rusty, barnacle-encrusted chain through *Sarakiniko's* fairleads. Later, as we went ashore for a farewell meal, he claimed that we had put *Sarakiniko* slightly down by the bow. I looked back.

'She's downcast that Anne is leaving,' I said. 'I suppose you wouldn't notice that she never abuses the boat.'

'I came quite close to it last night,' said Anne.

Donegal kindness can be almost bewildering. Martin Blake ran into us near the restaurant. He was driving his wife to Letterkenny in the morning and they would find space for Anne and Tony and their bags. This they did and, next morning, I returned to *Sarakiniko*, pined over another cup of coffee, and then resolved to get down to some revolting jobs like attempting to scour off underwater weed, leaning from the bobbing dinghy, and seek order from chaos by emptying and repacking the big stern locker. Days passed until Joan arrived, claiming that her ears were still ringing from the thunder of Lambeg drums for, waiting to change buses in Derry, she had watched the Apprentice Boys' parade pass. 'Remarkably stirring,' she said. 'They came in coaches from all over the North, I think; thousands of marchers and perhaps 50 bands. People just looked on; there was no cheering. Once or twice a fellow stumbled out of a pub to start shouting and then the police would guide him away.' She also brought news that our grandson, Alasdair Glennie, would join us at Portrush.

Sunday on the lough would, we thought, offer a peaceful contrast to the Derry drums. We would have a gentle afternoon sail, a night at a small anchorage called Port Salon, and then coast around the peninsula of Inishowen and Ireland's northernmost point at Malin Head. We had – Heavens knows why – an idealised image of cottages embowered by trees, a quiet pub by a mouldering pier, but Port Salon was not like that. Progress had been at work. An Admiralty chart cannot reveal the golfcourse and car-parks, the detritus of packaged food and the thump of music from car windows. I was too dismayed to lay out sufficient chain and the anchor soon dragged. 'Subconsciously you don't wish to stay,' Joan told me.

We left Port Salon next morning with the wind favourably in

the south-west and soon had Malin Head on the horizon. The land to starboard fell away for a time as we crossed an inlet some six miles wide and three miles long. This was shallow Trawbrega Bay, where a sandbar met the long hissing surf. Its name may be an Anglicisation of *Trá Bréaga*, the false beach. 'Often impassable,' declared the *Directions*. Near the shallows of the bar we could discern Five Finger Point where Grace O'Malley is said to have lost several galleys, though she managed to scramble ashore.

If I describe Inishowen as a rough diamond, it is solely because the most northern region of Ireland has something of that shape. Bounded by the two great sea loughs of Swilly and Foyle, if they nipped in a bit more near Derry the peninsula would become an island. The traditional rulers were the O'Dohertys, after whose overthrow the peninsula was granted to the Lord Deputy, Sir Arthur Chichester. It is an illustration of the betrayals and compromises of that age that Sir Cahir O'Doherty of Inishowen was foreman of the grand jury which found a True Bill of Treason against the earls after they left, on the flimsy charge that, in gathering at Rathmullan, they were levying war against the Crown.

In later centuries, the peninsula's comparative remoteness allowed illegal distillers to produce openly and undisturbed the famous label 'Inishowen'. The Inspector General of Excise estimated that, if the whole of Ireland had about 3,000 private distilleries, some 1,300 of them were located on Inishowen. Twenty-three corn mills were almost fully occupied grinding malt for illicit stills. Oats and barley were in such demand that they had to be imported from Scotland, Antrim and Down. Weekly whiskey fairs were held on each side of the Foyle. 'Inishowen' even reached Dublin. A Revenue official wrote in 1810 that the private distillers were 'well armed and would resist any force but the military, in which they would be joined by the whole population of the county'. He suggested that cutters be based in Lough Swilly and Lough Foyle and that, when the winter weather had passed, yet another vessel should patrol around the headlands so that the import of Scottish barley could be stopped. Anti-distilling legislation was enforced with determination through the early nineteenth century, and when a distiller could not be caught red-handed, his locality was punished with a fine. Livestock and other assets were seized for failure to pay fines and a famine in 1817 led to destitution. Troops were drafted to Inishowen and across the Foyle into the Magilligan peninsula, and illicit distilling was gradually suppressed except in the northern coastal districts.

The Catholic Bishop of Derry made trafficking in poteen a reserved sin in 1892, but this sanction did not prevent a boost to distilling during the First World War. Poteen making gradually died out when farmers' incomes increased, although fortunes are said to have been made during the Second World War in catering for the thirst of US troops based in Northern Ireland.

Could a benign government have built up a lawful industry? Giving licences to small stills would have been an administrative impossibility, but it might have been practicable to set up a local unit in each parish under rigid control and get the co-operation of the people in an industry which would provide both employment and public revenue. Had that been done, 'Inishowen' whiskey might now be a household name.

Ground swell rolled in as we closed on Malin Head, the creaking calls of hundreds of seabirds all around us. I was in a confidence-inspiring mood. 'Inishowen should be sheltered from the north-west by Greenland,' I said knowledgeably.

'How droll,' retorted the mate, 'and I suppose by Iceland too.'

Presently I squinted through the handbearing compass at the derelict square tower, locally the Tower of Ballyhillin. It had been Lloyd's signal tower, built about 1805 to report on shipping. The wireless station erected in 1902 by the Marconi Company superseded it. When the tower bore exactly south, I entered the time, 1005, in the log.

The traveller Richard Pococke came past here in 1758, taking his horse across a beach which offered smoother progress than the roads, and noting, in his precise way, how the birds followed to snatch at the sand-eels displaced by its hooves. 'It is in the degree of 55° 19',' he wrote of Ireland's northern point, 'and they told me they had not above two hours of night in which they could not read in the longest days and that the sun was excessively hot in summer.' He heard from fishermen that if they found a stone in a codfish, it was 'a certain sign of an approaching storm and it is supposed they swallow it in order to sink – that they may not be dashed against the rocks. It is supposed also they have a power of disgorging the stone.' The credulity of visitors has, I suppose, long tempted the locals.

North-east of us lay the last offshore acres of the Republic, Inishtrahull Island, uninhabited for over 60 years, apart from lighthouse men, who have gone now. Through the nineteenth century some 60 to 70 people subsisted here on fishing, smuggling and wreck. Christian remains go back to the eighth century, and there is a cross-inscribed mass rock from Penal times. The snug natural harbour on its north side, sheltered from the prevailing winds, must have made a convenient landfall for many a Viking bound on an Irish raid.

The accelerating tide took us through the reefy barrier of the Garvans. The chart warned of dangerous rocks – Blind Rock, the Breakers – and to starboard the black teeth of reefs which ran between us and Malin Harbour. We anchored in mid-afternoon off the pier at the fishing hamlet of Culdaff, where a solitary trawler under repair was named *Spiritual Vessel*, and next morning we rounded Inishowen Head wondering when we would spot the Foyle Buoy which is the seamark boundary of Northern Ireland. A secluded inlet with a sandy beach presently opened up. It was Kinnagoe Bay, where the 1,100-ton *La Trinidad Valencera*, one of the Armada's largest ships, had come to anchor on 14 September 1588. Having rescued the entire crew of another galleon in mid-sea, it was now overloaded, fast shipping water and beset by a south-westerly gale. 'They landed with rapiers in their hands,' wrote a survivor to Philip II, 'whereupon they found four or five savages who bade them welcome and used them well until twenty or more wild men came unto them, after which time they took away a bag of money.' After two days the ship suddenly sank, drowning 40 of the crew. The O'Dohertys of Inishowen, nominally in alliance with the Crown, tried to feed the remaining 350 men, but supplies were short, and the soldiers and sailors – Spaniards, Venetians, Neapolitans, Greeks and Dalmatians –

resolved to try to cross the Foyle and get on east towards Antrim and succour in Scotland.

Approaching Derry they were met by a large force of Irish soldiers in English pay under a Major Kelly. They surrendered on condition of being sent to Dublin as prisoners of war. They were then stripped naked, some 200 were killed and the others fled, most later dying of exposure. A few eventually reached Scotland. It is a poignant fact that *La Trinidad Valencera* was originally not Spanish but Venetian – she had been requisitioned in Sicily and forced into the Armada although Venice was a close associate of England. As Venetians, many of her crew would have expected good treatment. When Derry's sub-aqua club found some of *Valencera's* guns in 1971, at least one was Italian. Another was stamped 'Philippus Rex' and dated 1556.

Inishowen Head was our last contact with the Republic of Ireland's mainland. I wondered if the soaring gulls could see 'Éire' still outlined on the scanty grass. It had been imprinted on most of the Irish headlands in 1942 in a co-operative effort with British and American forces to minimise errors by their air crews. The Irish Army's General McKenna flew around the coast with British and American officers to familiarise them with the terrain, and each cape was given a number that was printed on RAF and USAF maps. When the Irish Cruising Club photographed the coast in 1993, 'Éire' was still discernible at Bray Head on Valentia and on Inishowen.

The wind fell very light as the entrance to Lough Foyle began to open abeam. A Canadian yacht came past, thrusting west under engine, a white bow wave showing the strength of the tide now favouring *Sarakiniko*. Inattentive for a moment as we raised our cups to them, I barely avoided a pot buoy swirling towards us. More appeared and, as the boat barely had steerage way in a current almost carrying her ahead of the breeze, I bent to the starting button and we came past the Foyle Buoy under power. Lough Foyle may seem spacious on a map but its approaches are constricted. To avoid the shoals to the east, the Tuns, and the long lines of sand dunes ending in Northern Ireland's Magilligan Point, shipping must skirt the Donegal coast past Warrenpoint and Greencastle by less than half a mile and follow a narrow channel as they move on to Derry city.

Joan was gazing astern. 'Some tide! I can hardly see that buoy we avoided.'

It was probably a tide like this that helped to end the siege of Derry, I thought. It can run up the Foyle at three and a half knots, and carried the relieving ships right through the boom set across the Foyle to cut the city off from the sea.

Derry was the last walled city to be built in western Europe, and the 105-day siege was the last great siege in British history. The origins of the conflict lay in Europe. In England, a nobility who feared that the Catholic King James II threatened English Protestant liberties offered their allegiance instead to the Dutch William of Orange. James fled to France, where King Louis XIV planned to invade Holland in a bid for European domination, and James subsequently landed in Ireland with a substantial French army. His progress to Dublin was a triumph. Ulster mobilised against him, and the climax of a bitter campaign saw the Jacobites camped outside the walls of Derry, where James joined the besieging army in April 1689. His offer of terms to Derry was met with the defiant cry: 'No surrender.'

Cut off by land and sea, the garrison of 7,000 men and some 30,000 citizens and refugees soon faced starvation. One account states that about 15,000 men, women and children died of hunger and fever. 'Scarce could be found room to inter them.' James's army set a boom of massive tree trunks linked by chains across the river to block relief by sea, but as the situation in the city grew desperate three ships and a longboat attempted to break through on 28 July 1689. The wind fell right away as they came up the Foyle but the flooding tide carried them on. It pushed the *Mountjoy* against the boom until the barrier smashed. The ships and crucial supplies reached the quays of an ecstatic city. The siege was lifted two days later.

The Battle of the Boyne in the following year, when King William of Orange defeated James II, was both a landmark in Irish history and the end of Louise XIV's European pretensions. James fled once more to France, no longer seeing Ireland as a springboard to recover his throne. The plantation of Ulster survived. And, as Joan had found, the apprentice boys who had shut the city gates against the Catholic forces are remembered each year in Londonderry.

Lough Foyle retained its strategic importance. Two hundred and fifty years later, shortly after the fall of France, the Royal Navy sought a base in Ireland for anti-submarine forces which needed to be located as far west as possible. They no longer had access to Lough Swilly, and the boundary line between the Free State and Northern Ireland which ran through Lough Foyle was under dispute. The Director of Anti-Submarine Warfare informed the Admiralty that the authorities in Belfast reported that 'Free State authorities have raised no objection to our using Londonderry and Lough Foyle as a base provided we go ahead and do so without referring the matter to them'. Indeed, when the Irish government was informed in early September 1940, they still made no objection. The destroyers, frigates and corvettes that soon spread across the Foyle were a spectacle greeted with silence by everyone in Éire. Except perhaps the mother of Lord Montgomery, future hero of El Alamein. She marked the passage of the British warships past her Donegal home by running to the shoreline and waving a large Union Jack over her head.

As we progressed down the lough we saw an object protruding above the Magilligan sand dunes. It was the Base Line Tower, landmark of an astonishing technical, administrative and cultural achievement: the first Ordnance Survey of Ireland. The project arose from the need for accurate maps for a new land valuation and was the first ever large-scale – six inches to one mile – mapping of an entire country. It began in 1826 by establishing the 'Lough Foyle Base' on level ground here at Magilligan; in effect a giant spirit level for the rest of the island. From this original line a net of triangles was devised over the whole of Ireland using obvious features like hilltops as ground stations. The survey was carried out with great dedication over a period of 20 years. For instance, a senior officer of the Royal Engineers, Joseph Porlock, lived under canvas at 2,000 feet in the depths of winter working on local triangulation in Co. Donegal. In his play *Translations*, a kind of parable set in 1830s Donegal, Brian Friel poses a hedge-school teacher, fluent in Latin and Greek, trying to come to terms with the pragmatic Englishmen who worked on the survey, but generally it remains a chapter of nineteenth-century history curiously unknown. As well as the geographical detail of the survey, a memoir was to be compiled recording the details of life in every Irish parish at the time. This project was only partly completed, but the unpublished memoirs still survive for much of Ulster.

Beyond the dunes we focused the binoculars on a strange image, a domed rotunda crowned by a form of Grecian urn. Perched precariously in striking isolation on a cliff edge, this, together with a ruined mansion inland, is almost all that remains of the great estate of Frederick Harvey, fourth Earl of Bristol and Anglican Bishop of Derry, a rich eccentric eighteenth-century traveller after whom every Hotel Bristol in Europe is named. The temple was dedicated to the beautiful Mrs Mussenden, the bishop's cousin, and the scandal of their relationship only ended with her death at the age of 22, just before the building was completed. We could discern the circle of classical pilasters supporting an elaborate frieze – no cliff on the whole coast of Ireland displays a more elegant seamark. Apparently the 'Earl Bishop' used it as a summer library. He was a man of liberal outlook and offered the crypt of the temple and £10 a year for a priest to say mass as there was no local Catholic church. Our approval of his instincts cooled a trifle when we subsequently learned that there is an inscription from Lucretius around the dome which translates: ''Tis pleasant to watch from land the great struggling of others when winds whip up the waves on a mighty sea.'

The holiday spots of Portstewart and Portrush lay ahead, almost running into one another behind long sandy beaches. Perhaps the din of a motor storming along Portstewart's hard sands induced us to hold on for the larger artificial harbour of Portrush, which lay under long neat terraces of Victorian boarding houses. It was a finely balanced choice for a holiday guide stated that Portrush Harbour now boasted 'an all-weather holiday paradise' which we felt might be more celestial than we deserved.

Having edged along the quay and moored by some half a dozen other yachts – a positive crowd after the waters *Sarakiniko* was used to – we joined masses of people ambling happily in the sunshine. Chattering whitehaired visitors poured out of coaches; clusters of men bent to their silent rituals on a velvety bowling green. Despite the pubs and the laser-strobed discos, I got the distinct impression that friendly Portrush, so far from newsflash images of Ulster, was not a resort where swaggering youths might bowl you off its pavements. The singlehander from the boat alongside later joined us in a convivial bar. He seemed disappointed that we were off to Rathlin Island tomorrow and would have to pass up a visit to the newest development outside Portrush: a leisure centre with 13 pubs. 'A vintage car hangs from the ceiling of one,' he cried, 'and another has Greek sculptures. And the car-park' – he jerked a thumb towards the quayside – 'twice the size of that harbour.' He slipped off the bar stool to go the phone-box, for he was an anxious man. His entry to a National Model Aeroplane event in England had to be telephoned through by midnight. We had heard in some detail of his three jet aircraft built with two stroke engines driving a fan. They could achieve 180 miles an hour within ten feet of the ground. It seemed a dangerous pastime to us, but who were we to say?

Next morning Alasdair joined as crew. It would not be our 13-year-old grandson's first taste of the open sea. Though his face occasionally acquired a pale shade of green, on an earlier crossing from Wicklow to Wales he had shared a watch like a true mariner and managed to smile when his tousled head was roused in the grey dawn. He was keeping the calorie level topped up with crisps now while patiently confirming that his mother had packed a vest and heavy sweater. Joan fed him a seasick pill and adjusted the straps of his safety harness. I double lashed the dinghy to the deck and stowed the refilled cans of diesel. Bangor in Belfast Lough would probably be our next convenient supply point.

The slopes of the Royal Portrush Golf Club lay all along the shore as we nosed around the grassy hilltop of Ramore Head. To

seaward a string of little islands drew past, the Skerries. A few
boats probing among them reminded us that this coast also
claims the finest sport fishing in Ireland. I think it must also display Ireland's most spectacular cliffside castle, Dunluce, tethering
on the edge of an isolated crag. Some of the castle actually fell off
the cliff during a storm in 1639, carrying away the kitchens, the
cooks and all the pots. Its bristling turrets and ragged gables
stood against the morning sun on a huge flat fist of rock. When
the drawbridge was up, Dunluce was only accessible by water.

We drifted in towards some rocks. 'These are the Storks,' I said,
'and if you look back now you can see that the Skerries and
Ramore Head would have sheltered Dunluce from the west.'

'Aren't you close enough?'

'Just a little bit more.' We could see the half cave, half natural
harbour, and a sloping shingle beach where galleys could be
readily drawn ashore. I had put the engine on for safety in case
we lost wind in the shadow of the cliffs. When Wallace Clark and
his stout oarsmen set off in the replica O'Malley galley from
Achill to Scotland, they brought their craft into this galley port at
Dunluce. *Sarakiniko*, however, needs four feet of water to float,
so I accepted the mate's misgivings and turned out to sea.

The Norman John de Courcy fortified Dunluce, as he did
several places around the north-east coast so as to maintain communications with England, but it is with the MacDonalds, Lords
of the Isles, that Dunluce and Rathlin Island are most closely
associated. By the 1550s they held considerable power
throughout Antrim. It was a more fertile place than most of their
Scottish islands, and the survival of the Scots colony there
depended on being able to bring reinforcements quickly from
Kintyre. Rathlin Island, only three miles from Ireland and 13
from Scotland, was a staging post and a springboard for attack.
Kintyre to the east and Islay to the north were each only a few
hours away. When fires were set ablaze on Fair Head or Torr
Point at Ireland's north-east corner, the men of Kintyre would
grab their weapons and rush to the galleys.

Through subsequent decades of pillage and bloodshed, the fortunes of the Scots and the English ebbed and flowed in this

corner of Ireland, with the O'Neills, the O'Donnells, McQuillans and other Irish clans coming in on one side or the other in bewildering combinations, intermarriages and treacheries. In faraway London the Elizabethan nightmare was always real: that English power in remote Ulster would be defeated by a coalition of Catholic warriors of the Isles, Mary Queen of Scots, the French and the Irish – especially if and when the Irish clans ceased to prey on each other.

The English developed ships that could carry guns effective against Scots or Irish galleys – one, which kept the north-east station for decades, became known simply as the Irish Galley – but there were no safe all-weather harbours on this coast, while in calm conditions a galley could just row away from danger. Thus, in January 1585, 24 galleys 'out of Kintyre' were seen off Ballycastle by an English commander who wrote, 'Our shipping here had sighted them but it was so calm they could not bouge.' He estimated that there were 2,500 men in the Scottish fleet, which landed in Antrim.

The English had pounded Dunluce into submission and installed a garrison the previous year, but the Scots leader, Sorley Boy MacDonald, later induced some of the soldiers to help his men mount the walls in baskets and recaptured it. In the spirit of the times he then wiped out the garrison and hanged the Constable, Peter Carey, from the walls. Sorley Boy repaired Dunluce using timbers and guns from the *Gerona*, when it was wrecked on the basalt reef at Lacada Point just to the east, but Dunluce later fell into decay when Sorley Boy's descendants, the Earls of Antrim, moved their residence to the Glens of Antrim.

'Bushmills,' I called, after the cliffs had given way to a tidy shoreline village. We could see on its outskirts massive shapes which were undoubtedly the distillery works. Bushmills is the oldest distillery in the world, founded in 1608, the year after the Flight of the Earls.

'This far out we won't even get a sniff – not that I mind,' I added generously. We were not planning to stop.

We were near the black and russet headland of Bengore when I saw groups of people wandering along a shore that looked like corrugated cardboard. Joan looked at it intently.

'Of course! It's the Causeway.'

'It's not very impressive,' I said, 'At least, not from out here.'

When we looked closely we could distinguish the tall tubular colonnades, a mass of basalt columns packed tightly together. From where we sat, we could easily imagine them as stepping stones leading from the low cliff-top out under the sea. I wondered if children still knew the legend of how the giant, Fionn MacCumhail, so scared his rival Angus, who had come striding across the Causeway from Scotland, that he scuttled back home, tearing up the Causeway behind him so that only two stubs remained, one here and the other on the Isle of Staffa at Fingal's Cave.

There are supposed to be about 40,000 columns left from the volcanic heave of ages past, most, though not all, hexagonal. This remote section of the Antrim coast became an instant tourist attraction after a description of the Giant's Causeway was published by the Royal Society in 1693. Early visitors came by horseback or boat; later the Belfast to Portrush trains were met by jaunting cars or horse charabancs, and in 1883 the Causeway Tramway opened, the first hydro-electric tram in Europe.

It was probably the Dublin artist Susanna Drury, painting from about 1733 to 1770 and whose romantic works were engraved and widely sold, who made the Causeway famous in Europe. Academic argument helped. In the eighteenth century British and French scientists disputed its origin, the Volcanists rightly saying that volcanic action caused these shapes, the Neptunists claiming that they were sedimentary.

Thackeray wrote of his visit here in 1832. He had come from the sea too, though not as comfortably as we did. 'Four rowers hurrooing and bounding madly from one huge liquid mountain to another – four rowers whom I was bound to pay.

'"Where, if you please, is the Causeway?"

'"That's the Causeway before you," said my guide.

'"Which?"

'"That sort of pier which you can see jutting out into the bay right ahead."

"'Mon Dieu! And I have travelled 150 miles to see that?'"

The *Sailing Directions* drew our attention elsewhere as we closed on Bengore Head by warning of 'its quite formidable tide race which can only be avoided by keeping two miles out'. There was indeed a rather sinister looking upwelling and swirling of water, but we skirted the race in one of its relaxed moods. When those chattering wavelets drew astern, Rathlin Island was waiting only seven miles away.

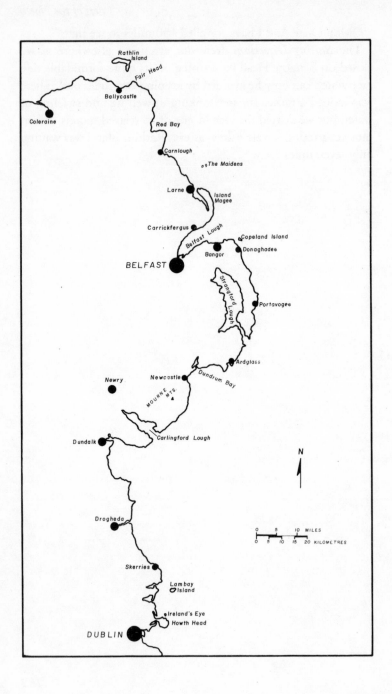

NINE

Hard Haul to Howth

'AN IRISH STOCKING the toe of which pointeth to the mainland,' Sir William Petty wrote of Rathlin in 1660. I prefer to think of the island as a sea boot floating in the mouth of the channel of restless tide-rips and eddies which runs between the mountains of Kintyre and the cliffs of Antrim. A billion tons of water run up and down this North Channel four times a day. The *Sailing Directions* explain the effect: 'streams frequently setting in opposite directions at the same moment with little diminution in force and, at the line separating one stream from the other, ripplings and overfalls of a more or less pronounced character which are dangerous to boats and small vessels.'

Hardly surprising then that Rathlin has acquired three lighthouses. At the toecap, Rue Point Light blinks across to the coast of Antrim. Another light which faces Kintyre in Scotland is sited near the island cave where it is said Robert the Bruce, in retreat from the English in 1306, drew renewed hope for the Scottish cause as he watched the persistence with which a spider built its web. The third is most remarkable. It lies on the west of the island and is visible along the south coast of Islay. Of all Irish coastal waters, Rathlin's are the most prone to fog, so West Light was built low on the cliffs. The 400-foot cliffs were cut back and an enormous concrete glacis constructed, with steps bringing you down to the six-storey lighthouse built at its base. You enter the lighthouse by the attic and descend to the lantern on the ground floor.

We had neither sudden fogs nor strong tides today; the sea winked in the sunlight as we reached Church Bay and made our way towards the island's box-like harbour. 'Low tide,' Joan called; 'we have to watch for the Bo,' a long curving reef running close to the inner piers. We turned and motored cautiously to the pierhead, where Joan and Alasdair eased the fenders between *Sarakiniko* and the hull of a fishing boat.

A Georgian manor spread out under a grove of trees on the shore. It looked incongruous on an island, its blank windows looking out to sea. This had been the home of the Gage family, owners of Rathlin for 200 years. A group of young people carrying wetsuits and helmets came clattering across the cobbles of the stable yard. Their smart launch began to purr at the harbour steps. We later heard that the diving school can offer some 60 wrecks for exploration.

Otherwise there seemed to be nobody about, but as we sat in the cockpit with iceless gin and tonic, a small ferry swung round the corner. Visitors spilled ashore, glanced curiously at us and stepped out briskly for the pub. Mainland Ballycastle, an important town and resort, is only five miles away.

The island has long been a stepping stone between Ireland and Scotland. 'Did you know,' I asked my crew, 'that one of the five great roads radiating from the royal court at Tara in Meath in the second century led to the coast near Rathlin?'

'Yes,' Joan said, meaning not that she knew but that she feared there was more to come, so I kept to myself the information that Rathlin has been inhabited for some 8,000 years and that the first arrivals had a corner in the market for porcellanite, the hardest stone in the British Isles and ideal for making axes. Until the bronze- and then the iron-makers ruined the trade, Rathlin exported polished stone tools throughout Ireland, Scotland, Wales and even south-east England. Later the iron-bearing Celts held the island for over 1,000 years; then the Vikings for another 400. They were defeated by the Normans in the twelfth century. Later the Scottish MacDonalds fought to win and hold Rathlin, until Queen Elizabeth took it with sea power and soldiers. She gave the island back to Sorley Boy MacDonald of Dunluce, hoping to win his allegiance, but later half-promised Rathlin to the Earl of Essex also. He dispatched ships under Francis Drake, who landed, claimed the island for Essex, and slaughtered the inhabitants.

The Scots won and lost Rathlin three times in 30 years, but

before Elizabeth's death Sorley Boy MacDonald had his grant confirmed once more. His heir, Randal McDonnell, was forced to defend his island inheritance in the law courts, when a Scot, Crawford of Lisnorris, claimed that the island was legally his. He had had the island granted to him by James IV of Scotland. It was a strong claim – if Rathlin had then been part of Scotland and within the power of James to bestow.

The lawsuit caused dismay. Sir Arthur Chichester, Governor of the massive fortress of Carrickfergus, wrote on 10 March 1617: 'If it be so we have run into great error for in the time of the rebellion [of Hugh O'Neill] we have often wasted it and destroyed the inhabitants by the sword and by the halter as we did the rebels in Ireland. The dismantling of it from the Crown of Ireland is a matter of State and not to be mined as a private debate.'

Amidst the arguments of archivists and lawyers, it was submitted that Rathlin must be a 'parcel of Ireland' because of the nature of its soil, 'which neither breeds nor nourishes any living thing venomous but is as clear of them as Ireland, while the isles of the Scottish and English in the same sea breed and nourish the snakes which was thought to be proof that the Isle of Man was British as appears by Giraldus'. Giraldus, a scribe and historian from Wales who had come to Ireland with the first Normans, had written that a dispute about ownership of the Isle of Man was settled by bringing venomous reptiles there on trial. 'They lived and as a matter of course the island was on this account unanimously adjudged to Britain.'

The Scottish claimant pointed out that some Scottish islands also enjoyed immunity from reptiles, to which Randal's lawyers retorted that this resulted from the holy aura spread by Irish monks. They won the case. Rathlin remained within the realm of Ireland and the ownership of Randal McDonnell and his wife Alice, daughter of Hugh O'Neill.

The common people of Rathlin, however, had short respite from misery. To settle old scores the Campbells of Kintyre killed every soul there on the excuse of helping the King in the Civil War. It was only under benevolent landlords, the Gage family who bought Rathlin in 1746, that the population recovered, reaching an overcrowded 1,300 before the Famine. By 1922 it had dropped to about 300.

We found a road leading by rocky outcrops where whins mingled with the heather. Rabbits ran ahead along a thin ribbon of asphalt. A car without a silencer clattered past. All around were remnants of the time when Rathlin was full of people: a deserted settlement by a reedy pond, stone walls still holding a flake of thatch, clumps of fuchsia and veronica surrounding broken cabins.

A few miles away Fair Head was a cliff wall above a slope of boulders. Torr Head peered beyond it, a signpost for us on our run south. Thirteen miles away we could see the houses on the Mull of Kintyre. This view of overlapping headlands and islands – Islay, Jura and Gigha faint in the north, Donegal due west – stirred a sense of shared histories. From here it seemed obvious that such narrow waters would always involve ties of land and family.

'Perhaps there should have been a greater Ireland,' I suggested, 'a federation of islands.'

'Never,' cried my Scottish wife.

On the way down to the pub we passed a fine limestone building, derelict and forlorn. An elderly man, walking unsteadily with the aid of his bicycle, told us that it was 'put up by the Gages to store the kelp'. He seemed ready to pause in life's race, and I believed his tale of a ship once run aground because of the kelp smoke when I recalled how we would sail past smoky shores in Brittany only a few decades ago. Kelp, a source of iodine, was a profitable industry in the early nineteenth century, and the practice of melting it down in kilns survived in Rathlin until after World War II. The wife of the island rector wrote in the 1920s of how men 'would cast off every garment except their breeches, get up on the rude wall of the grave-shaped kiln and poke and pound, working the heavy boiling mass'. Grinding labour, for they started at 4 am and worked all through the day.

We marvelled at the high-quality modern fencing running off the barren moorlands, enclosing unkempt fields of ragwort and thistle. Munificent grants from the European Union? Some sheep and cattle grazed the slopes but I saw no signs of cultivation. We did not spot a vegetable garden, nor even a potato patch, though the corrugations that ran across the landscape like ribbing on a pullover were reminders of where crops had been grown before. Islanders today do not seem to work the land; we had noticed this also in Inishbofin and Tory. 'It's easy now,' said a lady in the shop. 'They just get everything on the ferry from Ballycastle.'

But even basic facilities came later to this island than elsewhere, of course. Electricity only arrived in October 1993, welcomed by Dr Ian Paisley MP and the Fr Diarmuid Ó Péicín, Tory's saviour and director of the Irish Islands Trust. Power is generated by three wind-turbines which turn on the high ground at Kilpatrick. Their slender columns have been named Aedh, Conn and Fiachra. These were the children of Lir, who were changed into swans in these waters by a jealous stepmother. Three hundred years passed before they became human once more, now no longer children but old hags. They flew to Inishglora off Mayo, to St Kemoc, and became Christian before their deaths.

'I was born here,' said Mrs Dolores Kyle, chatting by the foreshore, 'and there are only ten of us natives left now.' There were about 100 people living on the island, with just ten children attending the local school. She showed us a plaque near by which recorded Richard Branson's unintended stopover when he was forced to ditch his balloon just off the island during his brave attempt on the transatlantic record in 1987. He returned to the island a month later and presented a cheque to the Rathlin Trust, present owners of the manor house, which still seemed to be waiting for a role which would best benefit the community. Meanwhile Rathlin grows more accessible, with a car ferry now running from Ballycastle on the mainland and another from there to Kintyre.

'I DIDN'T expect to see the Paps of Jura from out here,' Joan said, looking at the northern horizon.

'It quite spoils it to have three,' I said. 'Two would be remarkably realistic.'

We were bound now for Bangor on Belfast Lough where Joan and Alasdair would leave *Sarakiniko*, and Pat O'Donnell rejoin for the voyage down the Irish Sea. A light wind had been forecast but it was still calm as we puttered out of the harbour. The Viking prow of Fair Head rose in a wall of basalt to starboard. The Mull of Kintyre lay to port, and as its headlands came abeam, Ailsa Craig, that strange 1,100-foot pyramid in the Clyde approaches, emerged behind them. In the afternoon light even the coast of Galloway was a grey stroke to the east.

The tides flood into and ebb away from both ends of the Irish Sea, and a cunning mariner can be wafted south by a fading flood and pick up an ebb to carry him further down. However, you really have to be south of Belfast to play this trick. The wind was coming on the nose, so we stuck to the engine, plugging past neatly fenced farmlands running from the skyline into green combs by the shore. Here were fields made by a tidy, half-Scottish people, whose care was a pleasure to behold. They looked across the sea – the Waters of Moyle, they called it – to Scotland, while the Antrim mountains lay behind. There were few roads giving access to the rest of Ireland.

Here and there we saw a village nestling at the feet of the valleys. The Glens of Antrim was one of the last parts of Ulster where Irish was spoken. In the mid-eighteenth century Richard Pococke wrote that on this side of Antrim 'the people are all Papists' and almost all spoke Irish, though most knew English as well, while 'on that side from Ballycastle westward no one understands Irish'.

An occasional passing car defined the convolutions of the coast road, 60 miles of switchback splendour which Lord Northcliffe called the second finest coast road in the world, excelled only by the Grand Corniche. As it runs north the road eventually leaves the coast and climbs the hills in unbroken turns and arabesques. It opened an easy route for those who wished to see nature at her architectural best at the Giant's Causeway; they continued their journey on horses hired from the landlord of the Antrim Arms at Ballycastle.

Presently the recess of Red Bay offered a tempting anchorage – one of the best in Antrim – but a dip in the barometer hinted at stronger head-winds tomorrow so we went in on a failing tide to the diminutive harbour of Carnlough six miles further on. The narrow pierhead entrance was lined with black boulders on either side. The echo-sounder flickered alarmingly. Small trawlers, motor launches and a few traditional Antrim rowing gigs lay tied up in a web of mooring lines against the limestone blocks of the pier, which glistened creamy white in the twilight. We gentled up to a deserted trawler and Alasdair helped me take lines ashore.

We had found a snug hole, but the wind was getting up. I looked at the mast-top burgee and reflected that what was coming was implacably from the south, and Belfast Lough was nearly 40 miles away.

I crossed the trawler's deck in the early morning to the main street beyond the bridge. Carnlough boasted a fine limestone harbour, courthouse and clocktower, all built by the London-derry family. The stone was cut out of the rock-faces on the slopes above the town and carried by rail down to the quay. The Marchioness of Londonderry later financed a coaching inn, the elegant ivy-clad Londonderry Arms. We passed by the Bethany Christian Guest House, reflecting that it probably did not com-pete with the guesthouse opposite which displayed a poster: 'Support St Vincent de Paul.' Committed to a favourable tide already flowing south, we could not delay for either.

We bucked the perverse wind the following day, motoring through a blowing mist pierced occasionally by the seaward flash of the Maiden's Lighthouse. An old print shows two lighthouses, set on rocks half a mile apart. In the 1830s an assistant keeper on one fell in love with the daughter of the other lighthouse family. Her parents did not approve of the romance, though, and stopped the girl rowing across the narrow channel to her lover. They eloped in the end, and married in Carrickfergus.

We thrust south, past dangerous reefs. I did some arithmetic. The tide moved invisibly with us, carrying us along as on a travel-ator, perhaps at seven knots over the ground, the speed of an old lady on an ancient bike. Not bad at all, and the chimneys that Alasdair's youthful eyes spotted in the thick mist marked the power station at Larne. But even with this tide under us, we would be punching into the wind for another six hours. The mist thickened further. We lost sight of land when I turned to run along the peninsula of Island Magee. Muck Island appeared in the mist, shaped like a pork pie. The tide runs fast here – up to six knots at springs each fortnight – and there was nasty water running in front of us.

We had no choice but to buck against the grey breaking sea before an ebb tide turned against us. It was teeth-rattling progress now, for hour after hour, as short white waves tried to climb over the bow, *Sarakiniko* would occasionally leap off a wave top and crash into the trough. This sea was not dangerously high, but it was uncomfortable, and presently a slashing rainstorm tended to ease it. I went below to the chart table, walked the dividers across the mouth of Belfast Lough to Bangor on the south shore, and placed the points on the longitude scale. 'We'll be there in about two hours,' I called up to Joan. 'We should soon start getting shelter from the Bangor side of the lough.'

I offered beer and Coke to the cockpit.

'No,' said Joan, 'I shouldn't have had the first beer. Trying to crouch in the heads and remove oilskins is more than any woman should have to face.'

'I hope you don't lose your enthusiasm.'

'Enthusiasm for what?'

'Sailing. Irish harbours.'

'I wouldn't count on it.'

Island Magee went creeping past. At the start of the century the Irish engineer James Barton, associated with Hawkshaw and Hayter, builders of the Severn Tunnel, drew plans for a railway tunnel which would run under the sea to Stranraer. Professor Hall, Director of the Geological Survey of Ireland, concluded that the technical difficulties were surmountable, the sea-bed being water-tight horizontal layers of Silurian rock, in places overlaid by equally suitable beds of red sandstone and marls. Beaufort's Dyke would require the tunnel to take a dog-led bend to the north.

Ireland's tunnel project is now forgotten, but the Beaufort Dyke, whose undersea trench has been used as a munitions dump for over 50 years, is a continuing source of controversy. The quantity and type of munitions hidden there is unknown. Officially the British Ministry of Defence claims that just over 1,000,000 tons were jettisoned, including nearly 5,000 tons of five-inch rockets which contained poisonous phosgene. Critics, however, suggest that not only may chemical and biological weapons have also been included, but that much of the material was not actually dumped in the trench. Some 4,000 phosphorous-based incendiary bombs were washed on to the Scottish coast in 1995, possibly dislodged during the laying of a gas pipeline from Northern Ireland to Scotland. A survey by the Scottish Office followed the incident. Its report claimed that there was no risk to public or marine life.

After signing international sea dumping conventions, Britain last disposed of small munitions in 1976, but it is claimed that over 2,500 tons of concrete owned by the UK Atomic Energy Authority were dumped in this area in 1981. Uneasiness about toxic time-bombs persists, especially after the Irish public learned that Britain had in 1955-56 dumped about 71,000 tons of German nerve-gas bombs at another site 80 miles north-west of Ireland, admittedly into depths of some 2,000 metres.

Character-building wind and rain is all very well, but we were anxious to wrap a town around us. A racing fleet was out as we approached Bangor, spinnakers billowing in the fresh offshore wind, two of them free-style adaptations of the Union Jack. Beyond the piers we found the largest marina in Ireland, mall after mall of moored yachts, each rooted in its own reflection, mostly padlocked now for the week. With fenders out and mooring lines adjusted, one was suddenly relieved of the tension of decision making. We relaxed into that euphoric camaraderie one always feels at the end of a rough trip.

Bangor was still the popular seaside resort of Victorian times, like much of Northern Ireland a touch old-fashioned, carrying reassuring resonances of family values of the 1950s. I felt a fluid sort of person in this corner of Ireland, at home in an Irish ambience which carried flavours of England and Scotland. Should I really describe myself as Hiberno-British? Will multiple loyalties be acceptable and commonplace in the century to come? Are they the way ahead? The questions had no ready answers.

Here in Bangor every marina official, every passer-by and shop-keeper, was affable and chatty. We called to the headquarters of the Royal Ulster Yacht Club at the marina. When the Royal Yacht Squadron at Cowes blackballed Sir Thomas Lipton, apparently because he was a grocer, Bangor welcomed the Fermanagh man to the club, from where he issued five challenges for the America's Cup between 1899 and 1930.

The bow-mounted navigation light had been wrenched from its fitting by a steep sea in the Muck Island overfalls, so we sped to Belfast on the train for a replacement, coming into the city past the skyscraping gantries of Harland and Wolff. In the middle of the nineteenth century, after the Ulster Bank had foreclosed on its debts, Edmund Harland bought the shipbuilding yard for £5,000 and with his assistant, Gustav Wolff, secured an order for three steamers for Liverpool's Bibby Shipping Line. Liverpool was the gateway to a fast-growing Empire, while Atlantic routes were growing fast as a result of European immigration. Harland and Wolff supplied the ships for both. The yard designed record-breaking vessels for the White Star Line which made other North Atlantic liners obsolete. H & W's designer and supervisor, Thomas Andrews, drew many of the great ships which left its slipways, and died on the most famous of all, the *Titanic*.

Our trip to Belfast had to include a visit to the splendid museum which houses relics recovered from the Armada ships, *La Trinidad Valencera*, sunk off Inishowen, and the *Gerona*, wrecked at Lacada. The material which survived in the silt evoked a vivid picture of Spain. There were velvet collars and gold buttons, socks of woollen serge with double seams along the sides and silk tassels from the ends of powder flasks. There were juggling balls, a fine comb (lice would have been commonplace), and fragments from the stoppers of wineskins for, in normal conditions, the ration of wine was one pint a day. Divers recovered a poignant memory from the *Gerona*, a ring engraved with one hand holding a heart, on the other hand a buckle. It bore the inscription: *No tengo mas que dar te* – I have nothing more to give you.

Joan and Alasdair left for London. I fretted from shipping fore-cast to shipping forecast as I waited for Pat, and began reading the classic *Sailing Tours* by Frank Cowper. When he started cruising in 1878, there were three yachts at Yarmouth and three at nearby Lymington. Cowper felt their numbers would rise and set out on the self-imposed task of preparing reliable cruising guides for the British, Irish and French coasts. It involved several years cruising, without an engine, and resulted in five volumes still of practical value and of course compelling interest.

'I have never yet employed a pilot and up to the present have had no real difficulty,' he wrote. 'It was part of my scheme to do the work entirely alone, with the smallest number of hands. I have never had any other assistance in the management of my craft – which is a comfortable old cruiser fifty feet long overall by thirteen feet six inches beam and drawing six feet of water – than that of a boy whom I have picked up fresh for each cruise.'

With the prospect of nasty squalls and poor visibility in the offing, his views on the Ards peninsula were not encouraging. 'That coast is as nasty a piece of work as I have ever seen. It is low; the rocks are low and sneaking. There is none of the fine, bold, defiant air of other outlying rocks. None are more than a few feet above water when they do show, and that is not often at high water. Most are under the sea and lie a long way out. The highest rock,' he added gloomily, 'is Burial Island, only twenty feet.'

When Pat arrived off the Dublin train the outlook for the Irish Sea had not much improved, but we decided we would try to reach the fishing harbour of Ardglass some 40 miles down the coast, just west of the entrance to Strangford Lough. From there, though several horizons away, we could raise Lambay Island and the high Hill of Howth on a longish day's sail. The timing of our approach to Strangford, the Vikings' *Strang fiord* – violent inlet – was crucial. Every six hours the tide squeezes through the bottle-neck entrance as it fills and empties the 37,000-acre lake behind it, and at fortnightly spring tides and in fresh winds the full force of the half-ebb kicks up a roaring white water chaos around the entrance.

It was raining now. One always knew that there would be low points, times when it would be difficult to persist against fresh winds and choppy seas and bring this circle of Ireland to completion. In a mood of restless indecision we looked at the flaying trees on Bangor's Edwardian terraces and the angry cat's paws out on the water, trying to convince ourselves that the gusts could not be stronger than Force 6. I went to the marina office and copied the weather message posted there. 'A complex depression centred in the northern North Sea,' I recited to Pat, 'between Aberdeen and Denmark until noon tomorrow and then moving east and elongating to become centred from Poland to the Barents Sea.'

'Good man; you got it all. Now tell me what it means.'

'They translate it into south-westerlies Force 5 to 7, possibly gales Force 8, and in the following 24 hours the winds will be strong and gusty, decreasing moderate to fresh and going north-west.'

That night the wind racketed until dawn. I lay listening to the whine of rigging on nearby boats and the thrumming of their masts, but the 6 am forecast confirmed that the wind was turning north-west and therefore coming offshore; at least we would not have to beat against it. We cast off, feeling the tingling thrill that always accompanies departure. We would be in sheltered waters until we turned south, so a few hundred yards beyond the pier I brought the boat into the wind and reefed the sail, then unrolled some jib from the forestay. As I swung her across the offshore wind *Sarakiniko* went bounding ahead.

Presently we began the swing south-east into Donaghadee Sound, where the three Copeland Islands compress the tides, creating unwelcome passages of sea with off-putting names like the Ram Harry Race. The safe route through the sound is a mere few hundred yards wide and involves a dog-leg swing to starboard to take you past the Deputy Reefs on one side and the Governor Rocks on the other. But as we swung to starboard we lost wind from the mainsail, and a twelve-foot-high green buoy, set in a collar of white water, began to surge towards us at alarming speed. If we turned even more to starboard we would lose all drive from the sails. I dived at the engine button. 'More throttle,' called Pat. 'More, much more.' The swaying mass of iron swept past. We had entered a tide race.

The tumbling river of water ran down past the little port of Donaghadee. Soon we could see the harbour, a snug place which once flourished as the nearest Irish port to Britain 21 miles away. We laid a course well clear of Cowper's vicious rocks, 'like snakes in the grass, their ugly heads scarcely showing, the sea tumbling over them as if in league with their devilry....' I liked his strong views, even if he did call the shore behind 'a bleak expanse', when the Ards peninsula was traditionally one of Ireland's great corn-lands, with over 100 windmills animating the flat landscape. One still remains at Ballycopeland.

We kept a prudent distance out, sailing fast now in a fresh wind and reaching the South Rock lightvessel, 16 miles from Donaghadee. Further inshore I could see the old South Rock lighthouse surrounded by black reefs. It looked lonesome too. Built from granite blocks which had been carried here from Wales, Wexford and Newry, its first light shone in March 1797. By 1877, however, it was decided that the 60-foot tower did not adequately mark this reef-strewn area, so the lightship replaced it a few miles further out. The lighthouse remained in good condition until 1972, when the lead from the roof was stolen.

'Sixteen miles in two hours,' I called up to Pat, 'that's eight knots over the ground, but our tide is falling off now.'

He glanced at the sails. 'Wind's not too bad.'

Presently we could see Kearney, a fishing village which was notable in the later nineteenth century for supporting an all-woman fishing boat skippered by Mary Anne Donnan. Story-teller, midwife, active in linen manufacture, this remarkable woman, born in 1841, lived to the age of 99 years. Sir John Lavery painted her portrait, but she deserves wider recognition in the lists of outstanding Irish women.

As we altered course to starboard, visibility improved quite suddenly and the Mourne Mountains appeared in the distance across a very lumpy sea. Shallow water lay inshore, where a white tower capped in red marked the entrance to Strangford Lough. In there lay St Patrick's country. Tradition has it that, on his return to Ireland in 432 AD, he had meant to sail up the Ards peninsula, but the tide pushed him into the lough. He made the best of things by going up the little river Slaney, where he converted the local ruler and was given a barn in which he made his base. Today at Saul a memorial chapel and round tower commemorate 'the most ancient ecclesiastical site in the land.'

Hand over hand I went forward to check the forehatch and found a clip half undone and Pat's bunk exceedingly wet. *Sarakiniko* leapt off another wave top. The lower companionway step, basically a locker of tools weighing some 35 pounds, lifted from its two-inch-long clips and slid across the cabin. I reset it into its clips and went back to the cockpit.

Soon, though, the shoals fell astern, the seas moderated, and we could see St John's Point ahead on the east tip of Dundrum Bay, its lighthouse black with yellow stripes. A few miles short of the lighthouse we turned into Ardglass and pulled in alongside a pontoon, hungry, wet and elated.

This village of 1,300 people was once the busiest seaport in Ulster. In the 1840s it might have three or four hundred boats from Donaghadee, Carlingford, Skerries, Dublin, Arklow, the Isle of Man, St Ives and Penzance sailing in to sell their catch to carters travelling inland or to merchants with curing facilities or – for the most part in fact – to sloops and small craft waiting in the harbour to sail to the Dublin and Liverpool markets. The yachties will now add a cosmopolitan gloss, as the fishing port has acquired a new marina, but I have little doubt Ardglass will greet them all with cheerful aplomb. 'How ya?' was our greeting in the supermarket and from a man I met outside a pub. 'How ya?' smiled a solitary girl emerging from the post office. It seemed a shame to leave at 6.30 next morning, but the wind had at last turned north-west; tomorrow it should come across our quarter, a perfect point for sailing, and we would shape a bowline straight to Howth, leaving Carlingford and Dundalk some 15 miles inshore.

The wind held next morning, steady and fresh, sweeping us by the Mourne Mountains. They do not form a range, a line of heights, so much as a magnificent bulky cluster of steep summits. Scarves of haze still hid the towns – Newcastle, Annalong and Kilkeel – guarding the entrances to the mountain valleys. In better visibility we would also have seen the ruins of several coast-guard stations, for this was one of Ireland's most suitable retreats for smugglers. Lonely roads led quickly inland from the coast. Pack animals loaded with contraband at Newcastle would follow the aptly named Brandy Pad, now a walker's route, over the pass at Slieve Donard to Hilltown, a smugglers' hideaway. It is still a junction on the mountain roads.

The reduction in British naval forces after the Napoleonic wars gave smugglers further leeway; in 1819 it was estimated that some £3.6 million worth of goods arrived illicitly on the east coast of Ireland. There was little to deter them. Administration of the Preventive Water Guard, set up in England in 1809, was mis-managed. In Belfast the tide surveyor had no boatmen to row him out to inspect ships' cargoes. In Dublin, the superintendent of quarantine, or 'pratique master', was permanently absent in Canada; he had arranged for his annual salary to be collected and forwarded to him by a deputy who carried out his duties.

Smuggling was arranged much as William Maxwell had found it off the remote coast of Mayo. The ships were English, Dutch, Irish and American, run by individuals or by a 'company,' often armed and sailed by crews of up to 70 men. Huge profits could be made. There was a duty of four shillings on a pound of un-processed tobacco, which was bought at a cost price of eight pence or a shilling, and one boat might carry 1,000 bales each weighing 65 pounds. There was a brisk demand for tariff-free goods. An agent in Ireland distributed tickets for the merchan-dise to known dealers, while surplus tickets were sold openly in local shops.

When James Dombrain of the Preventive Water Guard was sent to Ireland to reorganise the service on the Cork coast, he established a new system of shore stations which worked in co-operation with Revenue cutters. The stations had at least one boat each, usually a 34-foot galley, which watched from the sea, while foot patrols explored the shore. Nightly patrols continued until 'good daylight', and the men were issued with a carbine, bayonet, pistol and cutlass. When smugglers moved their operations further east, a new Water Guard was established between Waterford and the Giant's Causeway, a coast some 300 miles long. By 1824 Dombrain was based in Dublin as Comptroller General of a force covering the whole of Ireland. It was renamed the Coastguard.

Coastguard men were not popular. Their dwellings were to be 'separate and unconnected with the people of the country', who saw them as Crown representatives and targets for political hostility. As happened with the Irish Constabulary, the men were discouraged from fraternising with locals. The policy did not always work. 'Fred Foot, boatman, removed to Portaferry. Married a native' reads an entry in an Out Station Book for Groomsport, Co. Down, on 14 May 1846.

By mid-century smuggling had declined considerably. The Coastguard was transferred to the Admiralty in 1856 and came to be regarded as a coastal defence force, available as a naval reserve in wartime, and the men were given regular arms training and an annual month afloat. Buildings were erected to standard Board of Works specification – 150 pen-and-wash plans for the buildings are still filed in the Office of Public Works in Dublin. After the Fenian troubles of 1864, gun loops were added to walls and doors, iron shutters to the windows, and internal doors connecting the terraced houses which provided accommodation for the coastguard men and their families. It was a lonely service, especially for the wives of men in the service.

If its history comes to be more fully recorded as part of Ireland's heritage, the achievements of the Coastguard Service, not just in preventing smuggling but in watching over and protecting seafarers, should never be forgotten. Today the coastguard stations lie abandoned and for the most part in ruins, for the service was terminated after the creation of the new state. It became the Coast Life Saving Service in 1923 and in 1989 the Coast and Cliff Rescue Service; later again it became the Irish Marine Emergency Service. But since the de-manning of the lighthouses there has been a new need for 'eyes' on the coast, and a new force, to be called the Coastguard once more, is now being established. But the service has not quite come full circle. The members of the coastal rescue units will probably be a mobile force using relatively few stations, and many will be part-time volunteers being paid compensation for their work.

Carlingford entrance appeared. It may be rock encumbered but it gives on to an eight-mile inlet which may be the prettiest on the easy coast of Ireland. 'The beauty of the place came on me as a surprise,' wrote Cowper long ago. 'I knew nothing of Rostrevor or Carlingford and was totally unprepared for the scene before me.' Richard Pococke seemed more interested in its industry.

'Carlingford,' he declared in 1752, 'is the port for Newry. They say that 400 vessels commonly come into this harbour every year.' Newry was a bustling place, described by a traveller as 'the fourth town in Ireland'. There were coal reserves in its East Tyrone hinterland, and from about 1725 more sophisticated methods of mining in the area around Coalisland. A cut had already been made to take barge-loads of coal from the Tyrone area to Lough Neagh when the Dublin government authorised a survey for a 'Passage of Boats from the said Lough to the Sea' – Dublin depended on massive imports of British coal, brought over in colliers which plodded across the Irish Sea. A canal to Newry was built over 18 miles of rough country. Using 15 locks, it was the earliest of all true summit-level canals, and by 1742 the first boats were taking coal to Dublin via the Newry waterway.

Newry could not yet handle larger ships, and subsequently a four-mile ship canal was built to link it to the sea. The town flourished as a result of its canal access to central Ulster, but coal supplies for Dublin failed to live up to earlier expectations. Lough Neagh, however, became the centre of a web of canals which gave access via the Bann to Coleraine in the north, Belfast in the east and, across the Ulster Canal and the Ballinamore Navigation, west to the Shannon. While the canals have long fallen into disuse, the future tourism possibilities for Ulster waterways are intriguing bearing in mind the success of the recently restored Ballinamore Navigation linking the Erne waterways and the Shannon.

Just to the south now the Cooley peninsula emerged, the legendary lands of the *Táin Bó Cuailgne*, where the Ulster warrior, Cuchulainn, battled with Maeve, Queen of Connaught, when she attempted to capture the Brown Bull of Cooley. Many rivers, passes and the fording points on Cooley can be identified from details in this first-century epic of warring between Connaught and Ulster, but we soon lost sight of these shadow lands as the coast receded behind the great bay of Dundalk.

We kept watches of one hour each, the deck heeling so that the helmsman had to peer under the belly of the jib. Pat suggested a distance check when we were three hours out. I took up the new electronic tool, the Global Positioning System. The hand-held GPS weighed nine ounces, and when I held it aloft in one hand and pressed a button with my thumb, it proceeded to lock on to up to eight satellites and give me latitude and longitude within minutes. It will do so wherever on the earth you may be. It also shows speed, course to steer and your likely time of arrival at your destination – all at the touch of a finger. So precise is the GPS that for security reasons its results are 'accuracy downgraded' by the US Department of Defence to plus or minus 100 metres.

The new device told us we were positioned dead on course for Howth Harbour and creaming along at 5.6 knots. We ate lunch in the cockpit, a spread of sardines on soda bread, and as we ate we argued over whether a solitary knob to the west might be a cloud or Clogher Head – some things had not changed. As more of Ireland began to appear out of the mist, we realised we were off Clogher Head, north of Dundalk.

The Boyne estuary and the plains of Royal Meath lay in there, and ahead we could now see Rockabill lighthouse sitting four miles out from the two granite islets of the Skerries, rising 30 feet above the sea, deep water between them. As we came abeam the wind began to die, but it had given us eight memorable hours furrowing across the water, revelling in the angle of the living deck and the tight efficiency of straining lines. Just six miles more to Lambay Island and another six to Howth. 'A few hours of motor will top up the batteries anyway,' Pat said consolingly, and he bent to the starter button.

Lambay. The Romans called it Limnos, and may have established a trading post on the nearby Irish mainland. The Vikings attacked in 795 AD and gave it the Danish name, Lambay. Frank Cowper asserts, however, that it is really Lambey, 'As Ireland's Eye is really Irelandsey,' the "ey" or "ea" being the Saxon for "island". So it is at Selsey, Guernsey, Chelsea, Mersea.' We were a mile off but thought we could identify Tayleur's Beacon just north of the island's small drying harbour. The *Tayleur* had been an emigrant ship which left Liverpool bound for Australia in January 1854. The wind was against them, fog closed in, and the ship's compass was defective. Widely off course, the ship struck and foundered, and most of the 620 people aboard were lost.

A black rainstorm built inland over Malahide. Sunlight spotlit the cliffs of Ireland's Eye against the dark background. I went below to fold up the charts and put those we would not need again under the bunks. We crept around the rocky little island and its martello tower, and saw a fleet of Mirror dinghies fluttering like red butterflies off the entrance to Howth Harbour.

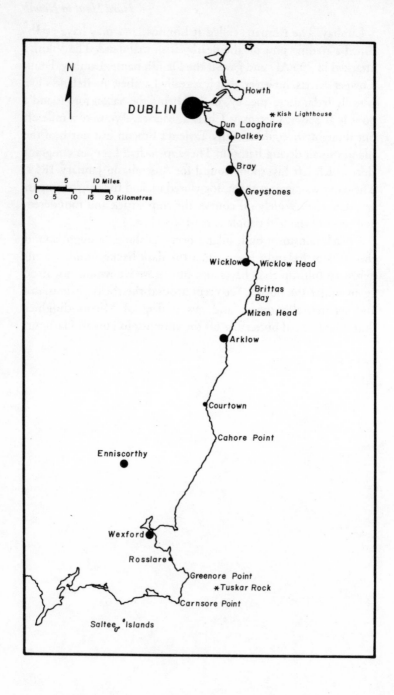

TEN

The Coast of 1,000 Wrecks

A PLAQUE AT the end of Howth's east pier marks the spot where
Erskine Childers' yacht *Asgard* came alongside in the early afternoon of Sunday, 26 July 1914. As Childers' friend Gordon
Shepherd was securing the yacht's lines to the quay, a company of
Irish Volunteers came swinging down the pier. They unloaded
the *Asgard*'s cargo of 900 rifles and 25,000 rounds of ammunition in under an hour.

The arms, which came from Hamburg, had been transferred to
the *Asgard* at a rendezvous off the Belgian coast several days
before. Childers then had to reach Howth on the flood tide on
Sunday, unload the guns and make a smart getaway before being
grounded on the ebb, when the harbour drained to mud. The
Asgard set a course for Ireland, sailing through frustrating calms,
severe gales and adverse winds, and a frightening encounter with
battleships of the British Grand Fleet on night exercises.

Childers and Shepherd were experienced sailors; indeed their
club, the Royal Cruising Club, had the year before awarded
Shepherd its premier trophy, the Challenge Cup, for having
brought *Asgard* from Oslo to North Wales in difficult conditions.
Since the outbreak of World War I, Irish fishing boats had been
subject to interception and search at sea, so Childers camouflaged
the gun-running operation as a yachting cruise and flew the RCC
burgee at the masthead. When the burgee was fretted by a gale,
he had Mary Spring Rice repair it before they arrived in Howth.
In a fresh north-west wind *Asgard* rounded the pierhead on
schedule, Mary Spring Rice standing on the bow, wearing a red
skirt as a signal to the Volunteers.

Asgard's cargo was only part of the arms run on to the Irish
coast in the spring and summer of 1914. The yachtsman Conor
O'Brien, a cousin of Mary Spring Rice, had also come alongside

the tug off the Schelt, just before the arrival of *Asgard*, and loaded 600 rifles and 20,000 rounds of ammunition on to his yacht *Kelpie*. Off the north Welsh coast he transferred the arms to another yacht, *Chota*, owned by the distinguished surgeon Sir Thomas Myles, who landed them at Rathcoole, Co. Wicklow, on 1 August. Some three months before, 30,000 rifles and some 3,000,000 rounds of ammunition had been brought ashore at Larne and elsewhere for the Ulster Volunteers. The country was gearing up for conflict.

O'Brien was one of Ireland's most colourful yachtsmen. In 1923 he set off from Dun Laoghaire on an east-about circumnavigation of the world in his Baltimore-built *Saoirse*. It was the first major voyage of any vessel registered in the new Irish Free State and won him the Challenge Cup awarded by the Royal Cruising Club in each of the years 1923, '24 and '25. 'In the early afternoon a fleet of yachts went out to meet him,' *The Irish Times* wrote on his return in June 1925, 'and he was escorted into harbour by about 200 vessels and greeted by a salvo of maroon as he was towed in by a motor launch. He was accompanied by a Tongan native who had come with him from the Friendly Isles.'

I last saw *Saoirse* in 1958, lost among houseboats in a derelict canal near Chichester, her rakish black bow far from the trade winds. Someone later gave her another lease of blue-water life, but a Jamaican hurricane did for her in 1979. *Asgard* is preserved in Kilmainham Jail Museum, where she is currently being restored, and opinion is divided as to whether the restoration should recreate the boat as a museum exhibit or a sailing vessel. Meanwhile the sail trainer *Asgard II* frequently drops anchor at Howth.

I went to the end of the West Pier in search of a very different fragment of Irish history, the footprints of King George IV, who came ashore here in 1821. I wondered how he could have left his stamp on Ireland for so long. After walking between trawlers and sheds, I met a fisherman who carried me to the edge of the quay where a stonemason had cut the imprint of two shoes into the granite blocks. They were elegantly, perhaps flatteringly, slim.

Dun Laoghaire, across the bay, had been miffed when the King chose Howth at which to arrive in Ireland, so he made amends by embarking from there on his return and renaming it Kingstown, which it remained until the change of government in the 1920s.

The royal visit forced Lord Byron into verse:

But he comes! The Messiah of Royalty comes!
Like a goodly Leviathan rolled from the waves.
Then receive him, as best such an advent he comes,
With a legion of cooks and an army of slaves!

At any rate, gratified citizens built that curious obelisk supported on four stone cannon balls and surmounted by a well-upholstered crown which now stands near Dun Laoghaire's modern ferry terminals. The novelist Thackeray, coming ashore here on a wet morning in 1842, found the monument 'hideous', stuck 'upon four fat balls, and surmounted with a crown on a cushion'. He thought these latter two 'no bad emblems' for the monarch in whose honour they were raised.

I sorted those elegant Irish coins depicting the elk, the horse, the bull and the salmon – soon to be superseded by the Euro – and made telephone calls to arrange a meeting with my brother Vincent and his wife Anne over at Dun Laoghaire. A few hours later I was creeping close up to the Bailey lighthouse as we rounded Howth Head on course for the other side of the bay. Here, we are told, St Nessan wrestled with the devil, and flung him against the cliffs so violently that his features were imprinted on the rocks.

The treasured Howth 17s were out as we left the harbour. These gaff-rigged keel boats, 17 feet on the waterline, started racing in Dublin Bay 100 years ago and are the oldest surviving one-design keel boat class in the world. They carry 335 square feet of canvas and need experienced handling, but their longevity is a tribute to Sir Walter Boyd, first Commodore of the Howth Sailing Club, who designed the original craft soon after the club was founded in 1895.

The Bailey light was still in operation, the Irish lightkeepers' last watch. The first light on this point was a coal-burning beacon set up in 1667; the first tower was built on Howth Head in 1790; and the existing tower, built lower down to escape fog and mist, dates from 1814. The Bailey was the final light to be automated

on the Irish coast. All Irish lights are now controlled and moni-
tored by the Commissioners of Irish Lights in Dun Laoghaire.

Dublin Bay opened up and, off to the west, the city lay
wrapped in haze. It is a shallow bay, and for centuries vessels
could not safely reach the city quays save in calm weather and
good conditions. By the mid-nineteenth century a great wall had
been built out across the shallows to reduce silting and encourage
scouring by the River Liffey. It incorporated a roadway and a
house at the end. The first caretaker, a Mr Pidgeon, developed
the place as a resort, and it later became a packet station and a
permanent hotel. However, Howth superseded it in 1813.

The government then established a fort at the end of the breakwater. There was a general belief that the Pidgeon House Fort was
to be a bridgehead for a British landing force or a refuge for the
administration in case of rebellion. In this century, the site
became an electricity generating station, whose twin chimneys
dominate the bay. By then the wall had been extended another
one and a half miles to seaward.

In my student days in Dublin I once cycled out all of three and
a half miles from the docks and had the illusion of being
marooned in mid-bay at the road's end, with Dublin, Dun
Laoghaire, and the crouching Gibraltar of Howth each about the
same distance from me.

Ahead of us now a superferry emerged from Dun Laoghaire. It
was like a block of flats built on a catamaran, spewing ribbons of
foam, and would reach Holyhead, 54 sea miles away, in little over
an hour. A conventional cross-channel ferry lying by the terminal
looked small enough to fit between this monster's keels.

Curiously enough, Dublin Bay first looked at the development
of catamarans as far back as the seventeenth century. In July
1663, Samuel Pepys wrote in his diary about the *Experiment*, a
vessel of Sir William Petty's 'built upon two keels – a model
whereof built for the King he showed me – hath this month won
a wager of £50 in sailing between Dublin and Holyhead with the
pacquett-boat, the best ship or vessel the King hath there... It is
about 30 tons burden, and carries 30 men, with good accommodation... this carries also ten guns, of about five tons weight. In

their coming back from Holyhead they started together, and this vessel came to Dublin by five at night and the pacquett-boat not before eight next morning; and when they came they did believe this vessel had been drowned or at least behind, not thinking she could live in that sea.'

Petty – best known in Ireland for having undertaken a land survey called the Down Survey – had already tested a smaller catamaran in a race held under the auspices of the Royal Society in wintry conditions off Dublin Bay in January 1663. A most detailed report of this first deep-water sailing match shows that, on each point of sailing, the catamaran was a winner. Petty built several vessels, and in recent years the sailing historian, Hal Sisk, has re-enacted the route of Petty's Dublin-built catamaran, *Simon and Jude*, in a boat constructed by a team headed by Howth shipwright John O'Reilly.

Travelling to Ireland from England was difficult because of the prevailing westerlies, but there was need for an efficient service between the capitals, London and Dublin. As early as the middle of the seventeenth century there were weekly packet services between Ringsend and Holyhead when weather allowed, and between Waterford and Milford Haven and Carrickfergus and Larne. By the end of that century an urgent letter from Dublin to London was expected to take from five to eight days, carried by post-horses across North Wales, where the roads were little better that mountain tracks in places. Ordinary passengers tended to use Chester, the main port for landing Irish cattle, which had monthly cargo services.

Thackeray travelled to Ireland in 1842. After a ten-hour ride on the Birmingham Mail coach, he reached Holyhead, 'to be thrust incontinently on board the packet; and the steward says there is no point providing dinner on board because the passage is so short. But, as the packet would reach Kingstown at midnight when all the world is asleep and the mail not be landed till 5 a.m., could we not now,' he asked, 'have one half-hour on shore before sailing? Even the steward agreed it was a useless tyranny and, after a little demur, produced half a dozen fried eggs, a feeble makeshift for dinner.'

After the 'black and cheerless' crossing, the passengers were awakened at five o'clock by the noise of the mail bags being unloaded. Thackeray was rowed ashore in the last boat and gave the steward half a crown for his services, whereupon he was advised that 'gentlemen usually complimented the stewardess with a shilling'.

The mail train from Euston arrived a few years later. From its initial run on 1 August 1848 right up until August 1939, when the service was suspended on the outbreak of war, the Irish Mail left Euston at 8.45 pm each day and delivered its cargo of letters in Dublin the following morning. Mail trains would run in from Cork, Limerick, Galway and Belfast to meet it and hand over their post for delivery to London on the return journey. Night after night on the Irish Mail, a chronometer was carried in a sealed package and delivered next day to the General Post Office in Dublin, to ensure that the Irish would always have the time precise from Greenwich. I have read that this practice continued up to the outbreak of war in September 1939.

We approached the great artificial harbour which Frank Cowper sailed into just over 100 years ago. 'Although there is a great deal of room,' he wrote, 'it requires judgement to pick out a snug place when it is crowded, as it mostly is during the yachting season after the Cowes Week is over.' Spires rose against the Dublin mountains, the steeple over the Mariner's Church, where naval units would parade to Sunday service, now marking Ireland's finest maritime museum. Near it I could see the lawns below the Marine Hotel where duty would once lead me to tea with a birdlike and petulant aunt.

Sarakiniko slipped between the granite arms of the breakwater, each almost a mile long. A spacious entrance, admitting nasty swell when the wind is in the north-east, but designed when steam power was a mere supplement to sail and helmsmen needed room to enter a busy harbour. Now launches sped through the moorings ferrying crews out to racing yachts, their topsides dancing in the sunlight. Jeering children sped by in a dinghy, faster and more fun than the canvas canoe with a lugsail and lee board which brought me on my first encounter with the sea, though one of the few hazards a small boat would meet in those years was the Mail Boat on its daily crossing to and from wartime Holyhead.

We put breast-ropes and springs safely out to a pontoon near the graceful Royal Irish Yacht Club, then stepped ashore to a town still full of Edwardian grace, despite the urgent development of malls, arcades and hamburger havens. Our lunch was a convivial success, beginning with plate-covering slices of smoked salmon. Topics ranged loosely and alcoholically, one anecdote waiting to interrupt another. There is a deadly pleasure in blathering on about the past – anaesthetic reminiscences. A good favourable tide for Wicklow ran to waste and it was three o'clock before we were out of the harbour and tacking across Scotsman's Bay towards the Martello Tower at Sandycove. It is now a Joycean museum, an essential stopover where the pilgrim may remember Buck Mulligan forever capering before Steven Dedalus, and Haines 'fluttering his winglike hands, leaping nimbly, uttering brief birdlike cries.' Below the squat tower is the Forty Foot swimming pool. Secluded, and notoriously cold, it was until recently the preserve of irascible old men who insisted on swimming in their tattered birthday suits, until Irish women invaded their waters.

We kept a sharp lookout as we crossed among the small breaking waves of Dalkey Sound, the tide against us, pulling lobster-pot buoys half under. A false wind emptied the sails. Just to one side lay terraces of velvet lawns, the tops of exotic palms peering over their low garden walls, affluent houses behind them focused on sun and sea. Further in were the lush suburbs pressing on the lanes of old Dalkey village. With its tiny harbour at Coliemore, it was once so important in Anglo-Irish commerce that seven fortified castles were built to defend the harbour from pirates by sea and the town from freebooters from the hills.

Two canoeists crossed our bow, reached easier water beyond the tide rip and made to beach off the little island of Dalkey. A few hundred yards wide, perhaps a mile long, the island once had a monarch of a sort. In the eighteenth century the 'Kingdom of Dalkey Island' elected its ruler annually and gave him the title

'His facetious Majesty, King of Dalkey, Emperor of the Muglins [nearby rocks], Defender of his own Faith and respecter of all others and Sovereign of the Illustrious Order of the Lobster and Periwinkle.' The ruler was anointed with whiskey at his coronation and appointed several officers of state. A spoilsport government suspected goings-on by a secret society and suppressed the Kingdom of Dalkey Island; however, a club boatman in Dun Laoghaire assured us that the fun continues.

Another Martello tower stands on Dalkey. These bomb-proof forts, some 19 ranging along the flat coast between Balbriggan and Bray, never fired a shot in anger. The towers are immensely strong, with walls some eight feet thick constructed of local stone. The ground floor was usually the ammunition room, the first floor held sleeping quarters, and a cannon set on a traversing carriage peered above the parapet: it had a range of about a mile. It is often said that they were named after a Captain Martello, but that is not so. When Royalist French asked for British help in Corsica in 1794, the Royal Navy sent two ships to destroy a tower at Martella Point on the island, but had to withdraw with severe losses. The tower was later captured from the land, and it so impressed the English that a model and plans were sent to the Admiralty in London. The ruin of the original still stands on Martella Point. Martella means myrtle, which grows profusely on the Corsican headland. Why Martello? Someone simply got the spelling wrong. As to the Dalkey tower we were passing, it is said that as a result of an administrative error its small garrison continued to draw full pay and rations for years after the British forces left Ireland.

We were now approaching an aspect of mountain and sea of startling beauty, reaching from Killiney Hill to Bray Head, a great sweep of scenery linked by a semi-circle of sand which runs south to the resort town of Bray. The cones of the Great and the Little Sugarloafs completed a composition which, in the age of Victorian tourism, inevitably led to comparisons with the Bay of Naples. The wind, favourable so far, began shifting and falling light, so we rounded Bray Head under engine, heeled to a stronger wind past the point and tacked offshore for a few miles until we saw flecks of white on the near horizon, the mark of shoals. We tacked again, running in to the long shingle beach at Greystones, wondering if this crab-like progress would fetch us to Wicklow in time for supper.

All the way around Ireland we had been free of the hazard of sandbanks, but they were a danger now as we sailed south-east. Though they were marked by buoys and beacons, the sands shift shape and position under the impact of storms, and the gaps between banks open and close unpredictably. They are difficult to chart accurately. Because the tidal stream turns earlier in the open sea than inshore, tides do not flow up and down parallel to the banks. As it runs north, the flood tide tends to ripple north-east across the shallows, while the ebb, coming south, can pull an unwary vessel south-west on to the sand, where the waves curl sullenly against the prevailing wind. Lying five, six, or seven miles out, these surf-washed traps ran all the way to Rosslare. We were to learn that even in fine weather shallow-draft fishing craft and yachts can readily go aground.

We left Greystones and carried on south past a monotony of low strands backed by the railway, plumbline straight and cutting off the sad bogs and reedy fields. The evening became quite glorious, the light changing continually, sending great shadows sweeping across the fields and hills, changing their shape. On the chart the banks became Bray Bank, Codling Bank, India Bank. In a few hours, when dusk drew in, buoys would be flashing red warnings along the entire coast.

Engine on rather guiltily for the last hour, we slipped in to the pier at Wicklow. A coaster lay by the wall and behind it some 35 yachts, clearly part of Ireland's racing circuit. 'Not there,' Pat muttered, 'they may be off at dawn. What about beside that sloop?'

I edged alongside and Pat stepped over the life-rails on to *Suju's* deck. A Labrador thumped his tail in welcome; the owner appeared from the cabin, teacup in hand. He was John Scott, carpenter, radio operator and robust crew for Wallace Clark in the Grace O'Malley galley on its journey from Westport to Scotland.

'We followed a few steps of your voyage,' I called across. I went below to get Wallace's book. 'Here it is,' I said, thumbing through the *Lord of the Isles Voyage.* 'John Scott, sailor and joiner, gingerhaired and close-cropped, drove over from his workshop in Donegal and at once made the sawdust fly.' John laughed.

'And you were still sawing and drilling in Clew Bay when the voyage began. One of the crew said, "Jisis, if I sit still for more than five minutes I reckon he'll have a cleat screwed to my shoulders!"'

John laughed. 'The real work was the rowing.' He raised his hands. 'The blisters eventually disappeared.'

We walked up along the old quays to the town, past grey sheds and derelict warehouses facing across the river. The tide was low, the River Leitrim slipping quietly through the seven arches of the bridge. We hurried on and found a place to eat. Next morning, I opened my eyes on an intensely blue sky set against the cabin window. On closer viewing, the sky turned out to have streaks of rust – it was the flank of a ship creeping slowly past. I scrambled across the decks of neighbouring boats and found John. He pointed to the massive bow-line of another ship moving astern of us: it had been lifted off the bollard on the quay and tossed into the harbour by some mindless fools we had heard last night. Fortunately, the ship was still held by a hawser.

Sailors love getting into harbour and then, after a very short time, want to be off again. But in Ireland word of your passage runs ahead of you, and a boyhood friend, Hugh O'Neill, was shouting from the quay. Ten minutes later the bay was a view from the windows of his home among the foothills of the Wicklow Mountains. Embraced in comfortable hospitality, we relished the luxury of carpets, armchairs and water hot from the tap. From up here the sea could be a void, an emptiness, something that simply marked the edge of Ireland. But by now it was our world, where we live days divided by the times of tides and shipping forecasts. It had a topography as intricate as that of the land, the names of its islets and rocks and shoals evoking history as vividly as placenames ashore, with accurate maps and signposts to find them. All this one felt more deeply after this interlude in the Wicklow hills; inside Ireland, looking out.

Pat gazed reflectively out on fields ripening to the harvest. In two days his farm would call him away and Tony O'Gorman, last on board in Lough Swilly, would come again. We had arranged for the changeover at Rosslare.

'Arklow tonight?' Hugh asked as we said goodbye at the quay-side ladder.

'No. We'll probably carry on to Courtown. Apparently the wind will pick up.'

At present there was just enough wind blowing out of the hills in the north-west to justify getting sail up. We drifted in the eddies and false airs off Wicklow Head and stood out to the east, boom rocking to and fro in the light following breeze. There are three light towers on the head, two of them derelict. When the first was built sailors found the sweep of its light partly obscured by the headland, so a second was substituted. This threw light on the areas which had lain in shadow but failed to reach the waters the first had illuminated. They will tell you in Wicklow, where good stories are appreciated, that officials finally left their Dublin offices, came and actually looked at the local slopes, and got it right third time.

Though we were still moving through the water, the changing alignment of the lighthouse and the old towers showed we were slowing. Then we began to go backwards in the quickening north-pushing flood, strengthening as it came around the head-land. The wind improved and we tacked back towards the coast. The binoculars picked out the North Arklow buoy off the end of the twelve-mile Arklow Bank. A feather of white out near the horizon gave away the presence of a dangerous narrow ridge, shallow and awash in places. 'Yachts should keep away from it,' the *Directions* warned, 'especially in calm weather and in fog or darkness.'

Presently we could count caravans, row after white row like evenly spaced dentures above the sandy lips of Brittas Bay. Beyond Mizen Head we could see Arklow harbour pier low in the haze. It is an old place – it is on a second-century map – and I cannot see Arklow without thinking of a cloud of sails now gone forever. In the early years of this century, scores of schooners and brigs of up to 500 tons were trading from here across to Britain and to France and Spain, and there may have been 150 fishing boats crowding the Avoca River when the four-acre tidal dock was opened in 1911. The approach to Arklow has always suffered from silting, and the bar was a particular hazard in onshore winds. Two long piers were built, giving the harbour entrance the appearance of a canal. Further up is the four-acre dock. Up until the 1920s, when the use of sailing craft declined, it would have been common to see sail boats being helped along by hawser from the harbour entrance to the quays at Arklow.

The Tyrrell yard, established here in 1864, was the foremost name in Irish shipbuilding for over a century. After her father's sudden death on board their schooner *Denbeighshire Lass* in 1886, 25-year-old Kate Tyrrell was left to run the family business. She skippered the *Denbeighshire Lass* herself for many years, trading with the Bristol Channel and Merseyside ports and even to Spain. The schooner was the first to fly the Irish tricolour. It was finally lost in the Bristol Channel.

Tyrell's built fishing boats such as the distinctive Arklow hooker and the Arklow yawl, some of which were still active up to World War II. It launched the *Avoca* in 1907, the first motor trawler to be built in these islands. The yard designed and built the wooden hulls which became the mainstay of the Irish fishing fleet in the 1950s and '60s. Tyrrell's was commissioned to build Sir Francis Chichester's *Gypsy Moth III* which was launched in September 1958. Later it built the *Asgard II*, its frames carved from local oak.

The Arklow trader *Kathleen and May* is preserved in St Katherine's Dock, London, while another is safe in the Ulster Folk Museum. The *De Wadden*, which carried its last cargo of motor cars to Scotland in 1961, became the star of the television series *The Onedin Line*, and now rests in Liverpool's Pier Head Museum. But old boats do not always retire so gracefully. When Arklow declined in the recession of the 1920s, redundant schooners were left to rot in an area of the river called 'the cemetery'. 'They tend towards the creation of an unsightly spectacle,' the local newspaper declared in 1934. Many became firewood in the fuel-short years of the war. Is it sensible today that Ireland

and the UK appear to be the only EU countries to insist that decommissioned fishing boats are destroyed – cut up with a chainsaw or burned? When John Heuston needed vintage vessels for the film *Moby Dick*, which was shot at Youghal in 1954, many could still be found at Arklow, but much of this seagoing heritage has since been lost.

A substantial reconstruction of Arklow Harbour was undertaken in the 1970s, and new ships and new trade now visits the town. It has always played a key role in sea-going trade; its fleet of 14 ships helped to sustain Ireland's economy during the last war. A critical shortage of vessels had arisen as no attempt had been made to establish an ocean-going merchant fleet before war broke out, when only 56 ships were available to safeguard Irish trade; these included three lightship tenders and a schooner built in 1859. The government established Irish Shipping in March 1941 and added some new ships to the merchant fleet. All through the war, the merchantmen operated in a war zone, and 135 Irish seamen perished. Shipping companies did their best to protect crews, but neutral vessels were not allowed to carry arms. Vessels were degaussed against magnetic mines. That did not save the SS *Ardmore*, blown up three miles south of the Saltee Islands in November 1940 carrying 500 cattle and pigs from Cork to Fishguard. All 23 crew died. *Isolde*, a tender for Irish Lights, was bombed a week later in the same waters, and in the following year German planes bombed and sank at least three, possibly four or five, Irish vessels off Wexford.

Irish ships actually rescued 521 seamen of all nationalities in those years. Most dramatic was a request from a German bomber to the *Kerlogue*, sailing from Lisbon to Cork in December 1943, to alter course to attend a German vessel. When the *Kerlogue* came upon the wreckage, its crew spent ten hours rescuing survivors. It reached Cork with 164 German sailors aboard. The year before, the *Irish Willow*, bound for Waterford, rescued 47 British crew from a torpedoed freighter.

Arklow was swallowed up in the haze. I began to concentrate on the line of shoals which marked the Glassgorman Banks, running close to the coast and parallel to the Arklow Bank six or seven miles out. The chart showed a depth of only six feet a mile and a half off Kilmichael Point, now emerging on our starboard bow. The wind was freshening, coming offshore. If we could run along the coast, we should be in easy water down to Courtown, and avoid making a detour across the Glassgorman Banks to deeper water. We carried on until, a mile or so past the point, white filaments of water rose ahead. Had the sandbanks shifted? Had we strayed too far out?

I switched on the GPS, fretting that it took up to three minutes to latch on to satellites. Then, with latitude and longitude scribbled on the log book, I ran the parallel rulers across the chart and pencilled in our position lines. They crossed directly on the Glassgorman Bank where the depth was charted as twelve feet. With some alacrity I twisted the knob of the depth-finder. The red cursor flickered. Here, possibly two miles from the coast, we were in nine feet of water. In this situation it is best not to alarm the crew, especially when the skipper is to blame. My self-restraint was justified. The depth increased to twelve feet, then 15.

Tea was indeed overdue. I put the kettle on and presently we could identify Courtown, about three or four miles inshore. The wind had increased sharply and the sea was dazzling in the evening sun. The Glassgorman Bank extended south of Courtown, but its tail had a charted depth of over 20 feet, so we crossed the eddies of sandy water once more, thrashing splendidly, heeled over until the water bubbled along the side deck and headed for the houses crouching behind the canal that leads into Courtown. The entrance is a hidden door in the coastline of hillocks, dunes and tufty trees. Against the evening sun you really only see it when you are yards from being shipwrecked on the beach, the aperture in the sands being no wider than a country lane. Then we were in, and as we plodded slowly down between the stone walls a voice called, 'Tie up to the old trawler with the swan.'

Round the corner a few acres of water opened up, more dock than harbour, quarried here as a Famine relief work in the 1840s and happily unmodernised. Yachts seemed to occupy all the available moorings as we circled, mystified, on the lookout for a swan, but all we could see were ducks. A few anglers gazed at us from the grassy banks, and boats and houses seemed locked in intimate tangle. Music belted out from an amusement arcade. At last we found the swan as a faded outline on the stern of a decaying fishing boat and tied up for the night.

We were in Co. Wexford. Around its south-east corner at Bannow Bay, three boatloads of Normans had beached their vessels in May 1169 and changed the course of Irish history. A major force soon landed at Baginbun Head, and within nine months they and their Irish allies had taken the walled town of Wexford from the Ostmen and subdued Dublin and much of Leinster. The county's air of comfort, neat domesticity and good husbandry reflects centuries of settlement. We were far from the harsh Atlantic counties which have only in our own time cut free from the gnawing fear of poverty.

Wexford has been called the 'Normandy of Ireland'. Mariners, however, know it as the 'graveyard of a thousand ships'. In this century alone over 220 vessels have foundered here, more than 800 if you include the nineteenth century, and these are simply the known casualties.

We made an early start and were clearing Cahore Point five miles south of Courtown by seven next morning. A complex of shoals lay ahead. A channel with the uninviting name the Sluice ran along the coast, so we made further offshore. Some two miles out we spotted with relief another red buoy – we had got beyond the edge of the shallows, the Rusk Bank, a five-mile sausage of sand where the depth dropped to four feet. The tide began to suck *Sarakiniko* down the Rusk Channel, an alley marked every three miles with a buoy. Ripples and waves broke out to seaward on a wretched place called the Money Weights Bank, which extends into the Blackwater Bank further down. Parts of the shallows dry out at low tide, several miles out from the coast. The sandbars run for ten miles, breaking off to create a gap for vessels making in to Wexford Harbour and then building up again where the Lucifer Bank waits on the other side. It is confusing and anxious water on a foggy day, but we had good visibility and picked up successive buoys without difficulty. The sea was gentle,

but 'Breaks' written on the chart showed where cross tides running against a strong wind could cause waves to curl and fall,
crashing on deck as solid water. Breaking waves can overpower a
boat; after all, one bucket of water is quite heavy.

When the *Pomona* was wrecked on the Blackwater Bank, the
London *Times* wrote that 'twenty-four hours in St George's
Channel are more dangerous that twice as many in the Atlantic
Ocean'. The 1,400-ton ship sailed from Liverpool for America on
Wednesday, 27 April, carrying 373 passengers, most of them
Irish emigrants. The captain cheerfully addressed them on deck,
saying that they might reach New York in 17 days. The boat
passed Holyhead and sailed south-west to clear around the lighthouse on the Tuskar Rock off the south-east corner of Ireland.
When the lookout reported a light off the starboard bow at about
midnight, Captain Marrihew assumed that they had reached the
Tuskar and ordered a turn to starboard into the Atlantic
approaches. But they had not found the Tuskar. The light came
from the Arklow lightship at the southern end of the Arklow
Banks, still some 30 miles from the Tuskar and only twelve miles
from the start of the Blackwater Bank. The *Pomona*, under full
sail and in heavy winds and sea, crashed on to the sands at about
4 am, heeling perilously and causing panicking crowds to rush
on deck. They were ordered below and the hatches battened
down.

The *Pomona* was scoured by breaking seas, but it was a new
ship and the oak hull stood up to the pounding for some eight
hours. When the tide rose the leaking vessel was driven across the
bank into deeper but slightly easier waters. Two of the three
masts were cut away and a lifeboat sent to the distant coast to
summon aid.

But the captain's next decision was unwise. Both anchors were
dropped in the hope that the vessel could be held while more
boats were lowered. If this had not been done, the ship might
have been blown the further few miles on to the sand dunes.
What next happened, however, was utterly shameful. The two
boats that got away were mostly occupied by the crew, who beat
each other and the passengers with oars as they fought for places.

One boat carrying 22 men – 17 crew – disappeared inland as soon as they reached the crowds on the beach. 'Except for one man,' a witness later testified, 'who waited to see if the second boat got safely ashore.' The second boat capsized.

As the *Pomona* began to break up, the emigrants, men, women and children, were left to die. One victim was Henry Lavery, whose widow died of sorrow soon afterwards. Of their three children, the youngest became the well-known Irish painter, Sir John Lavery, whose wife's portrait would one day adorn Irish banknotes.

'We saw a light which we presumed to be the Tuskar,' said the mate who had been on watch, but he admitted that he did not know the difference between the flash of the Arklow and Tuskar lights. The jury expressed surprise that, on a favourable wind, the ship had been so far off course, condemned the conduct of the crew and called for a Board of Trade enquiry. By early May this was sitting in Wexford Courthouse and noting that, in the twelve previous months, no less than 19 ships had been wrecked on the Blackwater Bank alone and that a Prussian brig, wrecked the year before, had also mistaken the Arklow light for the Tuskar.

For weeks the bodies drifted ashore, about 300 in all, some clutching children, some rosaries. At one time more than 60 lay awaiting identification on the little pier of Pollduff which we could now see nestling under Cahore Point. Three attempts had been made to launch the lifeboat from there, but the crew lacked experience. It was hauled on to Ballynowlan instead and local fishermen got it afloat, but the seas thrust it back on the beach. The lifeboat did not reach the wreck until Friday morning, towed there by tug. The only remaining mast appeared above water, the American ensign still flying. No bodies were seen. Divers were later to find many in the hull, one a woman whose seven children still clung to her in death. The captain's body was found tied to the stump of a mast.

The painted female figurehead of the *Pomona* and one of its anchors lie in the museum at Enniscorthy. A trawler's net in later years brought up what seemed to be the second anchor, and that is displayed in the village of Kilmore Quay. Apart from this we appear to have no other memorial to a sea disaster comparable to that of the other emigrant ship, *Tayleur*, whose 650 people were lost off Lambay Island only five years earlier.

Pat was shading his eyes. 'I can see the Tuskar now.'

His voice jolted me back to the present. The 100-foot-high lighthouse five miles off Carnsore Point hardened into reality. Close to the buoyed channel for the Fishguard-Rosslare ferries, the reef on which it stands rises about 30 feet above high water and big seas sweep right across it. It was a hazardous place to start constructing a lighthouse, but this was a death-trap for shipping turning the corner for Liverpool, Dublin and other Irish Sea ports after an Atlantic passage, and a light to mark the approach was vitally neccessary. Indeed, within weeks of work commencing on Tuskar in 1812, a West Indiaman bound for Liverpool struck the reef in fog. Five people drowned, but the workmen helped about 100 more to scramble onto the rock.

Later that year, in October, a gale struck the Tuskar. The seas increased for two days and smashed the workers' huts to pieces, washing men away. Those who were left fastened themselves with chains to the building blocks of the lighthouse, which each weighed two tons, but when seas tumbled these massive blocks over the men were either crushed or drowned. On the third day boats managed to collect ten survivors, but 14 men had been lost. Yet the great lighthouse, rather similar to the Eddystone, was completed in 18 months and got its light, the most brilliant then on the Irish coast, in June 1815.

Naturally the part of Ireland closest to France thrived on smuggling, despite the fleets of armed cruisers which hung around the coast. South Wexford's many windmills – one of the few surviving in Ireland stands near the village of Broadway – were used as signalling posts for smuggling vessels lying offshore. The *Wexford Historical Society Journal* records that 'when the sails were in their stopped position the goods could be safely landed. But when the customs officers were active in the vicinity, the sails were stopped in the upright position in the shape of a Greek or St George's cross.' And onshore, 'the mill could be a convenient "cover" for brandy, wine or tobacco until they could be transported inland in sacks of corn.'

Within six years of its opening, even the keepers of the new Tuskar light became involved in the business. In 1821 the owner of a cutter, the *Shark*, sailing from Le Havre with contraband, decided to moor at the rock and unload barrels of brandy and other dutiable goods before risking the approach to Wexford. He found the two keepers, Wishart and Hunter, willing to store his cargo for a suitable reward. The *Shark* was boarded when approaching Wexford; it had no illicit goods, of course, but its owner discovered that the Revenue cruiser would make a call at Tuskar Rock on the following Tuesday. Time was short. He borrowed a whaleboat and set out to retrieve his cargo, where he found the keepers had tapped the brandy and lay in a drunken stupor. Even the light was extinguished. The smuggler loaded the contraband, apparently without disturbing the sleepers, and wafted it away to safety.

This bold affair put at risk the Royal Squadron carrying King George IV back from the gratifying visit to the newly named Kingstown, when it failed to see any light at the Tuskar on its way to Plymouth. An enquiry resulted, the keepers were questioned, and all was revealed. Wishart was demoted to Second Keeper and later transferred to the splintered pyramid of Skellig Rock off Kerry, where he died in a fall from a cliff. His companion Hunter was also demoted, apparently to work for the service as a blacksmith in Dublin.

We held on now towards the flecks of white which we could see on the coast ahead, either the upper-works of ships or part of Rosslare's ferry terminal. A skein of birds skimmed low over the water, coming from Raven Point on the north boundary of Wexford Harbour. The polder area, famous for the flocking of migrating birds, was once called the North Slob. No PR man would stand for that, so it is now more happily named the Wexford Wild Life Reserve. There, in a few months, one-third of the world's population of Greenland Whitefronted geese would settle for a winter break.

Pat ignored the formation flight and bent over our chart, 'Wales to the East Coast of Ireland.' It had an inset for Wexford but no charted channel was shown – the banks shift too often. The bar, according to the *Pilot*, has a minimum depth of three feet at lowest tides but, given time and tide, the buoys which are laid and relaid to mark the shifting channels could guide us in.

'"Ruins submerged."' Pat put a finger on the middle of the entrance. 'And here it says "Ruins awash at High Water."'

'Yes,' I said, 'a village abandoned years ago.'

I was ready to scatter the seeds of freshly gleaned knowledge, and beside me, I thought, was a truly vacant plot. 'Waesfiord,' I said, '"fiord of the mud flats" for the Vikings. When ships were small enough to be beached, I suppose the mud didn't matter, but as they got bigger Wexford lost out to Waterford.' Pat, however, had turned to concentrate on a distant ferry doing a wheel-about as it left Rosslare. I carried on, reading from a guide book I had found.

'Grattan's Parliament made a law that the tonnage and crew size and port of registry of all trading ships should be declared, and in 1788 apparently 26 ports and 1,034 ships sent in records. Wexford just beat Waterford – 44 ships against 41 – but the Wexford vessels were small, all under 100 tons.'

He must have been listening. 'How many had Dublin?'

'Two hundred and forty ships, and Cork 99.'

Wexford should claim a distinction before it is forgotten: it was the final point of departure for the first ever steam-powered crossing from Ireland to Britain. In 1815 an engineer named John Dodd built at Glasgow an 80-foot steamboat, the *Thames*, powered by paddle wheels. After a hazardous passage he managed to reach Dublin, where he met the distinguished Isaac Weld, later to be president of the Royal Dublin Society. They decided to attempt a voyage to London. Thousands watched as the craft churned past Dalkey and, when smoke was seen off Wexford next morning, pilot boats, thinking it must be on fire, put out at once. 'The hopes of salvage were happily frustrated,' Weld wrote. After a night ashore while Mrs Weld rested from sea-sickness, the craft went on to Ramsey Island near St David's in Wales, where again boats put out on seeing the smoke. They carried on, and near Milford Haven saw the Waterford packet boat. Weld, deciding to send a letter to anxious Irish friends, gave chase to the packet and, to everyone's astonishment, not only overhauled the sailing ship but motored twice around it.

The paddle steamer reached St Ives and later Plymouth, 'where the port master had never seen a steam vessel and stood amazed'. Snooty naval officers in Portsmouth told them that steam power might have a future towing men-of-war in and out of port. They reached London. A report was made to the Holyhead Roads Committee. Within a few years, a number of little 100-ton steamers began to appear in the fishing village of Dun Laoghaire.

'Do you remember,' I said to Pat, 'when we sailed around Kerry, those stories about the privateer, John Paul Jones, during the American War of Independence?'

'Daniel O'Connell seeing Jones' ship as a child, and the Irish crew that escaped and rowed home when his ship was becalmed off Skellig?'

'Yes, but Jones and lots of other privateers – mostly French – probably made their richest pickings around here. He and John Barry of Wexford sailed a 200-ton cutter, the *Black Prince*, together. Barry set an eighteenth-century record with it: 237 miles in 24 hours.'

'I've seen Barry's statue on the Wexford quays,' Pat said. 'The Father of the American Navy, striding the wind, his cloak billowing out right in front of the Commodore Barry newsagents.'

Although John Barry was born in Wexford, he was taken to Philadelphia as a youth in 1760. He became a seaman and eventually owner of the *Black Prince*, a 24-gun ship which had originally been built for another Wexford emigrant, John Dixon, who first read the Declaration of Independence to the people of Philadelphia. When the War of Independence began in 1775, Barry presented his ship to the American Congress. Later he fitted out eight further ships for the improvised American naval forces and, in 1782, captured the first ever naval prize taken by the Americans – a fleet of nine vessels rich with cargo en route from Jamaica to London. When the prizes were sold at Lorient in France, £650,000 in gold enriched the American Treasury. Barry fought at the last, and inconclusive, Anglo–US naval battle of the war in March 1782. By now France had joined the War of Independence and, after the British lost Yorktown, it was Barry who carried a triumphant Lafayette back to France.

When the war ended, Barry returned to trading as a merchant sea captain, voyaging as far as China, but when the United States acquired six frigates and set about raising a permanent navy, he took command of the flagship, the *United States*. He was given command of all US ships in the West Indies, though he disapproved of the conduct of the undeclared war with France in 1798. This remarkable Wexford man died in 1801, only 58 years old. His ships had flown a flag of yellow silk bearing a rattlesnake and the motto: 'Don't tread on me.'

Rosslare pier was close now and Pat seemed preoccupied with the fast-moving ferry. I put the book away and forebore from mentioning that in 1852 another Wexford man, Robert McClure, found a critical part of the North West Passage, a hazardous strait some 600 miles north of the Arctic Circle, which still bears his name.

ELEVEN

Landscapes of Youth

WE SNEAKED IN to Rosslare and made to the far side of the harbour where some barges and tugs lay against a concrete wharf. Some dockers told us that *Tuskar Rock* would not be leaving tonight, so we went to tie up to her. She turned out to be one of a herd which presently included *Tuskar Star*, *Tuskar Dawn* and *Tuskar Pusher*, each tug with rudders as large as *Sarakiniko*'s deck and iron topsides festooned with lorry tyres.

Pat, whose time was now claimed by the harvest, waited until Tony O'Gorman arrived and then bade us farewell on the last part of our cruise, along the coast of Co. Waterford and on to Cork. Tony and I went scrounging on waste ground ashore, where we found a plank to hang protectively outside our own small fenders, and wondered why this pivotal corner of Ireland, the nearest to the Continent and so close to Wales, could not reconcile the needs of a ferry port with some basic facilities for yachts. We had seen something of Ireland's fragile coastal rim and readily appreciated that developments like golfcourses, caravan parks and yacht marinas all needed careful planning, but for the small-boat sailor something very modest could be done. Small boats don't demand very much. They can tie up to a simple pontoon which can easily be removed in winter.

Later, a 24-foot boat approached, crewed by a young couple from Wales. 'What's it like outside?' I asked.

'North-west Force 5, but gusting a bit more.'

'We're leaving early but come alongside us. We should have a quiet night unless the wind goes into the north.'

As we took their lines, maroons went off at the lifeboat station, and within minutes a dinghy sped out to the Rosslare lifeboat, which surged off, kicking up sheets of spray. Next morning a large yacht lay tied to the wharf: it had been rescued in a rising

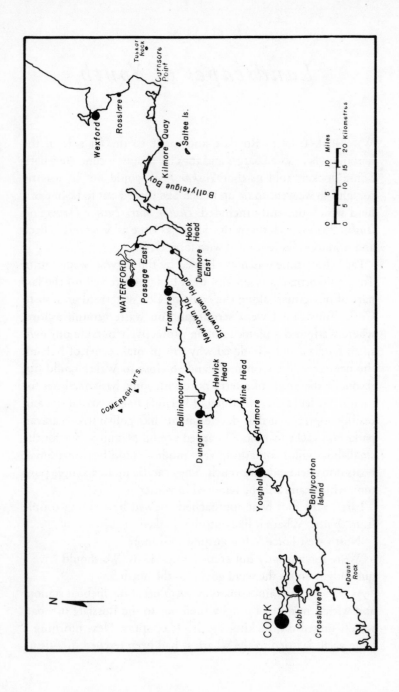

wind as it lay grounded on the Blackwater Bank. Its engine had failed, and the tide had taken the boat onto the shoals before the crew could get her under sail.

Tides keep unsocial hours, and we cursed the moon and its pull on the water which brought us stumbling on deck at 5.30 am, undoing slack and clammy lines. We needed to have the tide with us as we rounded Carnsore Point and turned for Dunmore East. I thought of Giraldus Cambrensis (Gerald of Wales), who first came to Ireland in 1183 and returned in the entourage of Henry II, and wrote so lyrically of tidal springs. 'When the moon is recovering her light and already beginning to grow beyond her half size, the western seas, through some secret natural causes, begin to be rough and tempestuous; they swell more and more from day to day in surging waves running up on the shore far beyond their usual limit,' because the moon 'is so much a source and influence on all liquids that, according to her waxing and waning, she directs and controls, not only the waves of the sea, but the bone marrow and brains of all living things, as well as the sap of trees and plants.'

We nosed past the pier, searching for the shipping-channel buoys that mark the avenue of deep water in from the Tuskar Rock, still half asleep but feeling that thrill which comes from stealing away on a voyage. The sea began to brighten. It was moving fast and running south towards Carnsore Point, Ireland's south-easterly tip, which the Greek cartographer Ptolemy called Hieron Akron, the Sacred Promontory, on the first known map of Ireland, drawn in Alexandria in the second century AD.

If we sailed outside the Tuskar, five miles to the south-east, then we would have a seven-mile haul west again before we could clear Carnsore. Did we really have to go beyond the Tuskar? I bent over the chart. A narrow bank of rocks, the Bailies Prong, ran for several miles mid-way between the Tuskar and Carnsore, and if we got out beyond the Bailies we could catch this tide down a narrow trough of deeper water between the rocks and the Tuskar. At the next red buoy, Tony wheeled to starboard out of the shipping channel, but despite a good sailing wind we ran the engine for safety. We had read that when a geologist was examining the sea-bed off Carnsore Point – investigations for a plan (happily scrapped) to build a nuclear power station there – he and his fellow divers found that tides here ran at up to eight knots. We could see foam tumbling from the Bailies rocks, and a prickle of unease ran down my spine. But we were well clear. A whistle buoy appeared, bent to the current, 'Mooing like a sick cow,' Tony said. We checked it on the chart and turned west, and soon saw the silhouettes of the Saltee Islands on the horizon.

Further inshore, the Black Rock shoals came abeam. They were marked on the chart, but the Long Bohur and Short Bohur remained submerged and only the falling levels on the dial of our depth-finder revealed how close they were. This seascape of rocks and reefs and treacherous currents was a shivery place. I looked to the compass with more care than usual, for the dead are dead because they were only a few degrees out in their navigation. Everywhere here you could feel the dead crowding in.

Tide rips and overfalls surround the Saltee Islands, three miles off the coast. A sea-scoured rocky moraine – called St Patrick's Bridge – runs out underwater from the mainland, and the trawlermen of nearby Kilmore Quay know the few safe gaps in it. We preferred to run through the sound between the two islands, where we were greeted by birds in squadron after squadron, wheeling and swooping above us. On Little Saltee the wreck of a red speedboat had been carried high into a tangle of rocks. Then the west side of Great Saltee emerged: outlines of fields, thickets of wind-tossed trees, a suggestion of buildings. The tiny islands sheltered pirates and privateers for centuries, supplied fresh meat and water to smugglers, and caves in which to store their contraband before it was transferred to the cellars of local castles and big houses. A complaint to the Privy Council in England in 1587 refers to 'Bands of Pirates... who appear to have made the Saltee Islands the depot for their ill-gotten gains. One of these, Alexander Voiles, robbed 46 tonnes of wynes from a French Vessel, some of which he sold to the inhabitants of Waterford and other places thereabouts.'

Great Saltee had a population of perhaps 20 and a detachment of three coastguard men in 1830, while only three people lived on Little Saltee. 'Stafford, Governor of Wexford, who betrayed the town to Cromwell, is said to have retreated to Little Saltee,' Lewis wrote in his *Topographical Dictionary*, 'and built a cottage which still bears his name.'

After the 1798 rebellion collapsed, two of its young leaders, John Colclough and his cousin Beauchamp Bagenal Harvey, fled to Great Saltee hoping to sail from there to France. A party of soldiers under the Chief Preventive Officer for the area, Richard Waddy, set off in a Revenue cutter in search of them. One account says that a soldier saw a tell-tale of smoke, another that soap-suds seeping from the mouth of a cave, where Colclough's wife was washing clothes, were the fatal give-away. The fugitives were arrested on 26 June 1798 and tried in Wexford next day. They were hanged the day after.

The Saltees are one of Europe's main staging posts for migrating birds, but the razorbills, cormorants, gannets and guillemots that fill the air with squawking are really only visitors in a princely land. Robed in a black cloak, white coat, red epaulettes and black trousers with a braided band, a self-styled monarch, Michael, Prince of Saltee, crowned himself here in July 1972. I have been told that Prince Michael in fact purchased the Saltees from the Irish Land Commission in 1943, and declared himself prince not long after that. A plaque in memory of his mother was placed near his throne: when Michael was ten years old, she had confided to him that he would one day be prince of the islands.

A few months after our voyage I found myself in Bannow. Shifting sands have ensured that nothing remains of Bannow town, but the ruin of a thirteenth-century church lies in the graveyard, and behind it a memorial building, large as a small cottage, was erected in 1980 'by John, Neil and Michael, Prince of Saltee, in memory of their mother and father'. I found the building locked, but cut on the gable wall were the names of Michael, Prince of Saltee, born in 1911, and Anne, Princess of Saltee, 1911–1996. They were 'Citizens of the World,' the stone declared, under an admonition of impressive simplicity that man should not forget God or his father or mother and should be kind and helpful to young and old. A carved crest showed two mermaids, one grasping an anchor, the other an oar and a shield, and each quarter contained a different kind of bird. The scroll beneath bore the words: 'God and Justice.'

It was now five hours since we had cleared Rosslare. We sat in the cockpit with mugs of coffee while Tony cut thick slices of barm brack, a delicious Irish speciality I describe inadequately as a cross between bread and fruit cake. Three miles north of us a church looming over the flat countryside made an excellent sea-mark for Kilmore Quay, with its new marina and old pubs which boast relics from scores of ships, amongst them the first gunship of the Irish navy, the *Muirchú*, which was given to the new Free State government by the British in 1921. She had formerly been the *Helga*, and had shelled the Four Courts and the GPO from the Liffey during the 1916 rebellion. Decommissioned in the 1940s and on the way to the scrapyard, she sank in about 200 feet of water just south of the Saltees.

Six miles to the south, I could see the red hull of the Conigbeg lightship, last of no less than five lightships which once guarded the south-east coast. Hook Head rose beyond the bow, some 15 miles away. We could see the lighthouse, gartered with two black bands. A pilgrim priest from south Wales, Dubhan, is said to have founded a monastery here and set up the first beacon, a fire fuelled by coal, pitch and tar. The monks tended the beacon for centuries, and the Normans built a tower for the light between 1170 and 1182. It was a striking engineering feat, 80 foot high, with limestone walls nine to twelve feet thick, and vaulted circular ceilings on the three largest rooms within.

The Tower of Hook, the oldest light tower in Europe next to the Pillar of Hercules which guides the mariner into Corunna in north-west Spain, lost its last keeper in March 1995. Lighthouses may not be around much longer, certainly not as we have known them. In a new age of satellite navigation, commercial shipping interests declare that lighthouses are unnecessary and resent their cost in light dues. I am sure that small-boat sailors will miss those long beams, stabbing the darkness of a dark coastline, or on a clear night seeming to polish the whole sky.

The cup-shaped bay of Ballyteigue lay between the Hook peninsula and the shoals and islets leading out to the Conigbeg Rock. Facing into the south-westerlies, it was a perilous place for a ship chased by a gale. 'A vessel from the westward must be careful to ascertain whether it is the Hook or the Tuskar before she alters course,' the 1887 *Sailing Directions* recorded soberly, 'an error in this respect having proved fatal to some vessels, while others have become dangerously embayed and entangled among Saltee rocks.'

At Bannow, on the west end of Ballyteigue Bay, some 30 men-at-arms, 60 mail-clad horsemen and perhaps 600 archers landed in May 1169, and set off the Norman invasion of Ireland. The Norsemen of Wexford surrendered the town to them. A further contingent of Normans landed on the headland of Baginbun, some two miles from Bannow, where you can still see a ridged embankment quickly built to repel an attack of Norsemen and Gaelic Irish chiefs. Finally, on 23 August, the Norman leader Strongbow rounded Hook Head with 200 knights and 1,000 soldiers and made a landing, crucially, on the Waterford side of the estuary, where the town lay directly open to assault.

We stood out to sea and finally tacked back, closing on Hook Head lighthouse, leaving creamy overfalls a few hundred yards to starboard as we reached the entrance to the estuary where the Barrow, Nore and Suir mingle at the gateway to Waterford. Edmund Spencer celebrated the fusing of the three sister rivers in *The Faerie Queen*:

All which long sundered doe at last accord
To joyne in one ere to the sea they come,
So flowing all for one, all one at last become.

In a faltering wind we crossed the estuary, the bulk of Credan Head hiding a view of Passage and the long bends to the quays of Waterford ten miles away. Cork and Limerick also lie on waterways withdrawn from the sea, but the way to Waterford has always seemed to me more beautiful, a landscape touched in places with the sadness of crumbling mansions, their ruined garden walls sloping down to the riverbanks.

As the estuary narrows and bends, the Atlantic swell dies away at Passage East, where a ferry crosses the river. Near here in 1171 King Henry II, anxious that Strongbow was becoming a shade too independent, arrived with 500 knights and 400 men-at-arms. More than two centuries later, Richard II is said to have landed in the estuary with 34,000 troops. It was from here, too, that James II took ship for Kinsale after his defeat on the Boyne in 1690. In the sixteenth century, the fort of Duncannon, three acres of military architecture, was erected to guard this important port against pirates. It is still an impressive sight, standing over the estuary on the Waterford shore.

A large red ship, the *Cattle Express*, went by. As *Sarakiniko* rocked in its wash, I recalled the steamers which used to take emigrants and cattle from the Waterford quays to Fishguard. Leaning over the rails, reluctant to go to my cabin, I would listen to the thump of the engines and the call of the curlews mingling with the maudlin singing in the bar. The lights would flash from Little Island below Waterford to Faithlegg, from Faithlegg to Snowhill and from there to Cheekpoint, and on by Passage and Crook and the ruins of Duncannon fort. As the ship cleared the Hook and began to roll, you would hear the lowing of the cattle down in the hold, and wonder if they, too, were thinking of the fields they were leaving. That was another time. Today, pontoons on Waterford's quays welcome sleek yachts into the heart of the city, while New Ross, not far away, is building a replica of a nine-teenth-century emigrant ship, the *Dunbrody*, with aid from the John F. Kennedy Trust and European Union regional development funds. Built in 1845 at Quebec for a small New Ross shipping firm, *Dunbrody* fetched timber from Canadian forests to the New Ross sawmills and returned to American and Canadian cities with emigrants. The new *Dunbrody* will symbolise the ships that once took so many away.

Sarakiniko finally approached Dunmore East. Alexander Nimmo designed its small artificial harbour in 1815, and his elegant Doric-columned lighthouse is still a gracenote over the much expanded fish quays. Village fishermen used the shelter of nearby coves for centuries before the quays were built, and if the wind is kind, they still offer a safe haven.

I could see yachts crowded together in a corner of the harbour, and my memory stirred uncomfortably. 'About 20 years since I was here,' I said to Tony. 'We had chartered a 26-footer in Wales. We had a fair wind coming across, and then we put the engine on outside that pier. We found it would only run in forward gear, and then it jammed at full throttle. The harbour was crowded too.'

'What happened?'

'We tried to brake by trailing a bucket. Some skippers seemed to panic as we approached, but we managed to stop. We were using small motor tyres as fenders, and every boat we came alongside on that trip got streaked black.' I paused. 'There's a yacht off the beach ahead. Let's try there.'

The yacht proved to be *Electron*, owned by Peter Price, Honorary Secretary of the Royal Cruising Club, so we anchored with particular care. To ensure we were holding I took a bearing on a gate-post and a small grey rock ashore. A few moments later the grey rock lifted a wing and flew off, but by then *Sarakiniko* had a secure foothold in my native county of Waterford.

We rowed the dinghy ashore through the indestructible litter of a busy fishing harbour. Boxes of silvery fish were coming off a late trawler. Dunmore's famous colony of kittiwakes, who should have been asleep, chattered in their cliffside nests. The wheat-fields beyond the village stirred in silk-like currents. With its thatched cottages and river setting, Dunmore is picturesque, but not so picturesque that it is uninhabitable. It was quiet now. 'It can be a madhouse,' said the owner of the pub where we ate, 'choc-a-bloc. Roads full of cars.' We were not sure whether he was boasting or complaining.

We motored past Portally and Rathmoylan next morning as the wind played fickle, and ran outside the Falskirt Rocks a few hundred yards offshore. Treacherous waves can sweep across this great plateau of rock, where the lure of fish, lobster and crab has tempted many small fishing boats to destruction. Was it Falskirt because its peril is hidden at high water? Near this hazard was Swine's Head, the origin of the name a mystery, though Flour Hole and Palm Oil Hole surely suggest bounty from shipwreck. It is an intriguing field of research before local memories fade.

A cluster of houses was just visible at the head of Ballymacaw inlet. The last recorded great auk in the British Isles was found here in 1834. It had been one of the first species of wildlife to be given legal protection – as early as 1794 – but already it was too late. A local farmer found one exhausted, and though he tried to revive it with fish and potatoes, the auk died. Later it was stuffed and mounted in Trinity College, Dublin.

Sarakiniko was still being carried on a favourable west-flowing tide, but we had to reach Dungarvan before the ebb drained the shallow harbour of water. The two great towers on Brownstown Head, eastern guardian of Tramore Bay, drew past, matching three more across the bay on Newtown Head. Tramore Bay looks remarkably like the entrance to Waterford estuary, a similarity which made it a trap for ships in hazy weather. 'A bay infamous for shipwrecks,' wrote Charles Smith in his *History of Waterford* published in 1746, 'for when the Hook tower could not be seen in heavy weather it has been mistaken for the harbour of Waterford....the wind blowing hard from the SSE to SSW, tumbles in a heavy sea which, joined to a great indraught towards that part of the bay called Rhineshark harbour, makes it almost impossible for embayed ships to weather the heads.'

In January 1816 the army transport, *Seahorse*, with the men and families of the 2nd Battalion of the 59th Foot, veterans of Waterloo, was driven by a gale on to the rocks near Newtown Head. Of the 292 men and 71 women and children aboard, only 30 survived, while Tramore people watched helplessly from the shore. They say you still sometimes hear the ship's band playing at the end of Tramore strand.

Lest the five towers on the bay's headlands did not give sufficient warning, a 14-foot-high Jack Tar, with black jacket and white trousers and a white gloved arm pointing eastward, was built on top of one of the towers at Newtown Head. We sailed close to the headland to get a better view. 'You'd have to be damn close in to see him,' Tony muttered. Absentmindedly I agreed, thinking of how, as a child, if you could hop all round the base of the tower, you would get whatever you wished for. As I cannot recall what I wished for then, I cannot say if it arrived.

Ochre sand dunes lined the beach of Tramore, and long rollers ran on to its three miles of hard sand. The beach made Tramore a resort as long ago as 1746, when Smith wrote his *History*. In those days, wealthy merchants would take a coach from Waterford to their summer houses at Tramore. Tourism began when the railway arrived in 1853, while coaches and charabancs brought day trippers from inland counties. Bathing-boxes lined the beach, and later coloured lights and incessant music drew throngs of people to the slot machines, bumper cars and dashing motor cyclists racing on the Wall of Death.

Past Tramore and along a coastline of which Robert Praeger wrote, 'Those who love the maritime scenery of Devonshire will find here an Irish analogue... flowery slopes, lofty cliffs and stacks and pinnacled islets with colonies of seabirds as well as choughs, peregrine and ravens; and an illimitable sea extending to the southward.'

The wind picked up, and live water began to run along our sides. Soft rolling land lay to starboard, the sun lighting small houses and patches of golden grain. Here and there a field stood out like patchwork in the uniform bottle green of nitrogen-fed grass. Behind this farming landscape the great Comeragh Mountains were wrapped in shrouds of mist. This was my place: a place of corries and precipices, loughs and streams and steeply pitched old fields, now reverting to fern and furze or disappearing beneath alien-looking forestry plantations. From the top of the Comeraghs you could see from Cork to the Dublin mountains in clear weather, and the ocean appeared to lie at your feet.

Tony directed me confidently between the dolefully named reefs, Carrickapane and Carricknamoan, and past the lighthouse of Ballinacourty. High water had passed as we turned into Dungarvan, and the ebb ran brown over two miles of shallows. We aligned the spires of Dungarvan on our bow. 'One eye on the church tower,' Tony demanded, 'and one on those poles in line on Ballinacourty golfcourse astern.' We drew past the massive ramparts of Dungarvan Castle, built for a visit by King John in 1185. It was besieged, surrendered and burned over the centuries, lastly during the withdrawal of anti-Treaty forces in the face of the Free State army in 1923. A memento of so much history, it seemed sadly neglected.

We reached the pontoons and, after a welcoming chat with members of the sailing club, hurried to place *Sarakiniko* on a mid-harbour mooring before the tide went fully out. As she grounded on her twin keels, oyster-catchers came picking through the mud, looking for scraps at low tide.

A lively modern town lies a hundred yards or so up from the narrow old streets and lanes around the harbour. It is many years since Dungarvan was one of Ireland's main fishing ports. On 15 July 1736, a fisherman named Doyle, trawling with a crew of seven in his twelve-ton fishing boat, *Nymph*, found the sea-bed some 30 miles south-east of Dungarvan littered with small stones and cockleshells. The bank marked the location of huge stocks of hake, ling, skate, bream and whiting, and Doyle, experienced on the New England and the Newfoundland Grand Banks, believed it might extend far into the Atlantic. He never found its true limits, but the Nymph Bank, as it is called, runs 90 miles south-west to Cape Clear. Some 36 hours after his discovery, the astonished man was back in Passage East, his boat so laden that he had to throw back huge rays which he knew would fetch high prices in the English, French or Dutch markets.

Dungarvan prospered. By 1824 it had 163 boats and some 1,100 men, women and children cleaning, salting and packing the catch; perhaps 5,000 people in all made their living from fish. Yet the Irish fishing industry of the time was severely criticised by Charles Smith for its practices. In the 1740s, he accused fishermen of being 'not only unskilled in the art of Navigation, but their Boats are open and too thin-skinned to bear or brook tempestuous seas, the terror of which, on going out of sight of land where they fear to be drove beyond their knowledge, is an invincible impediment to progress which might have long since been made.'

A conservationist long before his time, he condemned the trawl net used in Ireland, 'a Beam-trail or Trall on a pole up to thirty feet long so efficient that if a fisherman threw his knife into thirty or forty fathoms it would pick it up.' Drawn on the sea-bed for a mile or so at a time, 'it sweeps and tears away all the sea plants, moss, herring grass, etc. which some fish feed on. It disturbes or affrights the larger kinds of fish, as Cod, Ling, etc. in the same manner as if pursued by larger fishes of prey and thirdly, and worst of all, these Beam nets tear away, disturb and blend up the spawn of many kinds of profitable fish in a terrible manner and often many hogsheads of their spawn are drawn up in the Trail-bags so there may be distinctly seen several thousand embryos of young fish.' This way of fishing, he added, was prohibited in France, where laws also laid down the length of fish allowed.

JOAN, WHO had not been aboard since her rough ride with Alasdair from Rathlin Island to Belfast Lough, was to join us in three days. The wait gave Tony an opportunity for a visit home to Clonmel, while I idled around Dungarvan. I found myself in a tea-shop one afternoon, eavesdropping, as one tends to when alone, on a pair of elderly ladies bemoaning the modern age.

'The drinking!' said one. 'They get hundreds a week, of course. Oh, they can drink. Worse it's getting all the time.' She poured another cup and bent closer to her friend. 'I blame the parents. 'Tis hunted out they should be; hunted from the home.'

A young man went up to the till to pay while his mother gathered her things from their table. My neighbour missed nothing.

'Nice to have someone paying the piper,' she cackled to the young man's mother. The woman looked at her blankly.

'What piper?'

'Paying the piper. 'Tis lucky ye are to have someone paying for ye.' She turned to her friend. 'Sure the poor thing is deaf,' she said under her breath.

I enjoyed solitary strolls around the town and, in due course, found a bar, dark as Guinness, where men with raspberry-red faces and rheumy eyes sat in a row at the counter, drinks in front of them. I sat myself on a bar stool and heard of the local teacher, Marie Breathnach, who had recently become the first woman to sail solo around Ireland. Her small sloop got a special welcome in Portrush, Co. Antrim, her furthest point from home.

Two days later, Joan and Tony aboard, we cleared the

Dungarvan headland past the small artificial fishing harbour of Helvick, bound for Youghal and then Cork to close the circle of Ireland.

Watching the bulk of Mine Head – where lead and silver mines once contributed to the wealth of Richard Boyle, 1st Earl of Cork and father of the scientist – and the white lines of its lighthouse, it was almost too late when I spotted a figure waving from a small boat about half a mile to seaward. A net waiting to trap us: avoiding it took us on a two-mile diversion away from the coast, which we reached again at the round tower of Ardmore. It is said that the great St Declan may have baptised the first Christians in the south of Ireland here in 402 AD, some 30 years before St Patrick arrived. The round tower was probably built in the twelfth century when the renowned monastic centre was at its zenith. It vanished as *Sarakiniko* slipped west.

Sleepy Ardmore, so beloved of artists and writers, whose cottages turn their shoulders to the open sea. A few miles beyond we saw a wreck lying against the cliffs. *Samson* had been no ordinary ship, but a twin-funnel construction vessel with a crane longer than the ship's hull. Bound for Cork, a storm drove her in here in 1988. After the crew had been rescued, a local man abseiled down to the deck and claimed the ship as salvage. He stayed on board, enduring the battering seas to establish his rights of salvage, but no one considered *Samson* worth an offer, and the monument to his optimism will no doubt remain wedged here for many decades to come.

By late afternoon we were anchored alongside Youghal's crumbling quays and the blank walls of abandoned warehouses, *Sarakiniko* contending uneasily with a fierce ebb tide setting down the Blackwater River against an Atlantic swell coming up the harbour. It had been an anxious approach, for no less than seven salmon nets lay stretched across the harbour entrance, drifting disconcertingly in the ebb tide, and turning to skirt around the edge of each net led us closer and closer to the shallows of Dutchman's Ballast.

Youghal gathers in a compact bundle between the steep hillside and the wide river. It was a fine, walled town in the fourteenth century, trading with ports all over Europe: wine, salt and spices coming in; wool, fish, timber and farm produce going out. In due course it became part of Sir Walter Raleigh's 40,000 acre estate obtained in the Munster Plantations, and inevitably the story insists that here he planted the first potatoes in Ireland and smoked the first pipe of tobacco. Richard Boyle, Earl of Cork, bought Raleigh's lands eventually, and established, in the words of a contemporary, 'a very excellent Colony, consisting of veteran soldiers and many other persons, brought by himself from England.'

We walked along the quay and passed an Edwardian house, its garden wall running along the foreshore, where an aunt and uncle of mine had once lived in suffocating decorum, windows shut, roller blinds drawn against fresh air and carpet-fading sunlight. There would be tea around massive mahogany, a silent maid, and occasionally my uncle would cross the room and twist knobs on the wireless until, through the crackling and whistling, you could hear people speaking in England.

We stopped by the lovely St Mary's Collegiate Church, where Boyle's mausoleum displays the earl, his three wives and all 16 children. Outside, the sky looked changeable. I asked the man tidying the churchyard for his opinion on the forecast. 'The leaves are after coming on the breeze of wind,' he started, and while his remarks did not tell me much about the weather, I felt glad that homogenised Anglo-Americanese does not yet flourish in Youghal.

A plaque near the Moby Dick bar explains that John Heuston made his film here in 1954, and certainly Youghal's waterfront could readily become a look-alike for a whaling port in New England, but by the Market Dock there is a more interesting mural, of a vessel passing between two lighthouses. This was the *Sirius*, a schooner-rigged paddle steamer with 350 horsepower engines, used on service between Cork and London until it was chartered by the American Steam Navigation Company in April 1838 to challenge the Brunel-built *Great Western* on the transatlantic run. *Sirius* became the first vessel to cross the Atlantic under steam alone, carrying 40 passengers and a crew of 38, and beating the *Great Western* by 19 hours. Sadly, the ship's Cork-born captain did not long enjoy the achievement. In command of a successor ship, he and all aboard vanished on her second return voyage from New York. The *Sirius* too was wrecked, west of Youghal, on its Cork-London run.

In the 1870s some 150 merchant ships were registered in Youghal. The town's seamen had a special whistle, which they would use on arrival at foreign harbours to call up other Youghal men. The Flemings were one of the town's best-known seafaring families. It was a Fleming ship which found the *Marie Celeste* abandoned in mid-Atlantic in December 1872 and towed her to Gibraltar. There were two Fleming daughters, Kathleen and May, after whom the schooner *Kathleen and May*, now at St Katherine's Dock in London, was named, and Youghal's last sailing ship was called the *Mary Fleming*. A plaque on the quay records that she was 'Lost with all hands in 1936.'

Trade died when steam replaced sail, and river current and sea tides gradually built sandbars across the estuary. Behind me international trucks bore cargoes to and from the container ships in Cork. Juggernauts must be prepared for the unexpected in Youghal. A car went past, towing a fast-trotting horse on a very long rein, and the clatter of horseshoes on asphalt was still ringing in the air as tug and tow sped around a blind corner.

WE ROLLED uncomfortably, with a wind astern, past Ballycotton Island next day, its black lighthouse perched within a circle of white walls. Further in lay Ballycotton, home of some of Ireland's most notable lifeboat families. In February 1936, four Slineys and three Walshes from the village spent 63 hours on sea service in their efforts to rescue the crew of the Daunt Rock lightvessel off Cork. They went out in the *Mary Standford* to search for the drifting lightvessel and its company of eight in weather which saw spray lifting over the 190-foot lighthouse. The saga of the Daunt Rock rescue has been retold on film and television, but it was only one example of the services to seamen provided by this remarkable community. In later years, the *Mary Standford* was retrieved from the Shannon, where it had been used as a pilot boat, and restored to its former condition.

The lightvessel has now been replaced by a buoy at the Daunt Rock, which was just visible as we turned for the half-mile-wide entrance to Cork Harbour, one of the largest, most easily approached and safest harbours in the world. For centuries, sea-going ships anchored at Cobh – the Cove of Cork – to load or discharge their cargoes on to smaller vessels, which took them up the River Lee to the quays and warehouses of Cork. The merchant Francis Rogers described the scene as it might be found around 1700.

'Here are handsome quays where the smaller ships lie and load. This is a large and populous city, having many merchants and tradesmen in it. It is encompassed by a good wall of stone, but not many guns. They drive a very great trade to the West Indies with their provisions, chiefly by Bristol men who flock hither to load about September and October for Jamaica, Barbadoes, Antegoa, and the other islands of the West Indies, with beef, pork, butter, candles, etc. The inhabitants drive a pretty smart Gillycranky trade to France. This city is accounted the first in Ireland for trade; it has a very large market; the people are generally given to hospitality, civil and courteous to strangers; follow pretty much the French air in conversation, bringing up their children to dance, play on the fiddle, and fence, if they can give them nothing else.'

Cork became known as the 'Bristol of Ireland'. Arthur Young found it 'much the most animated, busy scene of shipping in all Ireland', and in 1764 it was said to export more provisions than any other town in the British Empire. The 1755 Lisbon earthquake cut trade for a time, as did the American War of Independence, starting in 1775, but at the height of the city's trade Cork merchants exported nearly 300,000 barrels of salt beef annually. Salted beef was an alternative to the English prohibition on the export of live cattle, and there were also exports of salt pork, butter, bacon, hides, rabbit skins, linen, wool and tallow.

This western harbour, big enough to shelter the entire British Navy, and with a productive hinterland, was the obvious supply base for fleets bound for America and the West Indies. Thackeray stood on the quays near St Patrick's Bridge in 1842, when some 40 ships lay at anchor along the walls, 'here a cargo of hides, yonder a company of soldiers, their kits and their Dollies, who are taking leave of the red-coats at the steamer's side. Then you may see a fine, squeaking, shrieking drove of pigs embarking by the same conveyance, and insinuated into the steamer by all sorts of coaxing, threatening and wheedling. Seamen are singing and yeehoing on board; grimy colliers smoking at the liquor shops along the quay...'

Over to port lay the yachting centre of Crosshaven, but we felt we should first sail past the waterfront of Cobh, a town which was the focus of the transatlantic liner trade for many years, but also the departure point for so many emigrants and convicts. Today it shows a smiling face to the harbour. Brightly painted houses lie near the water, while behind them narrow streets climb steeply to the Pugin cathedral. The first gives a touch of Regency Brighton; the cathedral suggests a town in France.

At Haulbowline Island, opposite Cobh, the oldest yacht club in the world, the Water Club of the Harbour of Cork, was founded in 1720. Its secretary and steward was called the Knight of the Island of Haulbowline and its highly exclusive membership was originally limited to 25. An account of its activities in 1748 rings odd indeed to modern ears. The club's heavy bluff-bowed vessels, depicted in the paintings of the marine artist, Peter Monamy, at the Royal Cork Yacht Club in Crosshaven, sailed in convoy under the admiral's command. 'When the Admiral hoists his foresail half up,' declares one of the complex sailing orders, 'it is for the fleet to have a peak upon their anchors, and when the foresail is hoisted up and a gun fired the whole fleet is to weigh.' No boat might presume to sail ahead of the admiral or depart the fleet without his permission.

The Cork boats, as an old account put it, 'did for painting and gilding exceed the King's yacht at Greenwich', but I wondered if the members could have had much fun. If you arrived late for the sailing rendezvous, which was fixed for spring tides every fort-night, you forfeited 'a British half crown for gunpowder for the fleet', which engaged in a deal of gunfire for signalling. Perhaps the most remarkable injunction was Rule 14, which declared that 'Such members of the Club, or others, as shall talk of sailing after dinner [shall] be fined a bumper.' It may be that this rule ensured the club had a constant supply of alcohol.

There is a gap in the records after 1765, but in 1806 the Marquis of Thomond and others arranged to revive the Water Club. Little happened, however, and the membership may have even dropped to eight loyal gentlemen. Then, in 1828, after a period of energetic rebuilding, King William IV granted them a royal warrant and the club became the Royal Cork Yacht Club.

In the 1830s, J. Caulfield Beamish of Cork, 'that true nursery of yachtsmen' in the words of *Hunt's Magazine*, designed a quite new style of boat 'aiming to produce the greatest speed with the least force and the greatest stability from form and not from ballast.' He discarded the bluff bows of the eighteenth and early nineteenth century in favour of a narrow entry. His boat *Peri*, built by Ahearn's of Passage, Cork, was a true innovation – 45 feet overall and twelve foot beam. Others followed from a yard at King's Quay, Blackrock: *Paddy from Cork* and *Big Paddy from Cork*. So notable was *Big Paddy* that the Commander-in-Chief, Portsmouth, decided that England's fastest naval cutter, *Emerald*, should be raced against her. On 13 and 17 July 1832, with *Big Paddy* deliberately carrying all the gear and equipment of a Revenue cutter, she so outdid the navy vessel on every point of sailing, both in easy water and in a seaway, that a race for a third day was abandoned.

When we had finished a brief tour of the harbour, we stopped at Crosshaven to pay our respects to the club. Notwithstanding its venerable ancestry, as host to events like the Ford Cork Week it remains one of the most prestigious and active sailing clubs in these islands. Seated in the hospitable clubhouse with my crew, Joan and Tony, my attention was caught by an old letter framed on the wall. It was an appeal made by some 30 ladies to the regatta committee in August 1831. They referred to 'females in the lower rank of life' being 'induced to take part in public Rowing Matches', and thought it difficult to see 'how any woman could so far forget her proper sphere' save, perhaps, through inducements or threats. 'Is it possible,' the women asked, 'that men of education and refinement could wish to lower our sex and take pleasure in seeing the coarse and masculine attitudes of a boatman assumed by a woman?' The committee were 'entreated as men of taste to desist' from these practices. It is not known if they did.

Tony and I assured Joan that *Sarakiniko*'s women had sailed with men of education and refinement indeed, and leaving him to draw the admission that neither she nor Anne had faced inducement or threat, I went to collect our celebratory drinks. The circumnavigation was near an end. Our nautical chatter carried on all through supper, but fortunately rules have changed in the world's oldest yacht club, and no one came to fine us a bumper.

Joan had to fly to London next day, and Anne and Pat rejoined to make a foursome for the voyage to Portsmouth. It was evening as *Sarakiniko* left the coast of Cork. The Great and Little Sovereign Islands, which had emerged from the mist as we approached Kinsale earlier in the summer, were in sight to the west. Our circle of Ireland was complete.

Ireland is a small island, growing more confident, prosperous and forward-looking by the year. One seemed to have been around it for a long time, stirred by a complex of emotions and memories, but it was time now to remove the tricolour from the crosstrees, where it had flown all through our voyage in Irish territorial waters. I clambered along the side deck, hauled it down and folded it carefully.

For several hours we could see the long double flash of the Old Head of Kinsale lighthouse glimmering over the stern, then it sank in the distance until it was merely a flicker from below the horizon. Wondering why I did so, I found myself watching it until it had gone.

Bibliography

Bardon, J. *History of Ulster*, Blackstaff, 1992

Beilby, A. *The Story of the RNLI*, Patrick Stevens, 1991

Boland, R. *Sealegs*, New Island Books, 1992

Bonner, B. *Our Inish Eoghain Heritage*, Pallas, 1991

Breathnach, R.B. *The Man from Cape Clear*, Mercier, 1975

Campbell, M. *Seawrack: Long Ago Tales of Rathlin Island*, Ballycastle, 1951

Chambers, R. *Granuaile*, Wolfhound, 1979

Chatterton, E.K. *Fore and Aft Craft*, London 1927

Clark, *Sailing Round Ireland*, North West Books, 1990

— *Rathlin: Its Island Story*, Impact, 1993

— *The Lord of the Isles Voyage*, Leinster Leader, 1993

Concannon, K. *Inishbofin through Time and Tide*, Irish Development Association, 1993

Coombes, J. *Utopia in Glandore*, Butlerstown, 1970

Cowper, F. *Sailing Tours*, Ashford Press, 1985

de Courcy Ireland, J. *Ireland and the Irish in Maritime History*, Glendall Press, 1986

— *The Sea and the Easter Rising*, Dublin, 1966

Enoch, V.J. *The Martello Towers of Ireland*, Dublin

Fewer, M. *By Cliff and Shore: Walking the Waterford Coast*, Anna Livia, 1992

Fisk, R. *In Time of War*, Paladin, 1995

Flanagan, L. *Ireland's Armada Legacy*, Gill and Macmillan, 1988

Flower, R. *The Western Island*, Oxford University Press, 1944

Harbison, P. *Pilgrimage in Ireland*, Barry and Jenkins, 1991

Heaton, P. *History of Yachting*, Batsford, 1955

Hayward, R. *Munster and the City of Cork*, Phoenix House, 1964

— *In the Kingdom of Kerry*, Dundalgan Press, 1976

Heraughty, P. *Inishmurray: Ancient Monastic Island*, 1980

Hill, G. *Facts from Gweedore*, Belfast, 1971

Bibliography

Hochling, A. and M. *Last Voyage of the Lusitania*, Longmans

Howarth, D. *Voyage of the Armada*, Collins, 1981

Huntford, R. *Shackleton*, Abacus, 1996

Irish Cruising Club, *Sailing Directions South and West Coasts of Ireland;*
    Sailing Directions North and East Coasts of Ireland, Belfast, 1993

Johnson, D. *Phantom Islands of the Atlantic*, Souvenir Press, 1997

Lavelle, D. *Skellig*, O'Brien Press, 1976

Lewis, C. *Topographical History of Ireland*, 1837

Lloyd, C. *English Corsairs of the Barbary Coast*, Collins, 1991

Long, B. *Bright Light, White Water*, New Island Books, 1997

MacLysaght, E. *Irish Life in the Seventeenth Century*, Irish Academic
    Press, 1969

McIvor, A. *History of the Irish Naval Service*, Blackwell

MacMullan, C. *Down Channel*, Rupert Hart Davies, 1986

Mahon, J. *Kate Tyrell: The Denbeighshire Lass*, Basement Press

Martin, C. *The Spanish Armada*, Guildford, 1988

Mason, T. *The Islands of Ireland*, Batsford, 1936

Mattingly, G. *The Defeat of the Spanish Armada*, Cape, 1959

Maxwell, W. *Wild Sports of the West*, London, 1832

Mizen Historical and Archaeological Society *Journal*, No. 3, Skibbereen,
    1995

Moody, T. and Martin, E. *The Course of Irish History*, Mercier, 1989

Morrisson, S.E. *The European Discovery of America*, Oxford University
    Press, 1971

Morris, J. *Fisher's Face*, Viking, 1995

Nolan, W. and Power, C. *Waterford: History and Society*, Geography
    Publication, 1992

O'Brien, C. *From Three Yachts*, Mariners' Library, 1950

Ó Cléirigh, N. *Valentia: A Different World*, Portobello Press, 1992

Ó Criomhthain, T. *The Islandman*, trans. R. Flower, Oxford University
    Press, 1985

O'Neill, T. *Merchants and Mariners in Medieval Ireland*, Irish Academic
    Press, 1987

Ó Péicín, D. and Nolan, L. *Islanders*, Fount, 1997

Otway, C. *Sketches in Erris and Tyrewly*, 1841

Pakenham, T. *The Year of Liberty*, Hodder and Stoughton, 1969

Pococke, R. *Irish Tours*, ed. J. McVeigh, Irish Academic Press, 1995

Praeger, L. *The Way that I Went*, Dublin 1937

Rees, J. and Charlton, L. *Arklow: Last Stronghold of Sail*, Arklow Historical Society

Roche, R. *The Norman Invasion of Ireland*, Anvil Books, 1970

— *The Saltees*, Dublin, 1977

Robinson, D. *The History of the Valentia Lifeboats*

Ryan, J. *A Wave of the Sea*, Ward River Press, 1981

Ryland, R. *History of Waterford*, Dublin, 1962

Sayers, P. *Peig*, trans. B. MacMahon, Talbot Press, 1974

Severin, T. *The Brendan Voyage*, London, 1978

Smith, C. *History of Waterford*, Dublin, 1774

Somerville-Large, P. *The Coast of West Cork*, Appletree, 1985

— *The Grand Irish Tour*, Penguin, 1985

Stagles, J. and R. *The Blasket Islands*, O'Brien Press, 1980

Stenuit, R. *Treasures of the Armada*, 1974

Synge, J. *The Aran Islands*, Maunsell and Co, 1906

Thackeray, W.M. *The Irish Sketch Book*, Oxford University Press

Therman, D. *Stories from Tory*, Country House, 1989

Watney, J. *Ireland*, Columbus Books, 1989

Westropp, T.J. 'Early Maps: 1300-1600,' *PRIA*, 1913

Whelan, K. and Nolan, J. *Wexford: History and Society*, Geography Publications, 1987

White, E.W. *British Fishing Boats and Coastal Craft*, HMSO, 1950

Wilson, T. *The Irish Lifeboat Service*, Allen Figgis, 1968

Woodham-Smith, C. *The Great Hunger*, London, 1962

Young, A. *A Tour in Ireland*, 1776-9, ed. A. Hutton, London, 1892